Seventeenth-Century English Romance

Seventeenth-Century English Romance

Allegory, Ethics, and Politics

Amelia A. Zurcher

palgrave
macmillan

SEVENTEENTH-CENTURY ENGLISH ROMANCE

First published in 2007 by
PALGRAVE MACMILLAN™
175 Fifth Avenue, New York, N.Y. 10010 and
Houndmills, Basingstoke, Hampshire, England RG21 6XS.
Companies and representatives throughout the world.

PALGRAVE MACMILLAN is the global academic imprint of the Palgrave Macmillan division of St. Martin's Press, LLC and of Palgrave Macmillan Ltd. Macmillan® is a registered trademark in the United States, United Kingdom and other countries. Palgrave is a registered trademark in the European Union and other countries.

ISBN-10: 1-4039-7752-6
ISBN-13: 978-1-4039-7752-6

Library of Congress Cataloging-in-Publication Data

Sandy, Amelia Zurcher, 1965-
Seventeenth-century English romance : allegory, ethics, and politics/ Amelia A. Zurcher.
p. cm.
Includes bibliographical references (p.) and index.
ISBN: 1-4039-7752-6 (alk. paper)
1. Love stories, English—History and criticism. 2. English fiction—Early modern, 1500-1700—History and criticism. 3. Politics and literature—England—History—17th century. 4. Love—Moral and ethical aspects. 5. Ethics in literature. 6. Love in literature. 7. Self-interest. I. Title. II. Title: 17th century English romance.

PR844.L68S36 2007
823′.08509

2007060020

A catalogue record for this book is available from the British Library.

Design by Macmillan India Ltd.

First edition: June 2007

10 9 8 7 6 5 4 3 2 1

Printed in the United States of America.

To my parents, Lynne Zurcher and John Zurcher

Table of Contents

Acknowledgments

During my work on this book I have incurred many obligations, which if I cannot requite I at least have the pleasure of acknowledging here. I take this opportunity, first, to record two very long-standing intellectual debts, to Jonathan Freedman and to the late Dennis Kay. Judith Anderson, John Boly, Ed Duffy, Constance Jordan, Steve Karian, Christine Krueger, the late Josephine Roberts, Tom Roche, and Will West all generously read and commented on portions of the manuscript at various stages; James Holstun offered some very useful words on James Harrington. My sincere thanks as well to Al Braunmuller, Larry Danson, Jonathan Goldberg, James Grossman, Devoney Looser, and Mark Sandy for all their help.

I am especially grateful to Margaret Reid for her generosity and her intellectual acumen, both as a reader and as a friend. I have been the beneficiary throughout the writing of this book (and for many years before) of Andrew Zurcher's meticulous reading, his assistance with all sorts of research conundrums, and his never-failing fellowship. Story Sandy and Will Sandy generously granted me more than a little extra time. I owe particular debts to Victoria Kahn, whose support has been unstinting from the very beginnings of my work on romance and without whose contributions of all kinds this book would be much poorer than it is; and to R. Clifton Spargo, whose intellectual rigor and commitment have been a model to me during the writing of this book and have stamped its pages, both directly and indirectly, in more ways than I can count.

A Whiting Doctoral Fellowship from the Mrs. Giles Whiting Foundation enabled me to undertake early research on this project, and a Mellon Postdoctoral Fellowship at the Newberry Library made possible a full year of research in very collegial surroundings, without which I could never have tackled these very long narratives.

Portions of Chapter 1, much revised for this book, appeared in *English Literary Renaissance* 35, no. 1 (2005): 73–101, published by Blackwell Publishing, under the title "Ethics and the Politic Agent of Early Seventeenth-Century Prose Romance."

Introduction

Despite the recent resurgence of scholarly interest in romance as a genre or mode, critics and historians of literature still know little about seventeenth-century prose romance. While the first published fiction by an English woman, Mary Wroth's *Urania* (1621), has garnered considerable critical attention in the last two decades, and John Barclay's *Argenis* (1621) has just received its first modern edition, few literary histories even allude to such ideologically and formally complex works as John Crowne's *Pandion and Amphigenia* (1665), Thomas Bayly's *Herba Parietis* (1650), or philosopher Robert Boyle's *The Martyrdom of Theodora, and Didymus* (first written in the late 1640s or 1650s), and recent histories of the novel dismiss the group of midcentury romances of which these latter three are examples as small in number and mostly imitative of French heroic romance.[1] The rich current of ideas linking Philip Sidney's groundbreaking *Arcadia* (1590) to midcentury romance has been little studied, and few accounts of midcentury thought acknowledge that prose romance was one of the most widely published literary genres in England at this time. Partly as cause and partly as consequence of this gap in our knowledge of seventeenth-century fiction, we also do not know enough, as a matter for literary studies, about the political- and moral-philosophical issues preoccupying prose romance. It is difficult to assert the importance of either to our understanding of seventeenth-century English literary culture without first assuming a similar importance for the other. But this book makes the twofold claim that prose romance is the dominant form of narrative fiction in the period, and that this is so in large part because the genre approaches with complexity and sophistication one of the most pressing issues in seventeenth-century English thought: the problem of self-interest.

A first look at seventeenth-century romance may seem to render such a claim improbable. Even in the 1650s, despite *Don Quixote*'s long, ironic shadow, English romance was still populated by the same knights and ladies on military and erotic quests who had characterized medieval chivalric romance. The genre imitated much older models in its formal techniques, and it obeyed a long-standing generic tradition of addressing itself thematically to the past. Perhaps it is all these adherences to convention that have misled many historians of the novel into assuming that in seventeenth-century England, prose romance was mainly a remnant genre. From this retrospective viewpoint, by the mid-seventeenth century romance had become divested of all real content now that the aristocratic ideology that produced it had become mostly obsolete, and it survived only in the enervated form of roman à clef or as mere imitation of French romance, its main function in the larger sweep of literary history to serve as an antitype for emergent, more authentically contemporary literary genres, especially the novel.[2]

To be fair, the relative critical neglect of prose romance has taken its cue not only from the novel's success at eclipsing older forms of prose fiction but also from romance itself, which has a long history of self-deprecation. In sixteenth-century England the ancient philosophical tradition of distrusting fiction intersected with the stigma against print in elite literary culture to define prose fiction in general, whatever its actual readership, as "low," material for an uneducated audience lacking a capacity for critical judgment and therefore tending toward uncritical (and socially dangerous) identification.[3] Educated readers of the time were aware of the extended neoclassical debate over romance in sixteenth-century Italy, in which defenders of the Aristotelian unities attacked romance—a genre never treated by classical poetics—for its proliferation of plots and characters.[4] And critics of romance also complained about its tendency to depart more capriciously than epic from the authoritative ground of history, a failing that identified romance in English eyes as matter for an uneducated audience, especially women, whose tastes were believed already to veer toward the fantastic.[5] For its own part, early modern romance persistently disavowed its own significance—explicitly, in its prefatory material; through its preoccupation with pastness, what Alex Davis calls its "temporal signature"; and, as I will discuss in a moment, through its generic habit of subjecting its idealism to irony.[6]

It has never been difficult to recognize romance's self-deprecation as in part strategic, a way to step out from under the weight of critical opinion even while acknowledging it, and certainly we no longer automatically dismiss nonelite literature as insignificant.[7] But the prevailing disrespect for romance in early modern England still serves as a model for our own sense that in the seventeenth century romance was located far enough outside the mainstream of literary culture to warrant today a concerted reading by only the tiniest of academic audiences. This commonplace assumption, I want to insist, is challenged by a sustained look at seventeenth-century romances themselves. To begin with, even the number of prose romances published in this period is in itself sufficient to demand our attention. Bayly's *Herba Parietis,* Boyle's *The Martyrdom of Theodora, and Didymus,* his brother Roger Boyle's *Parthenissa* (published in parts throughout the 1650s and as a whole in 1676), Crowne's *Pandion and Amphigenia* (1665 but apparently written a few years earlier), Nathaniel Ingelo's *Bentivolio and Urania* (1660, 1664), George MacKenzie's *Aretina* (1660), and the anonymous *Eliana* (1661), in addition to Barclay's slightly better known *Argenis,* Richard Brathwaite's *Panthalia* (1659), Percy Herbert's *The Princess Cloria* (published in parts throughout the 1650s and as a whole in 1661), the anonymous *Theophania* (1655 but probably written 1645), and of course Wroth's *Urania*—all of these are substantial and original narratives. And this list of works treated in this book does not include all the romances published in the seventeenth century, nor the several more that we know of in manuscript.[8] The production of original prose romance came to an end within a few years after the Restoration, but during the roughly forty-year period of their flourishing, English prose romances exerted a strong claim to be considered a distinct genre of seventeenth-century literature.[9] They gestured with generic self-consciousness toward a prose genealogy running from Heliodorus's fourth century C.E. Greek romance *Aethiopika* through Sidney's *Arcadia;* they demonstrated their cohesiveness as a group by frequent allusions to and revisions of one another, which suggests too that they expected a readership well versed in the genre; and they claimed romance's multiplicity as a virtue, distinguishing themselves from writers of other genres by their many overlapping modes of inquiry.[10]

One of the aims of this book, then, is to give a fresh and full account of a whole genre of imaginative literature in seventeenth-century England. As the debates and justifications in romance's prefatory material make clear, romance was a genre that in its own period was understood to be functionally synonymous with narrative fiction itself, and one of the reasons to reclaim seventeenth-century romance today is that it constituted an important chapter in the history of fiction, giving us, for instance, a much clearer sense of the complex mixture of good faith and pretense in the novel's later claim for its own newness. Even more broadly, however—and this will be my central argument—a substantial acquaintance with seventeenth-century romance brings into view a crucial chapter in a history that belongs not only to literature but also to sociology, political theory, and moral philosophy. Romance from Heliodorus on was preoccupied with the tension between contingency and design and, within that rubric, between divine providence and human agency, and Sidney's *Arcadia* inaugurated for English romance a tradition of employing the genre to take up specifically early modern anxieties about the ethics of political agency. In the seventeenth century, as reason of state theory was subsumed by the newly compelling concept of "interest," prose romance came to serve both as one of the principal midcentury grounds for the exploration of interest's political and ethical implications and also as a primary lens through which the problem of self-interest took shape. To read seventeenth-century romance now is thus not only to recover an important aspect of early modern thought but to see with particular acuity the mutually constitutive relation between genre and political and ethical philosophy in the period.

1. POLITIC ROMANCE

Prose romances took up many different subjects during the seventeenth century, and they treated the matter they did share—erotic love; weak, if not necessarily deposed, kings—in a variety of ways, but common to most of them, as I will show, was a broad conflict between the drive toward self-directed ends and virtue more traditionally construed. Self-interest is an idea perhaps particularly vulnerable, even today, to being understood as a law of nature rather than an aspect of ideology. But it does, of course, have a history, and its meaning has varied along with the ideals it has been made to oppose. In seventeenth-century romance its centrality proceeded especially from two factors: romance's long-standing preoccupation, so deep as to be formative, with the tension between divine providence and human agency; and, much more locally, the appearance in late sixteenth-century England of a set of ideas historians have recently called "politic ideology." For Philip Sidney these two factors converged, and in its treatment of self-interest his *Arcadia* became the inaugurator for a whole tradition of English romance.

As an idea, of course, self-interest did not suddenly emerge in Elizabethan England, nor in Renaissance Europe (although Norbert Elias locates the origins of what he and other social scientists have called the newly modern concept of "egoism" in Renaissance courts).[11] But the sixteenth-century context of ideas and institutions within which politic ideology located self-interest seemed to make this concept particularly compelling to late-humanist thinkers, both narratively, as an explanation for what drove human history, and ethically, as a diagnosis of what ailed court society. By "politic ideology" historians refer to what seemed in the latter half of the sixteenth century a newly destabilizing confluence of skepticism, Tacitism, and reason of state theory, first in Italian and French courts and then in Elizabethan court and university culture.[12] Late twentieth-century scholars initially approached this line of thought in England as an innovative theory of history, naming it after the new "politic histories," such as John Hayward's *The First Part of the Life and Raigne of King Henrie IIII* (1599, dedicated to the Earl of Essex) and *The Lives of the III Normans, Kings of England* (1613), that focused attention on the particulars of political conflict between individual actors rather than subsuming such conflicts within the sweep of providential design. In fact, however, politic ideas (and the term "politic" itself) quickly permeated a range of discourses in the late sixteenth and early seventeenth centuries, not only history but also drama (for instance, Ben Jonson's Roman plays), collections of essays by such figures as Francis Bacon and Robert Johnson, and finally prose romance.[13] Politic ideology clearly traced its origins to the spread of Tacitean and Machiavellian ideas in European political thought and then their rapid importation into England. Tacitus's *Annals* were edited in Latin in 1575 by the Dutch scholar Justus Lipsius and translated into English by Henry Savile in 1591, and Lipsius was also the author of the extremely influential Neostoic treatise *De Constantia*, a lesson in how to endure the politic realities of religious and political conflict during the Dutch and Spanish wars of the 1580s and 1590s, which was translated into English by John Stradling as *Two Bookes of Constancie* in 1594. Tacitean and politic ideas were taken up first and especially in England by the Sidney circle: Philip Sidney met Lipsius in Paris; his brother Robert's tutor was Henry Savile; and the English translation of Lipsius's *Two Bookes of Constancie* was dedicated to the uncle of Robert Sidney's wife, Barbara Gamage (who was Mary Wroth's mother). As a Stoic, and because of his cynical and bloody closet dramas, Seneca was associated with politic ideology, and Mary Sidney and other members of her circle translated Senecan drama in the 1590s. After Sidney's death Robert Devereux, Earl of Essex, inherited Philip Sidney's championship of the international Protestant cause, and even after Essex's execution for treason, writers associated with his patronage, including Francis Bacon, John Hayward, and Samuel Daniel, continued to investigate the possibilities of Senecan drama and Tacitean history.[14]

Recently scholars have begun to recognize the extent of politic ideology's influence by calling it "the new humanism," and one of its leading modern historians, Richard Tuck, justifies this label with the claim that in England and France it came to be "as powerful and soon as all-pervasive as the Ciceronian humanism of the Quattrocento had been" before it.[15] Both its adherents and its denouncers in late sixteenth-century England portrayed politic ideology as an immediate, temporally localized phenomenon, but viewed in a larger context it is clearly an aspect of what political historian Maurizio Viroli has described as the epochal ideological shift in Western Europe from politics to reason of state, from the Ciceronian vision of the state as governed by reason for the good of the many to a notion of political activity as a means above all of preserving the power of the ruling group or individual.[16] Often beginning with an analogy between the English court and Tacitus's imperial Rome, politic ideology challenged the traditional humanist notion of politics, as a noble exchange of views by leading scholars and humanistically educated courtiers for the purpose of educating the monarch, with the counterclaim that politics was a series of petty, chaotic wars springing from myriad clashes between individual courtiers. Fundamental to this view of social and political interaction was the idea that human beings were driven primarily by their own individual interests rather than by concern for divine will or the common good, an idea that historians such as F. J. Levy have argued both marked and furthered another related epochal shift in Western thought, from divine to human agency as the mover of narrative.[17] This is probably an overstatement—romance for one, as I have already suggested, had been preoccupied for centuries with the tension between providence and human agency—but Levy's argument reflects politic ideology's own sense of agency as a newly pressing problem, in conflict with traditional humanism's conceptions of virtue.

In particular, politic ideology assumed that self-interest was antagonistic, through its tendency to naturalize competition and social fragmentation, to any notion of the common good, and that in recognizing the power of the individual human will it necessarily challenged divine order. As a result, despite its frequent characterization as a form of political pragmatism—emphasizing, for instance, its own utility in educating its adherents "for the manage of civill actions"—politic ideology usually carried negative moral connotations.[18] Correspondingly, it was understood to dictate a social and political world governed by secrecy and dissimulation, by "the quaint practises of politicians," in the words of one English commentator in 1600, "wherein publike and open dessignes are oftentimes but shadowes of more secret proiectes, and these againe serve as foiles to more eminent intentions."[19] In late sixteenth-century England, when it was still felt to be new, politic ideology was usually portrayed as a mode of oppositional politics, a challenge to the dominant humanist model of the court and to the monarch who embodied it, and this perception was only strengthened by its association with the militant Protestant Sidney and Essex circles. The politic courtier, more concerned with his own interests than with the monarch's or God's, was always potentially a traitor, and therefore, even if politic ideology seemed to tell a demystificatory truth about human interaction and historical narrative, it nevertheless had to be formally repudiated, even by those who advocated employing its insights to get ahead.

Within the context of traditional Christian humanism in late Elizabethan and Jacobean England, then, politic self-interest was obviously problematic and easy to denounce, and the condemnations of "politic" and "dissembling" queens in Wroth's *Urania,* for instance, were echoed often in literature of the period. But insofar as politic ideas were also highly compelling, as was the case particularly for self-consciously modern historians and for those who wanted to challenge traditional structures of authority, it was necessary to walk a difficult line, adopting what seemed true or useful about politic ideology without seeming to issue too much of a challenge to official structures of authority and the notions of virtue that upheld them. And romance, I want to suggest, was uniquely suited by its generic history to recognize the complexities of politic ideology and to approach them with true ambivalence—providing something of a cover for would-be rebels toward authority but also, certainly by the 1620s (and even in the 1590s for Sidney), a real ground for the intellectual exploration of politic ideas.[20]

If epic, to use the metaphor that Spenser, in *The Faerie Queene,* builds from an ancient classical trope, is that genre in which characters and narrator sail resolutely toward a triumphant collective destiny, romance is built on the countervailing and just as ancient power of shipwreck. Epic, following the model of Virgil's *Aeneid,* takes as its work the harmonization of the hero's will with his and his nation's providential destiny, the elimination of all the distractions and hesitations that plague Aeneas in his march toward the future Rome, while romance requires the hero and heroine to surrender their desires in the face of random contingency, which then either prevails (hence romance's famous reluctance to end) or gets recuperated, through no act of the characters, as divine providence. To some extent, as David Quint aptly points out, romance does not just describe a different worldview from the one epic describes but is specifically epic's counternarrative, the story of history's losers over against epic's winners; and as such it also contains an element of ironic critique, expressed especially through those moments in romance when providence is felt to fail.[21] Providence, romance replies to epic in such moments, seems to work only sometimes; perhaps this means that providence is really luck after all, or perhaps, even more destabilizingly, that providence is a rationalization of victory and even a screen for the epic hero's exertion of will—which from romance's point of view may look much more morally ambiguous than it does from epic's. These ideas were implicit in romance's narrative structure as early as Heliodorus's *Aethiopika,* a seminal work that not merely incidentally underwent an enormous renaissance of popularity in sixteenth-century Europe, and they were central to Ariosto's pointed comedy in *Orlando Furioso.* By the time Sidney inherited the genre, romance seemed always already, even as it also upheld it, to have ironized the idea of providence as an explanation for history, and to have propounded the notion of human agency as a kind of open secret. Far from sounding the "death knell" of the genre, as some critics have supposed, this tendency toward irony about its own narrative principles was in Sidney's time a hallmark of romance, and was a good part of the reason for its extraordinary longevity as well as its suitability for taking up politic ideas.[22]

By the end of the sixteenth century romance had acquired another generic attribute that suited it to take up politic ideas: mirroring the duality in its approach to narrative causation was the more strictly formal duality signaled by its tendency toward political or social allegory and roman à clef. Romance inherited this tendency through two lines of influence. Heliodorus, as I will discuss in Chapter 2, offered on the very last page of *Aethiopika* a crucial clue to his own identity that recast his entire fantastic tale of love and deception as a quasi-political allegory about competition between what we would now call nations, a move that associated romance with roman à clef right from what Elizabethans understood to be its very inception as a literary form. Meanwhile, as Ann Astell has recently shown, on a separate trajectory romance became known as a frequent vehicle for topical allegory in medieval literary and political culture.[23] In the late sixteenth century this generic history intersected with the politic definition of allegory as the indispensable tool for anyone attempting to thrive at court—in George Puttenham's well-known phrase, the "Figure of false semblant."[24]

Allegory in this politic sense was not so much a form of polysemy as what Wayne Booth has called "stable irony," a way of saying one thing while meaning a particular different thing, and as the governing figure of a given narrative it became roman à clef.[25] In romance, I will show, by figuring the self (both writer and character) and its interests as the secrets behind more traditionally motivated fictions, roman à clef became itself a way of exploring the politic problem of agency—not a small part of the reason why romance was almost always also roman à clef throughout the next century.

I want to emphasize that in this respect my account of romance differs substantially from both Annabel Patterson's argument that the primary purpose of roman à clef in early modern England was to avoid censorship and Michael McKeon's judgment that in seventeenth-century romance roman à clef signaled epistemological naïveté. While Patterson is undoubtedly right that censorship was one of the factors driving roman à clef in the seventeenth century, her theory of functional ambiguity cannot do justice to the complexity of the semantic play within the form, at least in its manifestations in romance—it cannot, for instance, explain romance's tendency to generate multiple and even conflicting versions of the same "true" characters and stories, which in my view functioned not just as a cover for agency but also as an exploration of agency's nature and its ethics.[26] Nor does her theory make room, as I will explain in Chapter 1, for the intimate ethical relationship roman à clef meant to establish between author and reader. McKeon, for his part, draws an opposition between, on the one hand, moral truth and the traditional habits of allegorical interpretation designed to arrive at it and, on the other, what we would call factual truth and the genres of history that we now understand to be dedicated to producing it, and he argues that through its roman à clef form seventeenth-century romance showed itself to be confused about what distinguished these opposing terms (a confusion that the novel, by drawing a firm line between verisimilar fiction and factual history, would shortly sort out).[27] My argument suggests instead that within romance roman à clef was operating according to a different agenda, that rather than negotiate the distinction between fact and fiction its end was to mediate distinctions among different kinds of narrative agency.

Sidney's *Arcadia* is the first location in England where all these systems of thought—politic ideology, the generic conventions of romance, and romance's long history of affiliation with roman à clef—came fully together, both in the circumstances of the romance's production (or at least what Sidney advertised as these circumstances) and as a function of its content. In his dedication to his sister, Sidney claimed to have written *Arcadia* during the period of his rustication to her estate of Wilton for daring to offer the queen unsolicited political advice, and he further deprecated the work as a "trifle" despite the fact that at least in revised form it demonstrated a meticulous amalgamation and reworking of Heliodoran and Continental romance traditions for a new English context. Both of these facts furthered the sense already suggested by the Sidney family's established connection with politic ideology, that *Arcadia* was coded political rhetoric from a writer at once eager to declare his political opposition and careful to couch it in veiled terms.[28] These external linkages between romance and politic ideology were echoed within the romance itself: Sidney figured himself as the disaffected "stranger shepherd" Philisides, who in *Arcadia*'s Third Eclogues sings a famous song against tyranny, and in the conclusion, as I will discuss in Chapter 1, he offered a complicated parable that at once outlined the usefulness of romance's ironic treatment of agency for negotiating (at least in political terms) the gap between virtue and self-interest and at the same time pointed out the nature and extent of that gap with unprecedented explicitness.

To *Arcadia*'s immediate generic heirs, politic ideology was troubling for two main reasons. First, although self-interest might be a central, perhaps even *the* central, motivating force behind human behavior, insofar as politic self-interest contravened not only traditional religious and political authority on earth but also divine providence and the commonweal providence was vaguely supposed to support, with respect to morality it was probably irrevocably corrupt. Second, if people were all truly politic agents acting for their own ends rather than in the service of more communal ideals, competition and conflict between individuals threatened to become inevitable and ungovernable. In response, seventeenth-century romance followed Sidney both in diagnosing these problems for its own social and political contexts and in attempting to use the genre as a corrective for them. In Chapter 1 I show how in *Urania* Wroth brilliantly adapted roman à clef so that it pointed neither toward facticity nor toward transcendent moral truth, but rather toward fiction as an end in itself, as the continual process of generating another version of the author's self—a self that through its acknowledged estrangement from the real thing blocked narcissistic self-consolidation and autonomy without requiring the self-abnegation advised by more traditional constructions of virtue. As Wroth and Barclay also began to confront self-interest's social implications, both summoned quickly, as I show in Chapter 2, the emphasis in the Heliodoran romance tradition on chastity and singularity, the valorization of the peerless hero and the inviolate heroine, so as to make these problems disappear. Wroth, unusually, privileged endogamous relationships that preempted the aristocratic woman's entrance onto the marriage market and so promoted a metaphorical chastity, while Barclay narrowed authentic relationship to an identificatory friendship that effectively nullified the social risks of competition. Both these writers, like Sidney before them, invoked romance's generic attributes as antidotes to problems romance also raised, as if self-interest rightly construed were a containable threat.

2. From Morality to Ethics

For the first generation of Sidney's generic successors, the threat politic ideology presented was primarily to individual virtue: *Urania*'s and *Argenis*'s challenge was above all to certify the potentially politic agent as resistant to the moral failing (inherited of course, from many different contexts, but focused anew by politic thought) of self-love. Politic ideology's emphasis on the efficacy of self-interest made it more difficult to organize and regulate sociality in traditional ways, through hierarchy and mutual subordination to authority, and as a consequence *Urania* and *Argenis* sought to address politic ideology's social threat by, in effect, denying sociality, contracting the social world toward the limit of the single individual. But by the middle of the seventeenth century, as I will show in the second half of this book, this strategy would no longer seem tenable.

Reason of state theory was in most contexts a powerfully secularizing and rationalizing discourse, and historians have agreed that over the course of the seventeenth century its tenets became increasingly diffused and normalized in political and, more broadly, social contexts. One of its most influential formulations in midcentury England was via the concept of interest, which entered English thought and culture especially through the treatise *Of the Interest of Princes and of Christian States* (1634; first English translation 1640) by the famous Huguenot general Henri, duc de Rohan. In this peace offering to Richelieu upon return from exile after the failed Huguenot rebellion, Rohan drew especially from Guicciardini, who used the terms "interesse" and "ragione di stato" interchangeably to argue for an ostensibly anti-ideological, rationalistic conception of politics.[29] "The Princes Commaund the *People,* and the *Interest* Commaunds The *Princes,*" the duc de Rohan famously began, and then declared, in a formulation that would circulate for decades in England as the maxim "interest never lies," "the *Prince* may deceive himselfe, his *Counsell* may be corrupted, but the interest alone can never faile" (*l'intérêt seul ne peut jamais manquer*).[30] For Rohan, as for new humanist thinkers before him, it was no longer God's designs that rested in the hearts of princes but their own interest. Interest as such, he promised his readers, was the key opening all human motivations to comprehension, and it was available to anyone who would make the effort to observe carefully.

Rohan's emphasis on transparency and his relative lack of concern with moral virtue were significant contributors to interest's growing influence as a political concept in 1640s and 1650s England, and these aspects of his theory would later have a formative influence on the establishment of economics as a separate sphere of discourse. But Rohan's conception of interest also had another set of implications, less noticed by modern historians, that exerted a crucial influence on ethical theory at midcentury. Like politic ideology before it, Rohan's interest construed the political actor as one in a group, surrounded by peers in competition; unlike politic ideology, Rohan understood this sociality not as a secret but as the fundamental fact of politics. Moreover, for Rohan the other was no longer a mystery, nor could he be assimilated to the self; rather, by his possession of interest he was at once individuated from and made analogous to his peers, distinct from and yet interpretable by them. Sociality had come out into the open as an issue to be acknowledged and investigated, and this, I will argue, was the ground on which romance entered into its own wide-ranging exploration of interest as a problem. For romance, through its generic preoccupation with self-interest and politic ideology, virtue was increasingly an issue not for the agent in isolation but in her relation to others, measured not by the extent to which she aligned herself with divine will or other kinds of recognized authority but rather to the extent that she was generous (that is, un-self-interested) toward others. Over the course of the seventy or so years after *Arcadia*, I want to suggest, as both a sign of and an agent in the increasing normalization and expansion of politic ideas, romance as a genre enacted a shift from what for the purposes of this argument I want to call *morality*, a concern with virtue as a matter for the individual in relation to a set of mainly abstract ideals, to *ethics*, a concern with virtue as the measure of the self's tendency to respect the interests of specific other people.

In describing this turn in romance as a shift from morality to ethics, obviously I am not relying on early modern terminology, nor am I following standard moral-philosophical usage. In the classical philosophical tradition inherited by the Renaissance, the Latin "morality" emphasizes the social expectations that govern behavior, while the Greek "ethics" has more to do with individual character. John Stuart Mill speaks for the moral-philosophical tradition both before and after him on this issue in his argument that faults become immoralities only when they involve the breach of duty or obligation to others.[31] For my own, contrary distinction I draw especially on the work of Bernard Williams, who argues that our predominantly Kantian conception of morality as duty, designed specifically to overcome our inclination toward egoism (i.e., the selfish fulfillment of our own interests), obscures the broader and more efficacious notion of the ethical as that which "relates to us and our actions the demands, needs, claims, desires, and, generally, the lives of other people."[32] For Williams duty and obligation do not begin to encompass the nature of our shared life with others, and in fact, he suspects, they may as often refer back to the self as toward the other whom they are supposed to serve.[33] I do not mean to align Williams's version of Kantian morality anachronistically with morality as I have described it in Wroth and Barclay, nor do I necessarily follow Williams's judgments about the relative value of morality and ethics, at least with respect to the narrative I am constructing about the early modern period. But his sense of ethics as responsive to the other in a way that morality is not names a distinction with which other, more traditional moral philosophy is not concerned, a distinction that at least in an analogous sense, I will show, was made by seventeenth-century romance.

This shift from morality to ethics, as I have suggested, would seem to be a logical outgrowth of politic ideology and of reason of state more generally, in their increasing emphasis on human agency over providence and on sociality, but it certainly also had other, more local and material determinants. In English politics of the 1640s and 1650s, as has been well documented, the language of interest became attractive because it offered a way first for supporters of Parliamentary prerogative and then for people across the political spectrum (by 1647 the king himself was using the term) to conceive of the new, rapidly coalescing, but often unstable political groups that were making the old notion of political consensus untenable.[34] At least partly as a consequence of early Stuart political history, theories of tyranny in this period, as Rebecca Bushnell has demonstrated, became less and less about the moral character of the tyrant and increasingly about his violation of the liberties of others.[35] And recent work on the social implications of changing economic relations in the late sixteenth and seventeenth centuries also suggests, fascinatingly, that the unprecedentedly rapid growth of commerce in these years, both domestic and international, stimulated a sharply new sense of the social world not as a hierarchy but as a vast network of peer relationships between relative strangers. In such a world mutual trust was both more necessary than it had been before and also more frightening, because materially so much was riding on it and because one's peers were increasingly drawn from outside traditional kin and social groups—a situation that almost necessarily would seem to inspire increased conversation about the risks and rewards of social virtue.[36]

Within these multiple and sometimes overlapping social and intellectual contexts interest obtained many meanings, some of them contradictory. Interest was often identified with natural law, that desire or tendency that expresses most fundamentally the nature of a person or thing: it is the interest of a stone, it was frequently said in definitions of the term, to fall to the earth.[37] Interest was sometimes a synonym for passion, by the logic that such traditional passions as ambition and erotic desire were felt to be fundamentally self-interested; or, conversely, it was affiliated with rational and prudential calculation, in which case it was promoted as a discipline for passion. For some seventeenth-century commentators the notion of interest implied a fundamentally egoistic self, while others emphasized its etymological sense as *inter esse*, or being in-between, implicated in the affairs of others. Seventeenth-century romance might seem fairly narrow in its social reference, confining itself mainly to conventional stories of princes in love, but at midcentury it was exploring all these meanings for interest and more. Romance might suggest that the embrace of interest as a guide for action could conduce to virtue by curbing our most self-indulgent passions, or it might try to save a version of the autonomous sovereign self that did not by definition violate others. Still alternatively, it might argue that once we recognize the self-interest at the heart of our old models for love and friendship we must recognize ourselves as hypocrites. At its most radical, I will show, the genre reached toward an argument that the real measure of virtue was the extent to which the self serves the interests of another, even while finding itself unable to deny that self-interest was the most basic motivator of human behavior.

My argument for romance's turn toward relationship in the mid-seventeenth century runs against the standard history of the genre, in which early modern romance inherits from the medieval period an ostensibly feminine ethos of love and pity that is then overcome in the seventeenth century by narrative fiction's revalorization of more rigorous epic *pietas*.[38] In fact, as I will suggest in Chapter 2, as early as Ariosto romance had already brought pity into question, not for being too soft but rather for its hypocritical implication in self-interest. And if in the seventeenth century high epic was turning away from sociality, at the same time, as the less-canonical narratives treated in this book suggest, romance was already performing a critique of epic's rather belated response, implicating not only pity but heroic pietas as well in self-interest and searching for a construct of virtue it could endorse as more authentic. An understanding of prose romance's negotiations with politic ideas also complicates our histories of seventeenth-century English culture on several other, related fronts. To histories of the subject that argue for the emergence of an increasingly private, interiorized, and autonomous bourgeois self at about the time of the Restoration, midcentury romance would counter that the self's individual interests might be particular but were certainly not obscure, and that ethical life, at least, relied on the company of particular others.[39] Similarly, seventeenth-century romance offers an alternative to the Foucauldian paradigm of the self's construction of the other, so influentially stated by Stephen Greenblatt, as either entirely alien or identical (the self's ultimate goal according to this logic being to come to greater definition of itself), to suggest instead that the other might be simply proximate and that her interests (distinct from the self's, but not necessarily opposite or incomprehensible) might warrant attention as ends in themselves.[40]

Romance's involvement with politic ideas in the seventeenth century also has wide-ranging implications for our histories of self-interest as an idea. The fullest account to date of the new humanism, by Richard Tuck, reads politic ideas about self-interest forward into what it defines as their logical culmination, the Hobbesian notion of the state as a means for disciplining the individual self.[41] Meanwhile, canonical histories of self-interest generally open with the concept's high moment in the Scottish Enlightenment, casting an eye back toward the late seventeenth century as a period of origins. In these accounts the first French and English response to self-interest was resistance, which was challenged at the turn of the century by the increasing rationalization of the economic sphere (i.e., the sense that commerce, like nature, was governed by the immutable law of interest outside of any considerations of morality) and then definitively superseded by the establishment of interest as the most basic possession of the liberal subject.[42] The narrative link between Tuck's account and such conventional histories is prose romance: it shows us that self-interest as an idea was in near-continuous debate in England from the 1590s on and that it inspired far more than merely rudimentary and fragmented ethical reflection. In my view, romance also serves as evidence against the assumption shared by historians both of the new humanism and of the concept of self-interest (which happens to dovetail with the less precise but widespread arguments about the emergence of the bourgeois liberal humanist subject at about the time of the Restoration) that both ideologies led necessarily to the increasing consolidation of the individual subject. Certainly there is evidence for this conclusion, but seventeenth-century romance suggests that reflection about self-interest might just as significantly produce a sense of the self's ethical investment in others, and a notion of identity based as much in relationship as in self-discipline.

In closing I want to offer a few words about my relative neglect of politics in the most traditional sense of the term, which would seem more obviously the subject of these often explicitly topical allegories. Blair Worden has definitively demonstrated the depth and complexity of political meaning in Sidney's *Arcadia,* but even this admirably exhaustive reading would be enriched by a fuller consideration of romance's generic history.[43] In reading Sidney's inheritors, as may perhaps be clear by now, attention to genre seems even more crucial. Although Patterson must be correct that the allegorical nature of midcentury romance was intended to some extent to head off censorship, the correspondence between fact and fiction in these often manifestly transparent allegories is not formally very interesting in itself, nor, as Nigel Smith has noted, is there much to say about the explicit formulations of Royalist ideology in a romance such as Herbert's *Cloria.*[44] In the 1640s and 1650s romance did not for the most part try to develop a theory of the public or common interest (Harrington's *Oceana* is the obvious exception), engage political arguments against Royalism, or establish the principles on which a stable monarchy might be established. Rather, it took up the very timely question of interest in relation to issues the generic conventionality of which can mislead us into underestimating their potential for broad significance—erotic love, royal succession, and sovereign heroism. Sometimes romance's meditations on ethics did have obvious political applications, and sometimes its narratives about love and friendship gestured at Royalist political allegory, for instance, as I will discuss in Chapter 4, *Parthenissa*'s and *Aretina*'s stories of broken obligation. But for the most part romance's most energetic and complex arguments did not reduce simply or only to political allegory; on the contrary, as I have already suggested, political allegory in romance was itself one of the genre's several objects of ethical exploration, and we miss much of romance's point (as Barclay and Wroth cannot stop reminding us) if we read factual history too simplistically as its key.

I would add, finally, that romance's Royalism complicated as an aspect of its ethical exploration t of its one-to-one political allegory. Sidney beque a somewhat contradictory set of politics: he and versed in republican texts, and they looked back w republican Harrington would after them) to an e racy had more power in relation to the monarch; but at the Sidney's militant Protestantism sought ever-greater power for the virtuous queen, who at least theoretically could achieve an influence in this area not open to other political parties. *Argenis* would echo Sidney's political position explicitly in its powerful attraction to the political ideal of absolute monarchy even as it allowed ample space for the critique of tyranny, and *Urania* and midcentury romance would recast Sidney's political ideology in moral terms in order to suggest that the lover was a kind of tyrant or to criticize heroism as a form of social isolationism. The comedy of failed succession in *Pandion and Amphigenia*, or *Aretina*'s hint through some of its darker subplots that we necessarily fail our ethical obligations to others, or *Cloria*'s lesson in negotiation and self-discipline for its would-be monarch—each of these espouses a Royalism that could hardly be called uncomplicated. Through their ambivalences and complexities they translated Sidney's Tacitean, politic heritage for a new context, demonstrating the reach of reason of state theory and the extraordinary persistence of romance's talent for self-ironization.

Chapter 1

Allegory, Constancy, and the Politic Agent

Sidney's *Arcadia,* I suggested in the introduction, set up an association between romance and late sixteenth-century politic ideology by means of the basic facts pertaining to its production: that it was a politically coded narrative by the preeminent member of a family associated with the new humanism. But the link between romance and politic ideas that *Arcadia* bequeathed to seventeenth-century thought also had more substantive textual grounds. By presenting the providential design that wrapped up its plot as manifestly problematic, neither quite fair nor quite within the realm of the probable, *Arcadia* obliquely confirmed what readers would already suspect from reading the rest of the romance, that providence and the kind of romantic love that traditionally cemented social alliances at the ends of such narratives were only last-minute rationalizations for self-interested desire. Modern politic romance, Sidney taught his successors, could be self-conscious about its own generic conventions, ever aware that they were only fictions to cover up uncomfortable truths.

But *Arcadia* was not merely, or not only, demystificatory; even while offering the politic secret that love and providence were ideological fictions, it advised its characters and readers to assent publicly to them. If this double-sided recommendation, at once to believe and not to believe, was in its own context a canny solution to the problem of self-interest, it was also the source of a generative ethical uncertainty that was to become the central problem of seventeenth-century romance. According to the conventional humanist ideology of the late sixteenth century, self-interest was a form of passion, perhaps even the primary passion, manifested in a simple, self-serving urge to possess that in civil societies was curbed by the more communally oriented calculus of reason. From the very start *Arcadia* declined to endorse reason's power, expressing little faith in reason's ability to trump the self-interested desire that Sidney seemed to see almost everywhere he looked. But this did not necessarily mean a subject had to give himself over to passion's single-minded brutishness; instead, *Arcadia* argued, the enlightened courtier would construe self-interest in the politic way, as the secret everybody knows but no one actually speaks, and thereby put his self-interested desire at a safe and useful distance.

It is difficult to emphasize enough the impact on later romance of the space Sidney's treatment of self-interest opened up. In the most general terms *Arcadia* helped to enable a notion of interestedness as prudential calculation rather than as simply a rush to self-gratification, and thereby to make available the possibility of an agent directed by, rather than captive to, her own desire. But it also spurred in romance a flood of ethical debate, as writers in the seventeenth century found Sidney's knowing pretense untenable in the face of a problem that would come to seem so ubiquitous it could not be hidden. In response, romances from the 1620s all the way to the 1660s adopted a remarkably similar tack: spurning *Arcadia*'s pretense, they sustained its formal self-consciousness in order to take up directly, both thematically and also as a matter for romance's generic form, the ethical difficulties of self-interest.

Sidney's most meticulous and thorough respondent was Wroth, who set her 1621 *Urania* in a politic world that had taken entirely to heart *Arcadia*'s double lesson that self-interest is everywhere and that our claim to passivity in the face of providence or love is a useful lie. Wroth's initial innovation was that she refused to be complicit, on grounds I defined in the introduction as moral rather than ethical—not so much because it hurts others to be dissembled to as because complicity leads to self-deception, and self-deception to fatuous pride. As an alternative to Sidney's ironic blindness, Wroth developed for the subject a self-image at a precise remove from its self-interested desire, far enough to prohibit identificatory, narcissistic self-love, yet not so far as to permit dissimulation of that desire to itself or others. This moral-psychological response to the problem of self-interest translated in formal literary terms into a valorization of the literal, the letter or the image, as an end in itself, which Wroth realized by loosening the ties of her roman à clef form both to its real-life, biographical referents and to its conceptual meaning. Ultimately, I argue in the conclusion to this chapter, this construal of the literal as its own end was Wroth's most important revision of Sidney, as it recast self-interest as merely a subject for fiction, rather than as fiction's problematic motivation, and helped to define the romance writer as someone other than an ironic dissembler.

1. Acquisitive Desire and Agency in Sidney's *Arcadia*

Sidney's complex response to the politic problem of self-interest, I have suggested, not only primed romance to summon the problem of interest in all its seventeenth-century manifestations but also set up the terms in which the genre thought about love, virtue, and sociality for the next seven or eight decades. One of Sidney's basic tasks in his romance was to explore the problem of *cupiditas,* what we might call "acquisitive desire," the desire to obtain an object, which aims above all at self-gratification. An ancient formulation that in the late sixteenth century had new, politic resonances, cupiditas, both classically and in the Renaissance, took most readily the form its name suggests, of eros. Especially in the *Old Arcadia,* before his sister edited it for sexual decorum, but also in the *New Arcadia,* Sidney famously brought to the foreground the problem of cupiditas as eros.[1] In the *Old Arcadia* Pyrocles consummates his love for Philoclea before they are married (in the *New Arcadia* they spend the night chastely sleeping together), an event set up by an episode early in the romance (in both versions) when the prince slays a lion that was chasing Philoclea and then assumes the pursuit of the still-fleeing princess himself, along the way taking the time to appreciate how delightfully Philoclea's clothes have been lifted by the wind so that "much of those beauties she would at another time have willingly hidden were presented to the eye of the twice-wounded [Pyrocles]."[2] "Twice-wounded" drives home the point that Philoclea and the lion are in analogous relation to Pyrocles, that by means of a sly reversal the prince has shifted from pursuer to prey. Philoclea, as the second child of Arcadia's duke Basilius, is not a political prize for Pyrocles, who does not need a throne as he is already the Macedonian king Euarchus's heir, and this is part of the reason why the sex between them can be mutually pleasurable when it occurs. By contrast, Pyrocles' cousin Musidorus, over whom Pyrocles is "chiefer" (*OA* 9), has a greater need to marry up, and after his elopement in the *Old Arcadia* with Philoclea's sister and I heir Pamela, his own near-consummation of his desire on he ing body is accordingly presented as an attempted rape, foile by the arrival on the scene of some symbolically unruly commoners. And at the end of both versions of the romance, as if (in the first version) Musidorus's attempted crime has served as a gloss on what we might before have been tempted to interpret merely as a love scene between Pyrocles and Philoclea, both princes are declared by the judge Euarchus guilty of "ravishment"—a word that denotes sexual abduction—for attempting to take the princesses "from him that ow[n]ed [them], which was [their] father."[3] Political ambition, we are told, is analogous to, and indeed even actualized in, the impulse (in the first version) to rape or at least (in the second) to lay sexual claim, which is problematic not because it fails to consider the desires of the object but because it takes no account of others' claims to ownership and rushes headlong toward self-gratification.[4]

By figuring acquisitive desire as eros culminating in the drive to rape, Sidney expresses several of desire's most significant limitations within an early modern context. To begin with, rape, like Cupid, is blind, expressing an inability to see, or at least to recognize, other people. Like the Renaissance tyrant, the rapist lives in a society of one, simply appropriating what he wants rather than engaging in the negotiations required by a social system with mutual obligations and responsibilities. One of the ironic by-products of acquisitive desire, as its translation into the act of rape makes clear, is a devaluing of the object. Raped, Sidney's Pamela would lose her price on the market as a potential wife, and thus would be removed from circulation even more definitively than the tyrant's hoarded wealth. Outside of a social framework, we learn from Renaissance treatments of miserliness, objects lose their value. Spenser's figure of the miser Malbecco in Book 3 of *The Faerie Queene* suggests how the miser's acquisitive desire in turn makes the miser himself a mere shell, destroyed by his antisocial compulsion to hoard.

This self-defeating aspect of acquisitive desire, held at bay in the *Old Arcadia* by Pamela's last-minute rescue (though explored at length by John Crowne seventy years later in *Pandion and Amphigenia*, as I discuss in Chapter 4), is paralleled by the notion that cupiditas makes its characteristic subject, the would-be tyrant, into its slave. The canonical expression of this idea is *Arcadia*'s near-contemporary *The Rape of Lucrece*, in which the tyrannical Tarquin gives in to his lust to appropriate Collatine's possession, his wife, Lucrece, and finds that the real victim is his own soul, which has been inflicted with a wound that can never heal.[5] Overweening acquisitive desire, Shakespeare suggests by a familiar paradox, would seem to be a measure of the tyrant's power over other people, but in fact it signifies his inability to govern himself and, by metaphoric extension, other people too.[6] Sidney makes this point in *Arcadia* as well, in a comic rather than a tragic vein, when he has Pyrocles transform himself into a woman and Musidorus into a shepherd to get access to the princesses. To some extent these disguises are provoked by Basilius's withdrawal of his marriageable daughters to Arcadia, but Sidney also draws on the conventional notion that erotic passion effeminizes and lowers its heroic masculine subjects by suborning their will, an idea borne out in the *Old Arcadia,* of course, by Musidorus's attempt to rape.

Such, then, is the trajectory of acquisitive desire, which Sidney evokes with accumulating seriousness in the *Old Arcadia* until suddenly, at the end of the romance, the princes' transgressions seem magically to disappear—in an apparent narrative lapse that is actually, I want to suggest, Sidney's way both of highlighting and at least partly solving the problem.[7] Gynecia and Basilius, parents of the princesses, have each succumbed to cupiditas in their lust for Pyrocles, who Basilius believes is a woman. In order to block Basilius's tryst with Pyrocles and secure her own access to the prince, Gynecia has administered her husband a sleeping potion that by mistake seems to have killed him. When at the end of the narrative the king Euarchus (who also happens to be Pyrocles' father and Musidorus's uncle), arrives in the rulerless kingdom to judge Gynecia guilty of the duke of Arcadia's murder and to sentence her to death, Basilius wakes up and Gynecia is exonerated. But along the way the death sentence Euarchus has levied on Pyrocles and Musidorus for their acts of "heinous ravishment" is also entirely forgotten, and the chastened Basilius bestows on the princes instead the princesses they were earlier accused of trying to steal. The lesson of this story, the narrator tells us, is the moral power of providence, which in a world of "uncertain . . . mortal judgements" matches dramatic result to characters' original intention with much greater precision (416). According to narrative decorum, providence is reasserted here as poetic justice, restoring Gynecia's crime to the familial realm where it initially belonged as intention and where it can be matched and then cancelled by Basilius's own adulterous desires.

At first it might seem that the narrative also means to bundle the princes' transgressions into this plot, that Gynecia's return to comedy after her brief detour into tragedy is supposed to bring the princes along too. Against the grand scheme of providence, we might conclude, such human faults as acquisitive desire are essentially trivial. Like Gynecia the princes meant no real harm; perhaps they expressed their desires too vehemently, but their impulses matched providence's own trajectory, and the manifest justice of the providential end subsumes any mistakes in execution along the way. If we look more closely, however, this reading cannot entirely be sustained. Between Sidney's two plots there is a distinction in kinds of cupiditas: Basilius and Gynecia are comically deluded, and as a result their passions are absurd, unable to move their shared object and therefore powerless to do any real damage. Basilius's fatuous lust may confirm his unfitness to rule, demonstrated already in his decision to retire to Arcadia's forests, but in itself it has no real consequences in the public realm. The princes' passions, however, are not absurd at all, as their subsequent marriages to the princesses will prove; rather than being deluded, they see quite clearly that in a familial context they are appropriate husbands for the princesses, and in the public, political realm entirely plausible replacements for Basilius. Thus, their impulse to steal what they want is far more destabilizing than Gynecia's lust. And *Arcadia* does signal this distinction, not by any explicit statement but through its silence. Providence awards Basilius a fake death for his intentions, Gynecia a near-execution, but the princes' ravishment receives no providential rebuke, not even an ironic nod, nor does the narrator let them off the hook with any statement equivalent to his remark that Gynecia's fate proves the uncertainty of mortal judgments (416). The princes get what they want, yet without any explicit transition from guilt to fulfillment, as if the narrative is admitting its inability to fill this moral gap.

What does occupy the narrative space between Basilius's awakening and the concluding reference to the princes' marriages and heirs, rather than any expiation for or even mention of their intended crime, is a romance in miniature, the history of the sleeping potion that has caused so much trouble. Gynecia's grandmother, a "notably learned" princess of Cyprus, unable just like the princes to govern her passion and "answer the objections of Cupid," "did furiously love" a young nobleman of the court, who himself did not "dar[e] either to attempt or accept so high a place." To change his mind the princess concocted and administered the sleeping potion, had her beloved carried into a secret garden, and when he woke told him that unless he eloped with her she would publicly accuse him, in a direct allusion to Musidorus's and Pyrocles' purported crime, of attempting to "ravish" her.[8] The nobleman could find no alternative but to obey—"her beauty prevailed," says the narrator wryly—and eventually the couple was reconciled to the king, "after whose death they reigned" (415–16).

This miniature romance is the story of a man who, like Musidorus, marries onto the throne rather than acceding to it directly, and more importantly who seems to do so unwillingly, or at least without having to will it himself. As such it both recapitulates and revises the larger story that frames it. The love of the learned princess functions here in the same way providence does in the main narrative, displacing political and erotic agency so that the would-be prince is preserved from any accusation that he intended to steal what was not his by right. Perhaps Sidney meant by this repetition in miniature to draw our attention to the generic aspect of his narrative trick, to show us that it is the task of romance, which can fairly be summed up as a story of love governed by providence, to gloss over acquisitive desire and render its subjects harmless. By this argument romance would be a kind of social glue, a mode of acknowledging and at the same time redefining such potentially dangerous forces as political ambition as part of an elaborate and ultimately benign game.

But Gynecia's story would also seem to offer two other, more substantive and pointed lessons. First, by intensifying our sense of providence's, and romance's, artificiality, the inset story insists that acquisitive desire is everywhere, that Pyrocles and Musidorus are representative of us all. Whether he admits to it or not, Gynecia's learned princess says to her apparently reluctant lover, he has no choice but to be a usurper. Even the least (apparently) rapacious of princes is driven by his own interests, and if providence and love as conventionally understood are lies, what is left to lead him to the prize but his own desire? The other, more complex lesson concerns how to accommodate this acquisitive desire. Gynecia's princess teaches all would-be Musidorus figures—which we now know means everyone, or at least everyone who does not already have what he wants—that rape is the tactic of the foolish, weak usurper, the tyrant in training, who violently appropriates the objects of his desires because he cannot control his own passions. Far cannier, and more powerful, to recast usurpation as the accession to someone else's will—especially someone, as in this example, who insofar as she is virtuous is supposed culturally not to have much of a will, at least in the public sphere, and who thus functions as a nearly ideal cover.

Sidney probably meant here only to come up with a way of managing the acquisitive desire he could not see his way clear to denying, but the result is that in *Arcadia* he opened a suggestive space for agency. The tyrannical usurper may look like an agent, but really, we know, he is a slave to his passions, while the hereditary prince is the lucky pawn of providential order. But the educated Musidorus-figure, made wise by Sidney's lesson in politic prudence, can get what he wants even if he has not been ordained by birth order or some other manifestation of divine providence to receive it, and all without giving himself up to lust. To dissemble one's desire by hitching it to someone else's, by way of a brilliant sleight of hand on Sidney's part, is to separate oneself slightly from it, to loosen its hold and thus open a space for rational calculation that is at the same time—paradoxically, according to an old humanist ideology that puts reason and cupiditas on either side of a great divide—self-interested. And this is just the space of politic agency. The self-interested agent as Sidney imagines him is acquisitive but not quite passionate, liberated from grand providential design and also, by his dissembling, from the passions of others, which are now instrumental but never governing. In a new way, we can say, the agent has become free, responsible mainly to his own gratification. At the same time, in this capacity he is mainly secret. Cloaked in others' desires, he always dissembles his own ends, which perhaps, as the silent passivity of Gynecia's would-be prince suggests, he may not be able to speak even to himself. In effect *Arcadia* arrives at agency by taking what was for a long time a troublesome aspect of human will, acquisitive desire, and universalizing it, then hiding it from view.

Agency in Sidney is that which we cannot see but nonetheless know to be true—the most powerfully mystificatory kind of secret, which by definition operates just outside our ability to grasp it. Such a construction of agency was not at this time unique to Sidney, or to romance; Shakespeare's Iago, whom we might read as an extended meditation on this notion of self-interested agency that wraps itself in others' passions even while its motivations seem to remain opaque to the agent himself, is sufficient evidence to the contrary. But for Sidney, romance was integral to the formulation of self-interested agency, through its offer of a generic self-consciousness that Sidney extended to serve as a critique of romance's own premises, thereby leaving us in turn to posit politic agency as a first principle. By this linking of romance to questions of agency in a way that was not incidental but formative, both for romance and for the concept of agency in the period, *Arcadia* became the definitive modern ancestor of seventeenth-century romance, a precursor for all notions of interest and agency insofar as they would be connected to providence and acquisitive desire.

2. The Influence of Sidney: Wroth's *Urania*

If *Arcadia*'s conclusion asked readers to acquiesce to self-conscious artifice, to accept the romance's conventionally comedic ending as a sufficient answer to self-interest's disruptive power, by the early seventeenth century romance had begun to look more squarely at acquisitive desire, and in its anxieties and adaptations would reveal the truly destabilizing nature of the cultural ideas to which *Arcadia* was responding. To begin with an entirely canonical example (a narrative that probably had little direct connection to *Arcadia* but greatly influenced subsequent English romance), one of the complex rewards of reading *Don Quixote* (1605 and 1616) is to watch the ironic Sidneian balance with which Cervantes opens disintegrate in myriad ways. *Don Quixote* seems at first to argue for the benefits of a double outlook: we may have sympathy and admiration for what we read, as the priest's half-accomplished inquisition on Don Quixote's books demonstrates, but to believe it to be representative of pragmatic and self-interested modern society is ridiculous. What proves Don Quixote insane is not only that he acts as if what he reads is real, but also, more specifically, that he believes simply because his books tell him so that he was put on the earth to alleviate others' suffering. Here self-interest's opposite is not providence but the idea that we should sacrifice our own interests (in Quixote's case, a comfortable village life free from pain and want) to help others. At first Cervantes makes it easy to laugh at Don Quixote's absolute refusal to temper his idealist ideology with any recognition of the world's moral ambiguities, since his idealism requires him to remake in his mind what he sees all around him. But as the romance continues the hero's idealism comes to look less absurd. At the end of book 1, put in a cage by his affectionate neighbors to protect him from the harm to himself he seems actively to court, Don Quixote explains to Sancho that he must believe in the kind of evil magic that locks knights in cages, as in his own never-ending quest to thwart it, because otherwise he would have to confront a truth too horrible to accept: the casual indifference with which the average person ignores others' suffering in order to continue pursuing his own ends.[9] At some level Quixote understands that there are two contradictory ways to see the world, but his realization does not align him with the priest, the narrator, and all the other people in the world who love his idealism and yet laugh at its impracticality. Rather, Don Quixote advocates here what we might call a sincere lie; instead of hiding self-interest in plain view he banishes it from the world, and thus maintains—insanely, but in intention truly—a moral integrity to which Sidney's doubleness cannot lay claim.

Seventeenth-century English romance, we might say, picked up where the first book of *Don Quixote* ended, with the idea that although it may be insane to deny the reality of self-interest all around us, to go on to accept it may be immoral. Sidney's double view became in seventeenth-century romance not a solution but the expression of a problem, one that had to be addressed if the genre was not to come to an end with the kind of cutting insight Don Quixote offers (or would, if we weren't licensed to call him insane). Within the generic trajectory of romance there were two broad responses: to purge romance of its reflectiveness and generic self-consciousness, rendering internal irony impossible and thereby relieving the genre of any responsibility for revising its ironic approach to self-interest; or, more interestingly, to approach self-interest head-on. The first was the strategy adopted by the strand of romance that in form descended especially from Italian *novelle,* in which self-consciousness was often absent not merely from the characters but seemingly from the entire narrative. Whether deliberate or naïve, this turn away from the politic implications of *Arcadia* produced at its extreme something close to what we would now call "genre fiction," narratives so formulaic that they seem, at least in retrospect, to lack content. Examples might include the anonymous *Clidamas: A Sicilian Tale* (1639), heavily indebted to *Arcadia* in its plot, and some of the romances of Emanuel Forde, which remained popular throughout the seventeenth century but are what contemporary critics often have in mind when they dismiss seventeenth-century romance as an insignificant or exhausted genre. The second response might seem at first even more naïve: here, narrator and characters alike rejected Sidney's double view, taking on the ethical problems attendant on self-interest directly, as matters of explicit thematic concern, and with great sincerity. This move to an open investigation of self-interest and politic irony set up the wide-ranging and complex consideration of interest in midcentury romance; it can be traced most explicitly in Wroth's *Urania,* which at moments reads almost like a direct commentary on Sidney's ideas.

Urania raises the problem of self-interested agency most directly in the parable-like account of the princess Urania's conversion and rebirth, a narrative that clearly sets forth the romance's reading of politic ideology as moral dilemma. In the romance's very first episode Urania falls in love with the wrong man, one already under obligation to another woman, and several hundred pages later, at the direction of a benevolent sorceress, her brother Amphilanthus throws her off a cliff into enchanted water in order to erase such misdirected passion from her mind. Shortly afterward, while she is describing to Amphilanthus her sympathy for another friend who has also been crossed in love, her brother interjects, "'This . . . (by your favour sweete sister) prooves you love; the water it seemes, hath not so thorowly washed away your affection, but reliques remaine of the old passion.' 'No truly dearest brother,'" she replies, "'all those thoughts are cleane droun'd; but yet; I will goe on with my story.' 'Doe deare Sister,'" says Amphilanthus wryly, "'and begin againe at (But yet).' She blusht to find he had taken her, and yet daintily proceeded."[10] After Urania falls in love again, this time with the man who is to be her husband, she is discussing her passion one day with her cousin Philistella when Philistella suddenly says, "Let me be bold to aske this question; In this heate of love, did not your former passion never come glancing into your eyes? could you behold Parselius [the new love] with freedome, and Steriamus [the old] with affection?" Urania's reply is worth quoting at length for its remarkable ambivalence:

> "I will," said Urania, "(as to my confessor) tell you the truth; it was mee thought a wonderfull odde change, and passing different affection I did feele, when I did alter: for though I were freed from my first love, and had a power to choose againe, yet was I not so amply cured from memorie, but that I did resemble one newly come out of a vision, distracted, scarce able to tell, whether it were a fixion, or the truth; yet I resolved, and so by force of heavenly providence lost the first, and live in second choice, and this deare soveraigne good received I from Leucadia [where she was thrown into the water]." (331–2)

Through its main protagonist and Wroth-figure, the queen Pamphilia, *Urania* argues for the virtue of erotic constancy above all, and here the narrative clearly tries to sidestep the moral difficulties of Urania's change of heart by effecting it, in good romance fashion, via magic. But Wroth's characters also remain alert to the inadequacies of such a solution and want to press Urania on the role her own will plays in her change. Although he has earlier dropped her from the cliff with intense gravity, Amphilanthus now turns the issue into a joke at his sister's expense, "taking" her by leading her to qualify her own assertion that the magic sufficed to erase her love and then by drawing attention to her tacit admission. As in *Arcadia*, for Amphilanthus the assertion of human will over against providence is the secret everybody recognizes and enacts but nobody wants to admit. Passivity is only a cover for self-interest, a story Urania tells in public to maintain her reputation for virtue.

If Amphilanthus could be said to adopt here Sidney's overall strategy of recasting skepticism as an inside joke, Philistella, in a correspondence the gendered nature of which is probably not mere coincidence, mirrors *Urania*'s tendency to bring skepticism out in to the open. "Bold" in her curiosity, Philistella wonders if the waters really worked as a method of conversion, and Urania tries to answer her just as sincerely. In a series of pained contradictions and ambivalences, Urania explains that she has "received" her change, her "deare soveraigne good," by means of "heavenly providence," but on the other hand she has had to "resolve" (tellingly, she avoids assigning an object to this verb), and her love has been a matter of "choice." In her confusion over whether "it were a fixion, or the truth," "it" is ambiguous: is it her previous love, as she will shortly assert to Philistella, that was fictional, or is it the enchantment, as her ambivalence seems to suggest? As in *Arcadia,* the women characters in this episode cannot resist the realist insight that human will and agency have a large part in making plot happen, and they too suspect that at least part of the time providence's power is just a screen. Unlike *Arcadia* and Amphilanthus, however, and at least partly because change in love is so morally loaded an issue for women in an ideological context that defines them as irrational, bodily, and variable beings, Urania and Philistella cannot afford the luxury of framing this insight as a joke. For both women the questions of what the will can do and to what extent it can be defined as virtuous are to be puzzled over and brought into conversation, approached with seriousness and anxiety.

By this surprisingly precise rewriting of *Arcadia*'s concluding fable, Wroth recasts Sidney's ending as her own starting point. The would-be prince's passivity in the face of what looks like astonishingly good fortune, Wroth concedes to Sidney's text, cannot but be a screen for his pursuit of self-interest, and if this is true we cannot really believe that Urania's change is entirely the result of magic. But at the same time we must not simply wink at Urania's self-interest, because self-interest, as Urania conveys through her anxious hesitations and self-contradictions, is truly inadmissible—not just publicly or politically, because it might do damage to one's reputation and influence, but morally, in the sense that it vitiates the humility and self-abnegation on which women's characters are supposed to be founded in the world of *Urania.* To admit self-interest would be to claim not quite cupiditas (which *Urania* suggests is gendered masculine) but instead a sufficiency or autonomy of self in the face of God and men, a form of pride *Urania* cannot countenance. At the same time, Wroth also balks at the possibility of feminine self-abnegation with a vehemence that is close to feminist, in our modern sense. When Pamphilia cries to Urania that if she manages to go on after being jilted by her duplicitous lover she will prove that her love was "not for his sake, but mine owne" (470), Urania insists in effect that she would welcome some self-interest from her cousin, that Pamphilia must govern her passions like the self-sufficient queen she is and remember that the preservation of her health, beauty, and powers of judgment is more important than any lover (467–9). This sentiment, while it suits our modern individualist and feminist sympathies, also helps illuminate the stakes of giving up politic self-interest; sometimes, Wroth suggests, the alternative is not an eventually benign providence but the opposed interests of another person, and in this scenario traditional virtue may be equivalent to a loss of self.

Wroth's task in *Urania,* then, is to come up with a form of self-interest that steers between self-loss and too much self by means other than Sidney's ironic double view. Thematically she achieves this through her extended revision of feminine constancy, which she indicts for being if not a form of self-abnegation then potentially only another version of Sidney's fake passivity, and which she tries to salvage by developing for her characters a slightly distanced but not quite ironic self-regard. Formally her response is to adapt roman à clef so that it leaves Sidney's irony behind, a strategy by which she addresses in particular the problem of authorship's moral status, especially pointed for a woman in seventeenth-century English society but philosophically difficult for anyone in this period worrying about the link between agency and self-interest. I will elaborate these approaches to the problem of self-interest in a moment, but first I want to turn to a theoretical discussion of Renaissance allegory, in order to make clearer Wroth's range of options (and the range of options for later romance as well) in revising *Arcadia*'s compromise.

3. ALLEGORY AND IRONY

Broadly speaking, the post-Romantic critical tradition has tended to condemn literary allegory for drastically narrowing the space left to the literal, the images and plot the writer conjures on the page. Allegory, it is said, moves us straight to the conceptual, or, less often but by a similar logic, straight to history. Too much occupied with idea, or too slavishly devoted to fact, by this still mainly Coleridgean logic literary allegory makes no room for the exercise of the imagination, either writer's or reader's, and as such it is not really literature. It is a commonplace in popular criticism, and one related to this line of thinking, that fiction should make a world of its own, an alternative convincing in its complexity and depth, that fiction (or literature) finds its identity in its distinction from fact (or history). Of course, however, it is also one of literature's constitutive functions not just to *be* but to *refer,* both to conceptual meaning and to the material or historical reality to which it is related, and insofar as allegory's most basic function, literally, "other speaking" (*allos agoreuein,* speaking outside of the public assembly or the marketplace), is to express one thing by means of another, it seems fair to say that every literary work (indeed all language) is allegorical.[11]

For my purposes in this book, I want to define allegorical praxis, most generally, as the establishing of a literal realm (i.e., the fiction itself, the images and plot that the poet makes) that is primarily in relation to something else, rather than a world unto itself. In the early modern period, while imagination as such was still held to have a dubious moral value, this praxis was largely understood to encompass (though not to be exhausted by) what we now call the literary. Fiction (or, in early modern terms, "poesy") was significant, indeed definable as such, insofar as it gestured elsewhere, away from itself. And the elsewhere toward which it gestured, as we might expect from the view of allegory I outlined above, was broadly divisible into two kinds of knowledge: philosophy and history. In Francis Bacon's *De Augmentis Scientarum* (1623), to cite one of the most famous expressions of this idea, all poesy excluding drama can be separated into two kinds—either parabolical (Bacon's adjectival form for "parable"), in which "objects of the intellect are represented in forms that are objects of the sense"; or narrative, the "mere imitation of History," departing from "such as might pass for real" only by its tendency toward heroical exaggeration.[12] Poesy, that is, is an allegory either for intellectual concepts (in Bacon and in the work of most early modern theorists, usually moral-philosophical ones, teaching its readers to love virtue and shun vice) or for the facts and events of history. We can see the dominance of this model in the fact that during the mid-seventeenth century in England, by far the most popular forms of original prose fiction were the highly conceptual theological allegory (represented by John Bunyan's *Pilgrim's Progress* or Nathaniel Ingelo's *Bentivolio and Urania*) and roman à clef romance. Rather than reading romance in opposition to what in our terms is both the more purely fictional and the more realistic novel, I want to suggest, we should understand seventeenth-century romance as allegorical fiction located on a continuum between the conceptual and the historical, negotiating between and trying to carve out its own understanding of poesy's relation to these two poles.

Another opposition all allegorical fiction had to negotiate in the early modern period, one that proceeded from a different but related set of meanings for allegory, was that between identification and irony. In the long tradition of theological hermeneutics, allegory was chiefly polysemic, its multiple senses, though distinct, all pointing toward a single, unified meaning, and in the early modern period secular allegory frequently drew on this model; Spenser's Una, her name, clothing, and behavior all coinciding to convey the idea she is supposed to represent, would be a paradigmatic example. But the late sixteenth century also inherited from medieval roman à clef a habit of thinking about allegory as ironic, as expressing meaning either obliquely or by contrast, and this was the tradition seized upon by politic ideology, as is easily traceable in rhetoric manuals of the period. In the second, 1593 edition of *The Garden of Eloquence,* for example, Henry Peacham likened metaphors to "the starres of the skie," which "in respect of their perspicuitie, & light which they give" are "both the comfort of the night, and the beautie of the firmament."[13] Allegory, conventionally, was continued metaphor, "a signe compounded of many stars," or constellation, offering order in the midst of obscurity and serving as a navigational tool by which a reader might chart his course (27). In his dedication of the second edition to the politician Sir John Puckering, Lord Keeper of the Seale, however, Peacham employed a different metaphorical logic, promising that eloquence would bring "into open light" "the deepe understanding, the secret counselles, & politicke considerations of wisedome" with which Puckering was presumably occupied (AB3r). Darkness here is not an absence of wisdom but the place where wisdom begins, and figurative language, correspondingly, is not darkness's conqueror but its servant, making intelligible to the public its profound secrets. Peacham tactfully presumed in this dedication that Puckering's secrets were virtuous, thus releasing himself from having to consider any potential discontinuity between Puckering's intentions and the eloquent words Peacham was promising to help him employ.

George Puttenham's *The Arte of English Poesie,* first published in 1589, was not nearly as sanguine about its courtiers' intentions. Puttenham opens his third book, "Of Ornament," by comparing "figures and figurative speaches" to the cosmetics that "great Madames of honour" put on their lips and cheeks, and defines allegory, the "captaine of all the figures," as the "Figure of false semblant."[14] "The Courtly figure *Allegoria,*" says Puttenham,

> is when we speake one thing and thinke another, and that our wordes and our meanings meete not. The use of this figure is so large, and his vertue of so great efficacie as it is supposed no man can pleasantly utter and perswade without it, but in effect is sure never or very seldome thrive and prosper in the world, that cannot skilfully put in ure [*si*
> in somuch as not onely every common Courtier, but also the grav

> Counsellour, yea and the most noble and wisest Prince of them all are many times enforced to use it, by example (say they) of the great Emperour who had it usually in his mouth to say, *Qui nescit dissimulare nescit regnare.* (155)

Allegory defines the all-important gap between intention and speech act, and as such it is an ubiquitous attribute of the politic court, a tool without which it is impossible not only to "utter and perswade" but also to "thrive and prosper." The Tacitean tag at the end of the passage, repeated again and again in the seventeenth century, signals the intellectual context for this view of allegory, and reminds us of the connection between allegory and power: it is the ruler of men who most appropriately and effectively uses this "captaine" of all rhetorical figures.

Puttenham's manual was explicitly a tool for social climbing, and at this point he still seems cheerful about the lessons he is offering; there is no irony in the use of the word "vertue" to describe allegory's usefulness as a tool for dissembling. But later in the manual he shows himself to be far more equivocal, even despairing, about the political process and the figurative language that makes it run. In the last chapter of the work Puttenham presents the personified figure of Poesy as a social-climbing artisan, claiming that in his rhetorical manual he has pulled his subject "first from the carte to the schoole, and from thence to the Court, and preferred him to your Maiesties service." Poesy has been sufficiently "apparelled . . . in all his gorgious habilliments" that he will not slip up and "shew . . . himself a craftsman, & merit to be disgraded, & with scorne sent back againe to the shop," but "worthily retaine the credit of his place, and profession of a very Courtier, which is in plaine termes, cunningly to be able to dissemble" (250). But Puttenham next reflects that courtly dissembling is not just a language game but has real stakes, and when extended to the field of political action the gap between word and act comes to have moral consequences, forcing us to call courtiers hypocrites. Therefore, he counsels Poesy to avoid real politics and restrict himself to dissembling "only in the subtilties of his arte." If he succeeds at this self-limitation, he "need no more be ashamed thereof, than a shomaker to have made a cleanly shoe, or a Carpenter to have buylt a faire house" (253). Poesy, it seems, is returned to the shop after all, until Puttenham reverses himself a final time, reflecting that the true (i.e., the noble or aristocratic) poet speaks not like the popinjay or the craftsman, "by imitation artificially," but rather "by observation naturally." If poetry has to be taught, Puttenham maintains, it is merely artifice. From this premise, Puttenham is forced to resort to the nonconclusion that "it is not altogether with him [Poesy] as with the crafts man, nor altogither [*sic*] otherwise then with the crafts man." The would-be poet should try to learn the art of rhetoric, but unlike the craftsman he should drastically restrict its use, aiming to be commended "more by knowing of his arte then by unseasonable using it" (256–7).

The problem of truth that poetic (i.e., allegorical) language poses here intersects in complex ways with problems of status and ethics. Allegory stands for or sums up all figurative language in the gap it apprehends between word and meaning; at the same time it also epitomizes the court, which is rhetorically corrupt because it is socially corrupt, its inhabitants routinely saying one thing when they mean another. For Puttenham, anyone who uses allegory meaningfully is by definition participating in this social corruption. He hopes briefly that the *imitation* of courtly language, which is in fact all that is open to his tradesman audience since they have no real access to the court, might in fact be an escape out of hypocrisy into virtue, a turn away from the efficacy of real dissembling, but he also realizes that such language has no actual referent and is therefore just artificial, words without sense, like those of a popinjay or mockingbird. The courtly context of allegory apparently makes it impossible that one might mean what one says, that allegory might be polysemic. Instead it is ironic, in one of two ways: either it is an inversion of what is ostensibly said, an inversion governed by the intention of the speaker, or it is non-sense, with no connection to intention or to meaning.

Puttenham's model in conceiving the relation between irony and allegory is Quintilian's *Institutio oratoria*, which presents irony as for the most part a subset of allegory. Allegory, says Quintilian, conveys one thing "by its words" and "a different or sometimes even a contrary thing by its sense," and irony describes that situation where the sense is exactly contrary to the words.[15] Puttenham too begins with a definition of allegory as the "captaine of all other figures" (155) because it describes the quintessential figurative situation of saying one thing and meaning another, and like Quintilian he argues that irony is a subset of allegory, that particular mode of allegorical "other speaking" in which what is said is not only other than but exactly opposite to what is meant. But as the conclusion to *The Arte of English Poesie* suggests, irony will not stay in that subordinate position for Puttenham, not when he has originally defined allegory as fundamentally a mode of "dissimulation." If allegory is essentially polysemic, as it is in all its classic definitions, including Quintilian's, then all of its senses should supplement or fulfill, not contradict, one another, and

Puttenham does acknowledge this conventional expectation. At the same time his emphasis on dissimulation recasts allegory itself as a form of antiphrasis, in which what is said can at the very best only equivocally be also what is meant. Not only, for Puttenham, do sense and words in allegory not coincide, but literal and allegorical sense often cannot both be true at the same time, so that allegory turns out not to be polysemic at all. In essence, insofar as allegory is a mode of dissimulation in *The Arte of English Poesie,* irony is not so much a subset of allegory as the umbrella category under which allegory fits.

In his point about the popinjay Puttenham also intuited an idea that became commonplace after Kierkegaard, that although irony may be determinate, what Wayne Booth calls "stable"—that is, intentional opposite-speaking, either for rhetorical effect or as a mode of lying—it can also describe instead a failure or refusal of referentiality or even of meaning.[16] In general, though, occupied as he was with rhetoric as social transaction, Puttenham took for granted that as rhetoricians we need concern ourselves only with determinate, not indeterminate, irony. With every utterance, he assumed, a speaker intends to convey a particular sense, and allegory should always be decodable by the right tools, which for Puttenham were enabled by social stature and the inside knowledge such stature brought. Puttenham's view of allegory as predominantly a social and political tactic is hardly standard to post-Romantic readers, but it does share some now-canonical literary-critical assumptions about allegory, as a comparison with Coleridge's famous distinction between allegory and symbol will suggest. In Coleridge, who seemed forgetful of allegory's prior historical modes of reference, allegory begins in the wrong place, with mere "abstract ideas" that can at best be merely "translated" into other, equally shadowy terms, never brought into contact with the real. As a result, allegory's literal sense is for the reader merely a means to an end, a "picture-language," as Coleridge calls it dismissively, conveying abstractions by one-to-one correspondence. His ostensibly new concept of the symbol, in contrast, bridges the space between the real and the ideational; it at once "partakes of the Reality" that it also "renders intelligible," "enunciates the whole" and also "abides itself as a living part of that Unity."[17] Whereas the relation between the literal and the conceptual in allegory is thin and impoverished, leaving both poet and interpreter with little to think about or feel, the symbol comprehends a rich, organic relation between reality and idea (and the literal representation that mirrors it). We might want to say that Coleridge's interest in what he variously calls "Reality," "the Individual," and "the Temporal" (30) was so foreign to Renaissance habits of thought that Renaissance allegory could not make much sense to him on its own terms, but part of the reason his protest against allegory became so influential was that it astutely registered a tendency in allegory that theorists such as Puttenham also perceived (though Puttenham did not find it at all problematic): the tendency of allegory's literal sense, what Puttenham calls the words as opposed to the meaning, to act mainly as vehicle without accruing any life of its own.

Such an astute modern reader of Renaissance allegory as Angus Fletcher takes Coleridge's critique for granted, but he also sees the thin or one-dimensional relation between allegorical sign and meaning as an interpretable philosophical response rather than as mere evidence of aesthetic failure. Fletcher's contribution helps to put Puttenham's conception of allegory in a larger generic context. The allegorist, argues Fletcher, confronts a world of contingency terrifying in its randomness, and to oppose it he formulates the allegorical hero as a "daemon" proceeding inexorably, even mercilessly, according to a law of absolute necessity.[18] To the point is *Faerie Queene* 5's Talus with his iron flail, or "hoggish" Gryll;[19] in Spenser, Fletcher's thesis shows us, it is not so much that purely allegorical characters are defined by their actions as it is that their allegorical identity requires them to act as they do, and thus becomes entirely determinative of their role and fate. Allegorical figure or character, in other words, collapses into identification with quality or idea. Often in reading allegory we have a sense (in accordance with Fletcher's model) that the allegorical hero is an embodied virtue rather than a character possessing the potential to choose, and correspondingly (as Coleridge intimates) that as interpreters we have nothing to do. At the same time, there is always also in the execution of any allegory the potential for a breach between signifier and signified, and consequently for a reassertion of a sensuous world that defies allegorical (indeed all) structures of cognition and cuts the allegorical hero loose from referentiality (we might think here of Spenser's metaphor of the flooded Nile in *Faerie Queene* 1.1.21, generating multitudes of creatures for which we do not even have names). In effect, Fletcher's model revises the Quintilian definition of allegory by opposing allegory not to determinate irony but instead to Machiavellian contingency or *Fortuna*. The analogy such a redefinition suggests between allegory and Machiavellian *virtù* (irony and contingency, allegory and virtù being analogous pairs) will not entirely hold, if only because allegory in Fletcher's sense cannot accommodate the flexibility so integral to virtù. Yet the parallel between the two nonetheless sheds light on the intersection of two Renaissance habits of thought while helping to explain the intense appeal of allegory in this period.

4. THE ENGLISH CRISIS OF VIRTÙ AND ALLEGORY'S MEDIATING ROLE

In replacing determinate Quintilian irony, even if only implicitly, with contingency in order to make sense of allegory, Fletcher subscribes to the notion of irony as a failure of referentiality. But as I suggested, this is not the main definition we see in Puttenham, who for the most part understood the coincidence of signifier and signified to be on a continuum with the noncoincidence of signifier and signified. In his classic 1975 book *The Machiavellian Moment*, J. G. A. Pocock suggests that this difference depended on a distinction between Italian and English habits of thought. In Pocock's view the Machiavellian imperative to defy Fortuna was the most important characteristic of Renaissance Italian political thought. The tendency of the ancient Greeks to see politics as inherently ironic, producing results at odds with intentions, was carried forward in Renaissance Italy as a sense that the republic was continually beset by "a stream of irrational events conceived as essentially destructive of all systems of secular stability," and that any efforts to escape this stream were partial and transient.[20] Renaissance Italian thought, Pocock argues, constructed a conceptual polarity opposing virtù (in the Machiavellian sense) or sometimes virtue (in the moral sense) on one side to fortune as contingency on the other. In sixteenth- and seventeenth-century England, Pocock concludes, this was perhaps surprisingly not the case, partly because the English were more interested in legitimation of authority than in political action and also because of factors such as England's mixed government, its inheritance of a social structure founded on the hierarchy of degree, and its Protestant conviction that the nation was elect in the eyes of God.[21] Even as the hierarchical nature of English political society and its anxiety about legitimation within this hierarchy militated against any emphasis on virtù as the defining attribute of the individual politician, the concern with extra-individual structures of order substituted for the worry over contingency in the English political mind.

It is the function of Fletcher's allegorical agent to answer the problem of contingency, by opposing contingency's randomness with the daemonic necessity imposed on it by its figurative meaning. If Pocock is right that contingency did not represent the same threat to English as it did to Italian political thought, then English allegory in this period would have been free to take on a different function, one dependent on different notions of identification and irony. And politic ideology suggested what these might be. In England, where it translated especially as self-interestedness, virtù sometimes reversed its affiliation, joining irony's side: the salient feature of the self-interested courtier might be his single-mindedness, but he was also a double-speaker, cannily asserting his self-interested agency against the common interest he was also required to espouse. By remaining linked to virtù even as it shifted functions across cultures, allegory came to belong not only to the identificatory end of the polarity, at which signifier and signified coincide, but also to the ironic end, at which words and meaning, in Puttenham's phrase, "meete not." If the opposition anchoring Italian political thought was between virtù and contingency, the analogous polarity for English political thought was between virtue (a concern for the common good) and virtù (the individual's concern for his own good, also expressible as politic corruption); or, analogously for politic ideology, between the kind of language that consistently meant what it said and a politic, allegorical language that pretended to mean what it said while in fact meaning something else.

This switch created a problem for allegory, indeed for all figurative language, if we follow Puttenham's dictum that allegory is the captain of figures. For allegory was now sometimes on the wrong side of the moral divide, allied with irony rather than offering heroic resistance to it. One solution to this representational crisis was to reassert allegory's total alignment with the identificatory, a strategy adopted with rigorous thoroughness, for instance, in Nathaniel Ingelo's very popular 1660 romance *Bentivolio and Urania*. In his introduction to the second, 1669 edition of that work, Ingelo worries that the allegorical vehicle often takes on such density that the tenor is hard to find: most romance, he says, is like a vegetable with a "fabulous rind so thick, that few can see through it into the usefull sense."[22] Elsewhere in the introduction he offers a long metaphor in which Reason whips Fancy as punishment for the "long stories" and "Fooleries" with which it interrupts the steady accrual of meaning in most fiction (b3v). Populating his own, avowedly reasonable romance with such characters as Bentivolio (glossed in the margin as "good will") and Panaretus ("all virtues"), who progress from cities such as Argentora ("the state of covetousness") and Vanasembla ("the hypocritical state") to Theoprepia ("the divine state," etymologically "worthy of God"), not through any actions they take or symbolic ground they cover but simply by abstracted and contentless "travel," Ingelo leaves us in *Bentivolio and Urania* with a rare example of an almost pure allegorical subsumption of character into idea. The romance reads as though its author sensed that allowing his characters any life at all beyond the proclamation of their meanings would produce a distracting and seductive excess—a possibility so threatening that in the guise of Fancy it required suppression by force. Ingelo's perceived enemy was imagination rather than contingency (they are related, of course, in their unruly generativity and their resistance to control by reason), which is why, even as his romance follows the logic of Fletcherian allegory, it altogether lacks its rhetorical urgency and power.

Bentivolio and Urania was more popular than most midcentury romance—it went through four editions in a little more than two decades—and one reason was undoubtedly that in pushing its allegory toward the identificatory pole it seemed to be fulfilling the humanist requirement that poetry should try to inculcate moral virtue. The basic idea here was that poetry would not only persuade its readers to virtue but also, insofar as they read poetry repeatedly, make virtue habitual in them, leading them as if insensibly into the orbit of the ideals they read about—hence, for instance, a crucial part of Spenser's effort in *The Faerie Queene* to "fashion" his readers, as he says in the Letter to Raleigh, within the "discipline" he was trying to impart was his insistence that the process of reading should mirror structurally the thematic quest for virtue on which his heroes were embarked.[23] At this level Spenser's identificatory allegory might fit humanist goals for poetry by modeling the subordination of individual character to larger and more virtuous idea. At the same time, though, Spenser warns of the tendency for a character entirely identified with its allegorical attribute to turn into a demon or a cipher—such as the politically necessary but morally troubling Talus, again, or far less equivocally the spurned husband and miser Malbecco, who so thoroughly gives himself up to his possessive inclinations that in the end he "Is woxen so deform'd, that he has quight / Forgot he was a man, and *Gealosie* is hight" (3.10.60.8-9). In this example, identificatory allegory proves incompatible with the exercise of will, without which, in post-Reformation England, virtue was at best always questionable because one could not be said to have freely chosen the good. Ingelo reflected this tension between identificatory Christian allegory and free will in *Bentivolio and Urania*—a romance, as I have suggested, that might be read as an exemplum for identificatory allegory—in his vehement defense of the necessity for free will, denouncing those lesser discourses in which "the vertuous compliance of holy Souls with the Divine will [was] a meer Nullity" because characters were "meer Puppets drawn through all their actions with Homerical Wires."[24]

Given the moral limitations of both ironic and identificatory allegory, a third option for Renaissance romance also emerged, one that in a post-Romantic critical landscape does not get much attention but that is entirely consistent with the notion of allegory as sustained metaphor. In this view, allegory performs a mediating function between the two poles, gesturing toward both identification and irony but never surrendering to either, and thus establishing a sort of metaphorical buffer zone around the literal sense of a text. As the literal threatens to collapse into identification, either with the conceptual or with history, allegory so conceived defends representation's integrity, the inviolability of the space separating it from both alternatives. When, on the other hand, the literal threatens to become entirely detached from either meaning or history, turning all the way to irony, allegory asserts the legibility of the space separating idea or history from representation and thus mitigates ironic disjuncture. Allegory so conceived recognizes and helps maintain representation's link both to the conceptual and to history, while remaining distinct from each. This double function, I want to suggest, might be one of allegory's great strengths, lending it the ability to sustain two (or even more) senses at once—often of an experiential, historical world seeming almost sensuously apprehensible and a cognitive world in which ideas encounter, refine, and modify one another, but also sometimes of two cognitive or even two apparently sensuous realms. Concomitantly, as a literary mode it might work to persuade readers to suspend the drive for resolution, the desire either to identify the literal with the conceptual or historical or to sunder them.

Such a model, I want to maintain, was at least implicitly formulated in the Renaissance; it offers probably the best explanation for one of the most dazzling effects of *The Faerie Queene*, its evocation of separate worlds—faerie land, the English court, the conceptual universe of signs, the text that is given spatial and temporal existence by Spenser's insistence that the reader acknowledge her awareness of herself reading it—that all seem expressions or realizations of one another and yet still maintain their apparently autonomous existences. And in this light we might read Fletcherian allegory not as the norm but as a deformation of allegory, so anxious about contingency (that which is not subject to representation and must therefore be in a wholly ironic relation to the literal) that it cannot sustain the doubly mediating role my third model discerns in allegory and so collapses compensatorily into identification with the conceptual. If Fletcherian allegory does represent in this way a deformation of the form, such deformation has often also seemed allegory's most universal manifestation, as though *Bentivolio and Urania* represented the logical end of what for allegory is an inevitable trajectory. The problem with allegory, it is often said, is one of scale: metaphor writ small may be able to sustain the suspension of the literal between irony and identification, but when metaphor is extended too faithfully or over too great an expanse of a literary work its literal sense always recedes or is absorbed into its conceptual meaning. But there seems to be no formal reason why a metaphor sustained too long must tend toward its own constriction, as if figurative language followed a parabola according to which it continued to generate meaning until at some mysterious point it turned back and began to shut down.

I have tried to suggest instead that allegory's tendency toward irony or identification is governed by factors extrinsic to its own form—that politic ideology, for instance, cast seventeenth-century allegory as a mode of irony because it needed a way to figure the gap it perceived between providence and self-interest. If allegory's function in general is to present identification and irony, whether determinate or indeterminate, as opposite ends of a continuum, then where precisely a particular allegorical work or a set of ideas locates itself on that continuum must depend primarily on the ideological problems it is trying to solve. And seventeenth-century romance, which at first glance often does not even seem especially allegorical, conceived of its place on that continuum in a particularly complex and unusual way. In its dual effort both to acknowledge the persuasive ironic insights of politic ideology—that is, to accept to some extent the politic offer of virtù as a mode of agency—and at the same time to preserve for the agent some potential for disinterested virtue, romance was drawn particularly toward my third kind of allegory, the kind that balances irony and identification against each other rather than tending irrevocably toward either one; and it realized this version of allegory through its roman à clef form.

I want to close this somewhat theoretical discussion of allegory with a return to *Urania*, specifically to an episode that is so explicit about its revision of the relation between metaphorical tenor and vehicle that it seems almost to advertise itself as a paradigm for the model I have been laying out here. One of the main tasks of *Urania*'s book 1 is to subject Wroth's characters to the first of the text's four main enchantments, imprisoning them in an elaborate palace whose separate parts are figures for the many imperfect stages of love and from which its prisoners can only be released by the ascension to the throne of the "loyallest" lady and the "valliantest" knight, Wroth's author-figure/heroine Pamphilia and her sometime lover Amphilanthus (169–70). When the couple at last arrives at the palace, they pass easily, as in a masque, through the towers of Desire and Love, but when they come to the final tower, of Constancy, the narrative momentum gets suspended in a self-reflexive generic tableau. There the figure of Constancy stands "holding the keyes" to the gates behind which the other lovers are imprisoned, "which [keys] Pamphilia tooke; at which instant *Constancy* vanished, as metamorphosing her self into her breast" (169). Whereas in *Bentivolio and Urania* character is entirely subordinated to idea, in this strange scene idea is literally incorporated into character, almost as if Wroth meant to allegorize the movement of the conceptual back into the literal. Allegorical idea travels from a substantive (e.g., Constancy) to an adjectival function (constant Pamphilia), as literal character becomes the end rather than the means of allegory. This metanarrative moment intends to teach us, I want to suggest, the direction in which we are supposed to read roman à clef, not subsuming literal fiction within abstract meaning but rather embodying the allegory's more abstract senses by means of the literal. One of early modern roman à clef's more obvious functions, again, was its somewhat tactful avoidance of overtly topical reference, in my terms its avoidance of complete identification with its historical referent. But *Urania* shows us here that it was also a way to forestall, even undo, the collapse of the literal into the conceptual, to maintain for the literal an innovative and stubbornly persistent integrity.

5. Constancy and the Challenge of Self-Interest

If Pamphilia's odd anti-apotheosis at the end of *Urania*'s book 1 protects her from devolving into mere embodied idea, Constancy as abstraction, then the loyalty she assumes to her virtue also offers her a kind of self-consolidation from which she can defy contingency. Construed in this way, as will be readily apparent, constancy thus opens up a space of hypothetical freedom for the agent, by which she might steer between contingency's randomness and the fixity of demonic identification. But perhaps even more significantly, as I will show in this chapter, Wroth's use of roman à clef to configure the literal as an intermediate realm comes to have profound moral implications, supplying a salutary model for the relation of an agent to her self-interested desire.

Constancy is so crucial a virtue in *Urania* because, as the princess Urania's anxiety about her own agency would intimate, the most basic and pervasive threat in the romance is change, willed and also unwilled. Wroth articulates the problem through several discourses, the most obvious of which is gender. With disarming frequency *Urania* echoes prevailing ideas about the weakness of women by diagnosing inconstancy as the most fundamental of women's failings: so, for example, the key to the misbehavior of a "devilish" lady who locks virtuous knights in the dungeon of her castle is not Satanic determination but her quality of being above all "unsteady," "her head set upon so slight a necke, as it turnd like a weather-cocke to any vaine conceit that blew her braines about" (403). Not only Urania herself but all of the romance's virtuous female characters must defend themselves against the implicit charge of inconstancy, and indeed part of the reason Pamphilia's constancy is so heroic is that it so emphatically overcomes ordinary feminine weakness. Nonetheless, Wroth extends inconstancy to men as well, most notably to the emperor Amphilanthus ("lover of two"), whose serial infidelities are both the spur and the primary challenge to Pamphilia's virtue. In moderately progressive cultural-historical terms, the romance apparently argues that inconstancy is a human rather than a specifically feminine failing, and that women (at least exceptional ones) not only have the most stake in defying inconstancy but are the most capable of heroically doing so. This heroic constancy is clearly an elaboration and revision of Pamela's in *Arcadia,* an effort to extend Sidney's attribution of heroism to women, while perhaps also to refute *Arcadia*'s implication that the primary obstacle to women's constancy is their own or other women's failings.[25]

To understand constancy in *Urania,* however, we also need to consider contemporary contexts besides gender ideology, among them the discourse of politic ideology. Within the framework of late sixteenth-century politic ideology, inconstancy represented not moral vacuity where there should be principle but rather a drive toward Tacitean self-advantage, not an absence of self but, in a sense, too much self. We see this notion of inconstancy reflected in *Urania,* in which "politique" queens shift from lover to lover as they follow their own interests, and constant lovers find themselves required to assure their beloveds of the difference "betwixt fervent love, whose ends are love; and such, where only use and gaine attends desier" (303). In *Urania,* not only is inconstancy in love metaphorized as political, as for instance in the narrator's lament over "Uncertaine Tyrant Love, that never brings thy Favourits to the topp of affection, but turnes againe to a new choice" (124), but it is depicted as itself a primary political sin. In one inset story, a wicked queen conspires with a young favorite to assassinate her husband, the king, but once she and her son are "in full possession of all" (72) she flouts her lover's expectations of marrying onto the throne, and when her affections stray to a third man the lover betrays their previous crime. This queen, the narrator informs us, has two kinds of "ends," not only "lascivious" but also "politike"—the full meaning of "lascivious," not only sexual but corruptly sexual, directing us via parallelism to read "politicke" not only as political but as politic in the sense in which I have been using it, as corruptly self-interested (73).

Given the duplicity and inconstancy so consistently attributed to court culture by early modern commentators, Wroth responded in part as did most contemporary moralists and historians, by recommending within limits the acquisition of politic means of defense. A king endangered by a palace conspiracy can see "only with the eies of vertue" and therefore cannot "pierce into this plot" for his usurpation (55). The lady-in-waiting Lisia, one of the many figures for Wroth, does manage to recognize the plot to ruin her reputation when she is locked in a palace garden at dusk by an Anna-like queen, but remains foolishly innocent of the means to resist—at the garden door "I boldly put my key to unlock it, but it would not doe, mine was but single, my enemies double"—and as a result she is disgraced (560). With a little more canniness, both of these characters might have protected themselves from entrapment without compromising their virtue, and one of the benefits *Urania* offers is an education in recognizing underhanded courtly tricks. Part of its lesson is that doubleness is an attribute of social power; the ability of Pamphilia's fickle lover, Amphilanthus, to pursue more than one woman at once, after all, is bound up with the fact that he is the most politically powerful person in the romance. Practical Urania does not endorse her brother's infidelity, but in the face of its incorrigibility she regrets to Pamphilia that "ever that fruitlesse thing Constancy was taught you as a vertue" (470), and several times she counsels Pamphilia to forget her faithless lover and move on.

Still, *Urania*'s more characteristic response to inconstancy is resistance, figured most concertedly in Pamphilia's championship of constancy. To Urania's argument that Amphilanthus no longer deserves Pamphilia's love, Pamphilia retorts that she will never "let in that worthlesse humor change . . . till I can change my selfe, and have new creation and another soule" (459), and protests that "to leave him for being false, would shew my love was not for his sake, but mine owne"

(470). To match his inconstancy with her own, she suggests, would be to unmask her love as self-interest. And the narrator is unfailingly on Pamphilia's side, celebrating her heroine's passion as "not like the small corne that yeelds forth many staulks, and many eares of wheat out of one," but "one in truth, and being as come from one roote, or graine of matchlesse worth, brought forth but one flower, whose delicacy, and goodnesse was in it selfe" (317). What Pamphilia does, thinks, and is are all one; her passion for Amphilanthus comprehends everything about her, incorporating within itself all the ground that in others is vulnerable to capture by multiplicity and dissembling. Consequently the flower her passion brings forth—the sign, presumably, of her constant poetry as well as of her constant behavior—is as nonpolysemic as a sign can be, standing for nothing but "it selfe." Pamphilia's language, this almost unmetaphoric metaphor suggests, is ineffective in the same way her constant attendance upon Amphilanthus is ineffective, in that it is its own end rather than any kind of means. As such it is a reproach, a critique of the self-interested motives not only of the duplicitous Amphilanthus but also of all the ordinary people who cannot hope to approach Pamphilia's exceptional singularity.

But there is nevertheless a moral danger attendant on this kind of self-justifying constancy, the risk that it will turn back on the subject to foster pride, and Wroth's morally anxious romance figures this connection between pride and constancy almost obsessively. On the simplest level it puts forward the queen Nerena, whose aggressive constancy is the expression of her tyrannical will toward self-gratification. Nerena is already "absolute Lady" of an island when she finds herself in a "constant fury" of love for the prince Steriamus, and her misguided response to his indifference is to take a "Knight-like search in hand," in Pamphilia's scornful phrase, to track him down rather than waiting virtuously to see if he will return to her (192–4). Wroth's romance subjects the queen to several kinds of discipline for this mistake, including parodic worship by a crazed woodsman who dresses her up as a mock-Diana and eventually imprisonment by her subjects, but in the end she is unrepentant, declaring that she would rather be "thus miserable, then not absolute" (196). Nerena's singleminded devotion to the pursuit of Steriamus is the result of her constancy to her own image of herself as absolute, and both are aspects of her "over-running-weedy pride" (335), an infatuation with and hence an indulgence of herself. Nerena's story warns, rather broadly, that what looks like constancy to another might really be constancy to one's beloved self.

Wroth gives a subtler negative example in the nymph Allarina, who takes the wrong recourse when she is cast off by a jealous lover. At first she refuses to accept his rejection and protests her own love so vigorously that "the world was fild with my constancy," as she tells Pamphilia, but this public manifestation of her virtue does nothing to convince her lover, and at last she withdraws into solitude, "meekenesse my whole ambition, losse my gaine" (220, 223). Constant but not proud, she seems to have figured out how to avoid Nerena's mistake. But hers is a precarious state, and one day soon afterward she joins a crowd drinking ritually from a certain spring and finds herself "alterd in al things but my truth." Her "poore selfe" is "returnd to me againe, I did embrace it in the same true sort that love held me, and so we did agree. I love my selfe, my selfe now loveth me" (224). Lest we make the mistake of finding such a solution inspiriting, Pamphilia, her interlocutor, immediately rejects it for herself, and Allarina later renounces it too, realizing when she encounters her lover again that "wee are fine creatures alone in our owne imaginations; but otherwise poore miserable captives to love" (483). The sin that both Nerena and Allarina succumb to, as Allarina makes explicit, is self-love. Allarina is much less harshly punished than Nerena, but her failed attempt to be entirely self-sufficient, to bestow her "truth" or constancy on someone who is guaranteed to return it, is not really different in kind from Nerena's usurpation of the autonomous masculine role in order to defy the limitations placed on her by her culture and attain her own desires. Constancy's great danger, both these examples show, is that it is as likely to be predicated on an esteem for the self as for the beloved, which means that it is not different from self-interest after all.

Clearly *Urania*'s anxiety over women's self-sufficiency functions as a mode of policing the boundaries of gender—constancy needs to be reclaimed for women, but not at the expense of their humility or their respect for appropriate gender roles.[26] We should also understand Wroth's formulation of constancy, however, as a pointed entry into contemporary debates over Stoicism—not a surprising subject for *Urania* nor for seventeenth century romance in general given Stoicism's strong affinities in the late Renaissance with politic ideology. The Dutch scholar Justus Lipsius, as I noted in the introduction, was both the major Renaissance editor of Tacitus and the author of the influential *De Constantia,* published in Latin in 1584 as a response, he said, to the sufferings of the wars on the Continent and translated into English ten years later by a relative of Barbara Gamage, Philip Sidney's sister-in-law and Mary Wroth's mother.[27]

The connection Lipsius's career draws between Tacitean ideology and Stoic constancy was made by Tacitus himself, for instance in his story in the *Annals* of Seneca's death and his wife Paulina's fidelity to him, in which it is unclear whether constancy resists or is complicit with politic maneuvering.[28] Neostoicism was one part of the earliest manifestations of the new humanism on the Continent,[29] and in late sixteenth- and seventeenth-century England the association between Stoic and politic ideas became a commonplace.

Stoicism and politic ideology both had at their center the individual, private self, and though this emphasis was ostensibly toward different ends in each, Stoicism too came to be perceived as a mode of challenging authority, its withdrawal always potentially a tactic rather than a goal in itself.[30] In the 1599 edition of *Basilikon Doron* James I himself denounced "Stoicke insensible stupiditie," insisting that Lipisus was actually "inconstant," presumably to secular authority, and accusing him of being "proud."[31] The most concerted English opposition to Stoicism, however, came from the church, and tended to focus on the Stoic denial of passion. In a sermon in the early 1590s, for instance, Richard Greenham condemned "Stoicall apathie and want of feeling," calling men who affect Stoic constancy "past all feeling, and now more brutish and blockish then any brute beast . . . [they] neither tremble at Gods iudgements, nor reioyce in his promises," but "live like stockes, and die like blockes," and Joseph Hall declared that "I would not be a Stoic, to have no passions; for that were to overthrow this inward government God hath erected in me."[32] Underlying the frequent pun "Stock" for "Stoick" was a belief that good Christians come to God through love and fear, and that in freeing themselves from fortune by divesting themselves of their passions Stoics were thus turning away from God. The analogy between inward and outward governments seems to have been irresistible, hence the close link between religious and political objections to Stoicism.

In *Urania* the spring that inspires self-love in Allarina is presided over by a man "more servant to adoration then divinity," who promises that its "divine and sacred water" will deliver "Quiet of spirit, comfort in this life." Despite recognizing that the man "had said too much, since only one [spring] was fit to bee termed so"—presumably the "well of water, springing up into everlasting life" in John 4:14—Allarina drinks anyway "for novelties" (223). Afterward, when she is boasting to Pamphilia of her new self-sufficiency, Allarina declares herself "uncontrold of Fortunes selfe" (224). The suggestion is that Allarina's pseudo-priest is a Stoic sage, and that in joining the crowd at the well of his philosophy she is making not only a social but also a theological mistake, that to turn away from her passion for her beloved toward love for herself is also to turn away from God. This episode helps make sense of a strange moment elsewhere in the romance, when Urania concludes one of her arguments against Pamphilia's constancy with the admonishment, "besides tis a dangerous thing to hold that opinion"—that is, constancy—"which in time will prove flat heresie" (470). Pamphilia never flirts with Allarina's self-love, but Urania's warning against heresy at the end of an argument addressing Pamphilia's emotional well-being recalls us abruptly to constancy's religious and political implications, the challenge to authority that it always potentially issued.

One of the reasons constancy was a conventional feminine virtue in the Renaissance, and long before, was that it seemed to combat the fear of women's sexual agency, their supposedly innate tendency, in the words of Thomas Wyatt's lyric "They Flee from Me," to "range /Busily seeking with a continual change."[33] If erotic disloyalty, as Wyatt supposes, is at the very least an analogue for political disloyalty, then as a virtue constancy might seem to offer a counter-response to politic ideology, and upon a first look it seems that in *Urania* it will do just this. But in the late Renaissance the notion of constancy as a remedy for (women's) sexual and (men's and women's) political change conflicted with the politic construction of Stoic constancy as inimical to institutional authority, and unsurprisingly that conflict was clearly registered in this female-authored romance. Constant women in *Urania* are always potentially on the brink of declaring themselves independent, if not of masculine authority per se then of the gender ideologies that keep masculine authority in place. Like Milton's Eve they are in danger of finding their own reflections far more appealing than anything else they see around them, and like Milton after her, Wroth presents this tendency as narcissistically perilous. In the end *Urania* is caught in a bind: constancy, the remedy for politic change, on closer investigation appears to be mostly implicated in politic ideology, not only because it potentially offers a challenge to authority but also because it conceives of the individual, free-standing self as strongly persuasive, its particular ends likely to be felt as more compelling than the communal ends of any society or group.

Constancy is apparently attractive enough, or the prospect of its absence threatening enough, that despite its troublesome associations Wroth's romance cannot offer any alternative virtuous response to masculine infidelity and the callous and changeable fortune it seems to symbolize, at least beyond the isolated example of Urania's ambiguous rebaptism and her very ambivalently willed change. But even as she disciplines her Stoic women lovers Wroth is careful to avoid subjecting them to the faithless men who will not own them, choosing instead to stage their allegiance to the deified figure of love itself. After Pamphilia first hears Allarina's declaration that "I love my selfe, my selfe now loveth mee," the queen wonders how it is that her ordinary subject Allarina can master love when she herself feels so bound by it, and orders herself to "Scorne such servilitie, where subjects soveraignize . . . either command like thy self, or fall downe vassall in despaire." But this metaphorical assertion of rank and the "great spirit" that accompanies it is suddenly interrupted by a resurgence of passion:

> "Yet when all this is said, and that the truest knowledge tells me these [vows to command] are true, my wounded heart with bleeding doth professe vassalladge to the great and powerfull might of love. I am a prisoner, guard me then deere love, keepe me but safely free from yeelding, and keepe me, as thou hast already made me, thine." (225)

As Pamphilia vows absolute fealty to a composite deity, part Christian God, part feudal lord, part courtly love's *bel ami*, her paradoxical plea to love to keep her "safely free from yeelding" ingeniously inverts the virtue of chastity, redefining the act of "yeelding" not as putting herself under another's power but as denying that power and taking refuge in an illusion of self-sufficiency. Amphilanthus may leave her, but even so, as long as she stays in love Pamphilia never escapes subjection, and therefore she is protected from what opponents of Stoicism fear is a natural tendency to claim autonomy and thereby to challenge authority. Lest she worry about how to reconcile this subjection with the social and political power she asserted initially (which as queen and poet she must claim), the reformed Allarina later assures her that "the greater your minde is, and the braver your spirit, the more, and stronger are your passions, the violence of which though diversly cast, and determined, will turne still to the government of love; and the truer your subjects are to you, the firmer will your loyalty be to him" (483). Although the logic is somewhat out of order, the general idea seems to be the paradox that the greatest and bravest spirit, as a consequence of her great passions, is also both the most compelling ruler of subjects and the most firmly subjected of lovers—the strangely wishful thought that from those most equipped for defiance the least threat will come.

6. Alienated Self-Regard

Constancy, then, is very useful in *Urania* for resisting contingency, figured in Pamphilia's narrative especially as masculine variability, and thus enabling at least the potential for agency. Despite its status as the romance's most celebrated virtue, however, constancy is also dangerous, because it threatens to slide so easily into self-love rather than sustaining devotion to an external ideal. And it is in the face of this moral predicament that *Urania* invokes its allegorical form as an oblique but effective solution, in the conclusion to the narrative's second major enchantment, which reads conceptually as a revision and even an overgoing of the first. In the lead-up to this second enchantment, Pamphilia and a retinue of ladies are motivated by a wanderlust even the constant Pamphilia cannot deny, and after they recklessly set sail with no particular destination in mind they find themselves stranded on an apparently uninhabited island. Exploring, Pamphilia comes across a "round building like a Theater, carved curiously, and in mighty pillars" (372), and upon entering the ladies find "as magnificent a Theater, as Art could frame," with an elaborate throne in the center. "Instantly the sweetest musicke, and most inchanting harmony of voyces, so overruld their sences, as they thought no more of any thing," and as they surrender to this masque-like spell the gate locks behind them so that "all thought in them [was] shut up for their comming forth thence" (373). Wroth amplifies this self-containment in the next paragraph: "All the comfort their owne hearts could imagine to them selves, they felt there, seeing before them, (as they thought) their loves smiling, and joying in them; thus flattering love deceiv'd the true, and brought contrary effects to the most good" (373).

The problem this episode allegorizes is not that the ladies fail to recognize their lovers' inconstancy or that happiness in love is just a delusion—many of them are happily paired back at home with men who try to rescue them as soon as they hear of their enchantment and to whose sides the women are restored as soon as the spell is broken. Rather, the ladies' delight in "flattery," even to the point of failing to notice their lovers' absence and their own imprisonment, suggests a revision and complication of Pamphilia's critique of constancy: here, even reciprocated love tends toward solipsism. Inside the theater the ladies replace their lovers with their own self-gratifying projections, quite gratuitously and without any awareness that they have done so. Not only heroic constancy but also ordinary mutual love, free of the stresses of infidelity and the resulting urges toward heroism and martyrdom, is here implicated in the pleasures and moral failings of self-regard.

To help make sense of this problem we might invoke Bernard Williams's notion of "moral self-indulgence," which he defines as a "second-order motivation" describing an agent's desire to further his own image of himself as a virtuous person by acts that are only ostensibly in the service of others.[34] The morally self-indulgent person, argues Williams, asks not "What does the other require?" but "What can I do to express my own disposition as a generous person?", betraying a "reversal . . . between self-concern and other-concern," a "misdirection . . . genuinely of concern" (47). Williams's model does not issue much of a challenge to the Pamphilia-figure constant in the face of infidelity, who seems already to have internalized his critique. Where the model seems more surprising in its relevance to Wroth is in regard to the second enchantment, which reveals uneventful mutual love, love that elsewhere in the romance is depicted as morally unproblematic, to be based in self-regard as well. Both Wroth and Williams, we might say, worry that politic ideology is actually right, that even the ostensible lover of others lives necessarily in a solitary world, accompanied only by instruments of her own self-realization.

For Williams, the problem with self-preoccupation is especially that it substitutes for genuine other-concern. For Wroth the emphasis is somewhat different: the self-preoccupied agent in this episode is caught in a delusion. By its nature a form of cupiditas, erotic desire casts the world as a false projection of self, all of its ironic difference obscured by a megalomaniac process of identification. Wroth's solution is not to assert the difference of the other from the self, but instead slightly to estrange the self from itself, as if to block the primary and most unthinking act of identification. In the terms of the second enchantment, the ladies need to see that they are in a theater, acting in a masque—to perceive the frame around the action, and thus to take up their function as audience as well as performers. *Urania* brings this point home in the conclusion to the enchantment, which can only be dispelled by "the sweetest and loveliest creature, that poore habits had disguised greatnesse in" (373)—that is, by a character playing a part. The primary liberator turns out to be the princess Urania, stolen from her royal parents as an infant and raised as a shepherdess. Although by this point she has been returned to her rightful parents and her story has already been recounted several times in the romance, she must rescue the trapped lovers by restaging her discovery of her true identity—by finding and opening a book containing her own biography. And the entire enchantment turns out to be itself a piece of theater, staged by a man who aided Urania when she was a kidnapped infant in order to gain public acknowledgement for his virtue. All of this emphasis on performance and recapitulation, Wroth implies, is a corrective to the self-flattering ladies, who will be able to free themselves from delusion only if they can achieve the kind of ironic distance on themselves that acting in a drama or reading about oneself in a roman à clef can provide. Self-indulgence proceeds here not from too much attention to the self but from attention of the wrong kind, from a surrender to desire precluding Urania's self-conscious awareness that she has always already been a character in a romance.

In the second enchantment, as in her accounts of Pamphilia's struggles and her antitypes, Wroth is outlining a moral paradigm, a blueprint for how to construct a virtuous self. Her starting point, I have suggested, is not Williams's other-concern, nor any abstract, pre-Kantian precept, but rather the nature of the self's relation to itself. Narcissism is her characters' great pitfall, but the involvement of self with itself is also in a sense what founds morality, because it is the ground on which the agent faces her purest, most direct challenge from desire. Self-interest would like to be all, to claim everything as its own, and the self's primary moral task is to preserve some corner for disengagement, some aspect of the self that simply observes. The Freudian resonances of my reading here are strong. In his famous essay "On Narcissism," Freud argues that any "ethical ideas" about which a subject does not have "merely intellectual knowledge" but "recognizes . . . as a standard for himself" and "submits" himself to are present to him exactly insofar as he has embodied them in an ego-ideal.[35] This ego-ideal, moreover, although its formation is prompted by the critical influence of people and ideas outside the self, is in essence a substitute for the infantile ego, and the subject's allegiance to it a "displaced" version of its primary narcissism (94). Freud suggests that all ethical deliberation that is not merely speculative but has as its end a determination of behavior, even if it seems to proceed by discussion of precept, is originally implicated in self-regard, and that self-regard is furthermore the structure through which ethics comes to have meaning for the individual.

Freud's concept of the ego-ideal brings into clearer focus the second enchantment's revisionary task. Constancy to another who seems only intermittently to solicit it, I have suggested, seems so untenable for Pamphilia that she constructs an abstract, external ideal on which to bestow her fidelity and to which she can subject herself so as not to be accused of self-interest in turning from her lover. Now we might read the slightly alienated self-consciousness advocated by the second enchantment as a further revision of that abstract ideal, an effort to find for it a compromise position closer to the subject herself, hence to mitigate her subjection, but not so close as to threaten a collapse into identificatory self-unity. In effect, Wroth posits her own version of Freud's ego-ideal, one next to which the self still appears reassuringly weak and incomplete even as it also powerfully, and much more subtly than constancy, accommodates the subject's primary narcissism. Wroth is walking a thin line here, thinner than Freud's: she needs to answer her culture's moral strictures against feminine narcissism and self-sufficiency while at the same time separating herself, at least slightly, from feminine subjection. We might define her solution as a sort of distanced narcissism—a recognition that in the Jacobean court and country-house society to which she belonged, the only relationship a woman could have that even began to honor her desire for autonomy and agency was with herself, but at the same time an acknowledgement of the serious moral pitfalls of such a relationship.

If we are seeking a pre-Freudian model for this conception of morality, as I have already indicated, it might rest for Wroth in the relation of the allegorical text to the reality it purports to shadow. According to the allegorical schema for roman à clef I have here outlined, it is the dual function of the allegorical representation to set up correspondences among real, literal, and conceptual and at the same time to block complete identification between literal and real, or literal and conceptual, and thus to maintain the integrity of the literal as a distinct sphere. Analogously, self-consciousness in Wroth's moral system—which is figured, strikingly, as the product of acting in a masque or reading a book, engaging with some sort of representation—holds the agent aloof from identification with the self as instantiated wholly by its self-interested desires, while refusing to cede the self entirely to subjection by love or any other abstract precept. Self-consciousness, like the literal, is a fiction in the etymological sense, a "made" or constructed vantage point mediating between self as a perfectly nonsignifying agent of its own ends and self simply as idea. In the second enchantment, we might say, allegory becomes moral paradigm, a template for the subject's self-conception.

7. VIRTUE AND TRANSPARENCY

The strikingly revisionary nature of Wroth's adaptation of allegory becomes clear by comparison with the standard use of roman à clef in the period, described most succinctly in recent years by Annabel

Patterson's theory of "functional ambiguity." Patterson reads roman à clef as the product of a kind of tacit contract between writers and the state, by which writers agree only to imply to their audience rather than to voice directly their criticisms of the conduct of public affairs, and in exchange receive immunity from the censors who would otherwise "be *required* to make an example" of them.[36] In the first part of this chapter I suggested that in *Arcadia* Sidney enlisted a similar strategy in a broader sense, using his roman à clef form not only to comment on particular topical events but to publish for others the inescapable reality of self-interest even as he seemed at the same time (tactfully, ostensibly virtuously, and strategically) to obscure it. Wroth's innovation is to internalize this same strategy, removing it from its usual social context to confine it within the purview of the single self. In *Urania* self-interest is not a social threat, requiring roman à clef to mediate a relation between the real and the represented in order to establish an understanding between writer and audience; rather, it is a threat to individual morality, and in response Wroth marshals roman à clef as an analogue for self-consciousness, a model for forestalling narcissism. In *Urania,* that is, it is not the writer's relation to others but the subject's relation to herself that is structured (as if) by allegorical representation.

But surely, any reader aware of the controversy over *Urania*'s publication would want to object, roman à clef in Wroth's romance also has a social function. Through her allegorical narrations of real events Wroth clearly meant to criticize court and gender politics, and her technique of multiplying and diversifying her portraits of real people, for instance, though it may have been meant to contribute to the moral goal of self-estrangement I delineated above, must also have been meant to disrupt the correspondence between historical person and representation and thus to protect her from censure. Interestingly, however, Wroth also tells us all but explicitly that insofar as she does have a social intention in deploying roman à clef, its emphasis is the reverse of what we would expect from Sidney or Patterson. Near the end of the romance she recounts the story of Pelarina, who has Wroth-like penned a fictionalized account of her passion "in an idle Booke" and left it for her lover to find. To her astonishment he declines to play her game, refusing "by word nor writing" to acknowledge what she has written, "not honouring me so much, who was his slave, as to finde fault, or to seeme pleasd" (533–4). Pelarina has issued her lover an appeal, and his refusal even to acknowledge it is presented as outrageous, a cruel denial of her very presence. Roman à clef does mean to convey tactfulness on its writer's part, Wroth says here, but a tactfulness consisting not in any willingness of the writer to dissociate from or disavow the meaning of her words; rather, Pelarina's circumspection functions rhetorically as an intensifier, an assurance to her lover that her words are entirely sincere.

In a social context, this episode suggests, the risk posed by self-interest is not too much identification but none at all. When Pelarina writes obliquely to her lover she is not worried that her obliquity will be obscured, that he will make an identification between her words and her true feelings, but rather that her allegory will be rejected entirely. Her response to his deliberate neglect of her book is shame, because in refusing to receive her desire he casts it back on her and forces her to own it all. In politic terms she wants too much, and she wants it all by herself, in the terrible isolation produced by the ironic relation between her own interests and those of her lover. Pelarina's shame demonstrates something that scholars of early modern culture are only recently beginning to see, that women in this period may have been exhorted to see their silence or their obliquity, in certain cases, in as morally problematic a light as their speech.[37] By the logic of politic ideology, obliquity in general and roman à clef in particular, after *Arcadia*, are vulnerable to the charge of concealing self-interest, and Pelarina thus becomes guilty even in her social isolation. What this means in *Urania* is that self-consciousness as a remedy for narcissism is not morally sufficient, that Wroth must take another step to indemnify her characters' virtue. One solution might be to dispense with desire entirely, but for all the reasons I have been discussing—anxiety about hubris, a sense that traditional modes of renouncing desire such as Stoicism are in bad faith, or perhaps just a fundamental belief that desire cannot be denied (and it is significant here that even such a figure as Allarina does not deny desire, only redirects it toward herself)—*Urania* refuses to do this. Wroth's tactic instead, which is strikingly similar to that proposed by the discourse around the concept of interest a couple of decades later, is to construe true desire as entirely transparent.

The paradigmatic example of this move occurs not incidentally at the exact midpoint of the romance, the opening of book 3, when *Urania*'s arch-beloved Amphilanthus and his friend Polarchos are wandering through a forest when from a distance the two men spy what seem to them to be two perfect pastoral lovers. Rather than interrupting the scene the two men stand apart and watch, "admiring" the lovers "as much, as either had in former times themselves, when first in love, calling their passions round about them, wrapping themselves in them, as in their mantles." When first in love themselves, the narrator says, both men had apparently known to stand apart in order to "admire" themselves as objects of wonder—behavior that might seem self-absorbed if the second enchantment had not taught us the opposite, that in fact such self-distancing is the only ethical response to one's own desire. Now the men's witnessing of this tableau recapitulates that earlier situation, except that this time the image is at a greater distance from the perceiving self.

At first Amphilanthus's identification with what he sees at a distance spurs him to consolidate and conceal himself, to wrap himself away from view in his own remembered passions. But then Wroth's model shifts. Continuing to gaze at the lovers, Amphilanthus becomes

> so much love it selfe, as he might be compar'd to be it selfe, as neere as a round glasse made of the clearest temper, and fild full of the clearest water; turne it any way, you see thorow it, yet both seeme one colour, and clearenesse in agreeing; so did the clearenesse of his love shew through him, or was it selfe onely love, and purely cleare, no vacant place, least turning of the glasse might make a bubble to appeare a change; no, he was round and true. (343)

What Amphilanthus does here can still be described only as identification, but paradoxically, in this identification he seems to lose his particular identity, his own love (the purity of which is thus guaranteed) turning entirely to a medium for the transmission of the image. A "glasse" in early modern usage is not only a vessel but a mirror, and by the episode's logic it is as if Amphilanthus as mirror stands at a slightly oblique angle to the lovers who are not quite himself, thus passing the image on to us as secondary audience rather than reflecting it back toward itself according to the more typical, circular model. In this episode the estranged—here we might call it the secondary—self-image does not just correct the self too wrapped up in its own love, as in the second enchantment, but actually replaces it, becoming itself the representational end for which the author is merely a medium. Rather than assert the existence of an authorial self beyond representation, then, this model dissolves that self, insisting that what is real is only what is translatable, conveyable by multiple signs—in other words, entirely image.

To convey this central lesson Wroth picks the most unlikely and most challenging of all her characters. Amphilanthus is a man, and therefore already less disposed than women by the rules of gender to discipline his desires. Of all the male lovers in the romance he is the least constant; and not incidentally he is also the least self-aware of all Wroth's major characters, virtually without conscience. Even at the very end of the romance, in the process of forsaking a new lover to return to Pamphilia for the last time, he engages in no self-scrutiny and feels no remorse, his decision coming to him like "drops falling on soft stones" that "weare in to them at last" (659). At the same time, of course, like Pamphilia he is also a love poet, hence his susceptibility to the tableau he witnesses. Even the most intractably un-self-conscious character, Wroth thus insists, can be morally justified by entering into the project of representation; even in this most difficult case, a sympathy toward what one sees and a recognition that in relation to it one is essentially a medium have the power to purge the subject of all that prevents him from being "round and true." In the end this is Wroth's real revision of Sidney, her alternative answer to the problem of self-interest. Representation in *Urania* does not serve self-interest but instead functions to render it insignificant, even ephemeral. Indeed, by replacing self with image the representational act takes away self-interest's putative ground, and in a sense makes both desire and the image that conveys it into goods in themselves, their own ends. Or rather, it makes them the subject's ends: roman à clef's goal in *Urania* is neither to deliver the self nor to hide it (which, as I have been arguing, is actually another mode of delivery), but rather to engage the subject in the task of continually searching for, generating, and replacing itself by images. The moral self as Wroth defines it seeks always to be signifier rather than signified; it is, above all, a communicative entity.

Ultimately *Urania* privileges the literal as a means of disappearing the overweening self, that self which in its hubris declares its mysterious essence the impossible endpoint of interpretation and the true object of all its own desire. From our post-Coleridgean vantage point, according to which allegory seems to have more to do with abstract concept than with persons, this move may seem odd, but in fact such disciplining of self may be one of allegory's characteristic uses. In concluding this chapter I want to offer two suggestive examples, one Wroth's near contemporary and one our own, as a way of pointing to a context for *Urania*'s treatment of allegory beyond *Arcadia* and politic ideology. In his book *Literal Figures: Puritan Allegory and the Reformation Crisis in Representation*, a study of the fortunes of allegory as a rhetorical mode in the early modern period, Thomas Luxon tells the story of several Civil War Protestant radicals who, taking to heart Thomas Cranmer's argument that the devoted reader of scripture may be "altered and transformed into that thing, which he readeth," believed that they themselves had become the new Christ, body and soul. Luxon describes the radicals' mistake as a form of "hyperliteralism," an emphasis on the literal over all other allegorical senses, but it would seem more accurate to say that these Puritan radicals wanted to do away with the literal so as to become the thing itself.[38] Longing for and claiming to have achieved a world that no longer needed the letter, they argued that presence had finally become immanent. Outraged religious authorities offered the response we would expect, that for the radicals to claim themselves as Christ was an act of almost unimaginable hubris. As discipline, they reasserted allegory: in this unredeemed world, they argued, all we have is the literal, God's word, and until Christ came again the radicals would be lucky even to be counted as allegorical signs themselves. Luxon goes on to show that this marshaling of representation to defer presence is the quintessential function of Protestant allegory, which in his words tried endlessly in this period to "other" the body and its claims to material presence (26). His picture of the theological imperatives behind allegory reminds us that Wroth's use of allegory to banish self-interest was a secular adaptation of an older and more widespread theological habit of thought.

Clearly my own reading of seventeenth-century allegory is informed by the self-conscious linguistic turn of late twentieth-century literary theory, but the texts I have been discussing in this chapter are also oddly anticipatory of it, and so the other example I want to cite is Paul de Man's use of allegory to rebuke Coleridgean symbolism's excessive fondness for subjectivity and the self. In his essay "The Rhetoric of Temporality," de Man indicts symbolism as an attempt to extend the subject's domain over the world, an effort to redefine the object as an aspect of the subject so that in the end all the subject's relationships will be only "toward itself."[39] He reserves his most withering scorn for Coleridge's "reducing" of the relation between human being and God to "interpersonal relationship," which Coleridge also compares to the relationship between a "favorite dog" and its master—as if God and dog were equally just projections of Coleridge's own personhood rather than qualitatively separate, and very different, entities (198). What Coleridge in his hubris denied, says de Man, is the truth allegory is forever trying to impart, that we encounter the world only through language—that is, through signs—and what's more, that signs have no access to the real but are in relationship only with themselves. Symbolism is a fallacy that expresses the self's characteristic desire for presence; allegory, contends de Man, siding with Luxon's 1640s religious counterradicals, insists on the truth that all we can really know is the letter, and by doing so recalls the overweening subject to his necessary estrangement from the world. De Man has much more to say about allegory in his essay, but in this respect his argument is uncannily similar to Wroth's. Allegory's function for each writer is to divest the self of any ground on which it might establish a reality separate from its image and from images in general, and by doing so also to prevent it from construing its desire, in its particularity and limitedness, as in any way significant.

It is difficult to decide how we should value such a function. Luxon's sympathies are with the Civil War religious radicals, because their belief in the real presence of bodies, not just letters, appeared to bestow dignity on the poor, who owned little more than their own bodies, and on women, who were often understood to consist of nothing more than body. He indicts the "allegorical ontology" of Reformed Christianity for always displacing or deferring significance, the political effect of which, he suggests, was to confirm the traditional, existing distribution of authority and to de-emphasize the physical, material suffering of those without power (26). In effect Luxon argues that in the early modern period women and the poor had every right to their self-interest as a minimal counterbalance to their oppression, and that if allegory's function was to deprive their self-interest of legitimacy then it was an unethical form. As twenty-first century readers we might want to say that Wroth's women characters, too, could have used more self-interest rather than less, and that the problem of self-interest that allegory tries to solve in *Urania* is not as pressing as the problem of women's self-abnegation to which it may contribute. Sidney and de Man, however, both suggest contexts in which to see self-interest as an urgent moral problem and give us added reason to concur with *Urania* in understanding the enlistment of allegory as a good-faith response. Perhaps the merit of allegory is in part to weaken the persuasive power of the overweening self and to help us imagine a world driven by something other than, or at least in addition to, acquisitive desire. How we value allegory, Wroth's *Urania* suggests, as an aspect of Renaissance thought and perhaps in other periods as well, depends considerably on how we value self-interest.

Chapter 2

Incest, Rivalry, and Succession: Romance and the Problem of Sociality

Wroth, I argued in Chapter 1, explored at length in *Urania* the threat politic ideology posed, as a potential stimulus to narcissism and hubris, to the moral status of the individual self. In itself, of course, politic ideology would seem to pose a social threat too, insofar as it destabilizes providentialist order and pits the self-interest of each agent against that of every other. And romance, as I have characterized it thus far, with its long-standing generic interest in narratives of succession and erotic competition and its particular affinity in the late sixteenth and seventeenth centuries with politic habits of thought, would seem in turn primed to take up these social problems. As I will show in Chapters 3 and 4, this does turn out to be the case, as the romances of the 1650s and 1660s focus explicitly and with unprecedented intensity on the conflict between self-interest and the self's care for and obligations to others. But the major romances of the early seventeenth century and Sidney's most immediate heirs, *Urania* and John Barclay's *Argenis*, look at least on the surface quite different, reading relationship primarily through the natural and seemingly a priori hierarchies and affinities of the extended kin group. While this fascination with endogamous relation may seem on the face of it to mark a lack of regard for the social implications of politic ideology, perhaps even a turn away from them, in fact it is an indirect mode of addressing them—something that begins to become clear, perhaps a bit paradoxically, only when we recognize Wroth's and Barclay's complex marshalling and revising of generic tradition.

If Wroth and Barclay are not so much unconcerned with as reluctant to acknowledge the destabilizing power of rivalry and competition in their stories of love and succession, they are backed by a powerful narrative tradition. As Vladimir Propp reminds us in a classic essay on the *Oedipus* cycle, there is no act of succession not implicated in violence, even the succession of a most loving father by his most obedient son, but it has also been the function of Western succession narratives from Oedipus onward to obscure this violence, to depict it as unwilled (or, I would add, as in *Hamlet,* to displace and overmotivate it).[1] Similarly, Fredric Jameson argues in *The Political Unconscious* that peer rivalry is actually the constitutive social condition of romance, that the genre came into being in twelfth-century Europe specifically to define self in opposition to foreigner and to formalize and regulate the relationship between them. Following upon the class consolidation of the feudal nobility, says Jameson, twelfth-century aristocrats suddenly saw their own doubles everywhere they looked, and were for the first time faced with the problem of "how my enemy can be thought of as being *evil* (that is, as other than myself and marked by some absolute difference), when what is responsible for his being so characterized is quite simply the *identity* of his own conduct with mine."[2] In response, this population formulated romance as a way to stage its own class cohesion and to displace evil onto a realm more remotely other, the realm of the supernatural. For both Propp and Jameson it is thus the constitutive function of aristocratic European narratives about political and social rivalry, whether inter- or intragenerational, to obscure or formalize impulses toward rivalry, to protect against the kind of ungoverned free-for-all to which early modern politic ideology, for one, might seem conducive.

"With this development," Jameson concludes his account of twelfth-century romance, "something like a history of the form"—that is, of the genre of romance—"may be said already to have begun" (119). Clearly Jameson's account captures something fundamental about romance (hence the attractiveness of this particular narrative to scholars of early modern fiction, who in making use of it have tended somewhat ironically to pluck it out of its larger argumentative context).[3] But such a conclusion seems wishful in its attempt to pin down generic origins. As one kind of counterargument I might cite Heliodorus's Greek romance *Aethiopika,* which as I will demonstrate shortly was already taking Jameson's opposition between familiar-'ty and foreignness as its pretext in the fourth century C.E. My aim 're is not to advocate that in order to give a more accurate account 'omance's origins we simply substitute the material conditions that animated twelfth-century romance with those that gave rise to *Aethiopika*. Indeed, Heliodorus's material context is so much more shadowy than that of twelfth-century narrative's, and so few of its fellow romances have survived, that it would be impossible to do so. Rather, I want to suggest that by the time of written record, genre was already not just a response to history but was operative itself as a form of history, and that it therefore becomes exceedingly difficult, if not impossible, to step outside it, to posit genre, as Jameson does, as a "solution" to social contradictions (118) without recognizing it as also a formulator of them. When in early seventeenth-century England Wroth and Barclay were faced with the challenge of politic ideology (itself not exactly a new set of ideas, as I have argued already, but a re-presentation and recombination, perhaps an intensification, of ideas that romance, for one, had been interrogating for centuries), their apprehension of it was mediated through romance's generic history, and we cannot understand what they made of a relatively locally situated, particular set of conditions or ideas without taking into account too their narratives' place in the romance genre's version of history.

In positing generic practice as to some extent distinct from more local considerations I do not mean to portray it as monolithic or transcendent. One of the most telling, if also simple, ways that *Arcadia* intervened in romance's succession narrative was by depicting Basilius as weak and fatuous, as if to forestall any real intergenerational struggle. Sidney also went to great lengths to avoid rivalry between peers, differentiating between and meticulously balancing the assets of his central pair of princes in order to ensure that they would have no reason to compete for the same prize and (in the *New Arcadia*) revealing Pyrocles' rival prince Amphialus to be Oedipally unwilling, his compulsion to unsuccessful rivalry ultimately a tragic flaw rather than a social problem. Both of these tactics are consistent with romance's effort to downplay social violence, but in their self-consciousness, I want to suggest, they also represent an excess, a sort of overresponse—one that we might plausibly understand, as it extends a generic trajectory, to be also motivated by an anxiety over politic agency. *Urania* and *Arcadia* dramatically elaborate what we might call the "Basilius syndrome" in Sidney through their weak and dying father-king figures, but they do not resort to Sidney's rather summary balancing and Oedipal tactics to preempt the problem of intragenerational peer rivalry. Instead, both romances enact a marked recuperation of one particular generic ancestor, revising Heliodoran chastity, which as a conventional romance value was satirized and ultimately repudiated by both Ariosto and Cervantes before them, as rivalry's counterbalance. In effect Wroth and Barclay reanimate what elsewhere in the early modern period is dismissed as a hoary, naïve generic convention, reminding their readers anew of its vitality and complexity and laying the groundwork for midcentury romance's sincere exploration of the idealism Sidney found himself unable to countenance.

1. Peers Who Are Chastened

In the "Apologie for Romances" prefacing *Aretina; Or, The Serious Romance,* published in Edinburgh in 1660, George MacKenzie offers a select list of romance-writing predecessors, what we might read as a basic genealogy for seventeenth-century romances "Written originally in English," as *Aretina* advertises itself on its title page. MacKenzie cites with defensive zeal the "thousands of Ancients, and Moderns, Ecclesiasticks, and Laicks, Spaniards, French, and Italians" whose romances offered precedents for his, but to describe the particular tradition in which *Aretina* was positioning itself he lists only "the famous *Sidney, Scuderie, Barkley,* and *Broghill*" and then "that noble Romance, Written by a Bishop, which the entreaty of all the Eastern Churches could never prevail with him to disown."[4] MacKenzie's "Barkley," of course, is John Barclay, whose *Argenis* was first published in 1621; Broghill is Roger Boyle, Baron Broghill and shortly to be Earl of Orrery, who published *Parthenissa* in installments throughout the 1650s; Sidney and de Scudéry are more familiar to us, as they are regularly included in our own canon of early modern fiction (although MacKenzie probably refers here not to Madeleine de Scudéry but to her brother Georges, whom most English people in the seventeenth century believed to be the real author of the pair). The one exception in MacKenzie's list of rough contemporaries is the "Bishop" Heliodorus, who although not named directly nevertheless receives pride of both place and attention. MacKenzie refers here to a legend widely circulated in the Renaissance, in Montaigne's *Essays* and in Burton's *Anatomy of Melancholy* among other works, that Heliodorus lost his position as Bishop of Tricca because he refused to repudiate *Aethiopika*—a narrative MacKenzie uses as an anchor for his argument in the "Apologie" that if romance has always been besieged, its history of besiegement is nevertheless a highly distinguished one.[5] The preeminence of British names on this list (arguably three of the four modern writers) confirms that in seventeenth-century Britain, English romance was not felt to be derivative of the French—if anything, the opposite was the case. And the fact that all of MacKenzie's examples are specifically prose romances suggests the importance of prose as a generic marker at midcentury and warns against subsuming these works in a larger category including drama and verse. Still, the list's most significant detail is its claim for Heliodorus as romance's preeminent classical model.

Aethiopika first appeared in the Renaissance in Greek, in 1534; Jacques Amyot's French translation was published in 1547, Stanislaus Warschewiczki's Latin translation in 1551, and Thomas Underdowne's English (via the Latin) not until 1587 (although not surprisingly, *Aethiopika* was already well known to Sidney and his contemporaries in the 1580s).[6] *Aethiopika* was a model for early modern romance in several ways, most significantly, perhaps, in the evidence it provided that romance could be a morally virtuous genre (probably the reason that MacKenzie felt it to be such an important precedent for his own "Serious Romance"), through its thematization of chastity persistently assailed but never overcome. The event initiating the whole action of Heliodorus's narrative is the birth to the black Ethiopian queen Persinna of a white daughter, Chariclea, a long-awaited heir whom Persinna is nevertheless forced to foster outside Ethiopia because she fears being accused of adultery—in this case of violating not only sexual but also ethnic or national purity. Here and throughout the romance, the challenge posed by Chariclea's narrative is the Jamesonian one of how to construe the dividing line between self and foreigner and then how to accommodate oneself to what has been deemed foreign. Eventually Chariclea returns to Ethiopia and marries the Greek prince Theagenes, a descendant of Achilles, with whom she has fallen in love during her exile, and what is ostensibly achieved is an interpenetration of two cultures, a recuperation in a public and officially sanctioned sense of an alliance that in the privately transgressive context of Persinna's (symbolic, if not literal) adultery would have been inadmissible. The lesson conveyed is apparently the Jamesonian one that in the face of the chaotic likeness of what we had assumed to be different (here the instant affinity between Chariclea and Theagenes, and, of course, the inexplicable similarity of Chariclea's skin color to Theag es'), what we require is formal, publicly recognized relationship at once sanctions mixture and defuses it of real threat. Thi likely also the lesson of Odysseus's famous dream-rebuke elsewhere in the romance, when Homer's hero warns telling descendant that if the descendant does not explici edge the presence of the ancestor he will be forced

ancestor's story. Formal recognition of the historical or cultural predecessor is better than stealthy usurpation because it confers on the descendant a space for the establishment of an independent identity, one beholden to but also safely distinct from the predecessor's.

There is, however, another way of reading what goes wrong for Persinna, one that on its face is more naïve but also more challenging to the symbolic mode of accommodation I just described. At the moment of Chariclea's conception, black Persinna is looking at a picture on the wall of the hero Perseus escorting the naked and dazzlingly white heroine Andromeda down from the rock on which she has been chained, as a sacrifice to a monster holding her country in thrall, and Persinna's ill-timed gaze apparently transmits Andromeda's white skin to Chariclea. Modern commentators have wondered whether Heliodorus's contemporaries really would have believed such a story, but this seems beside the point: the force of the episode is as an allegory for the way that the viewer, whether she intends it or not, appropriates what she sees.

It is customary to interpret the scene in Persinna's picture as erotic, and doubtless for a viewer taking Perseus's perspective it is: as Perseus well knows, he has just inherited this young woman from the monster he has vanquished, and the naked body he sees before him (along with all the royal status she conveys) is about to become his possession. Several centuries later, via Ovid's version of the Andromeda story, Ariosto was to make pointed fun of such a perspective in paired scenes in *Orlando Furioso* 10 and 11. In the first, Ruggiero rescues naked Angelica from her chains on the rock but fails to kills the Orc threatening to ravish her, only to be inspired by her resemblance to his beloved Bradamante to rape her himself (his failure is the result only of a sudden bout of impotence); in the second, the sadly belated Orlando does succeed in killing the Orc but rescues someone else's lover instead of his own and is left alone afterward to wonder whether Angelica has faced a similar fate. Ariosto's parodies both expose and frustrate the cultural logic by which "rescuing" the woman from the monster is really a means of taking the monster's place.[7] One of their effects is to send us back to see the scene from Andromeda's eyes, to entertain the possibility that even after Perseus kills the monster, her shame and vulnerability persist. Heliodorus, I would argue, had already acknowledged this perspective through the echoing shame he assigned to Persinna at the birth of her white child, and he had also already rendered it even more complex, as Persinna in *Aethiopika* is at once both victim and appropriator, both Andromeda and Perseus, guilty of an act she did not intend but that she effected nonetheless.

Furthermore, her own visual appropriation of Andromeda, unlike Perseus's, is actually harmful to her, causing her to conceive a child whom she cannot acknowledge.

Aethiopika's corrective, its answer both to acquisitive desire and to more ambivalently willed appropriation, is chastity. Chariclea's great and exceptional virtue as heroine throughout the romance is the chastity her mother enjoins upon her as she gives her up for fostering. When Chariclea agrees to leave Greece with her suitor Theagenes she enjoins chastity on him as well, a directive not repeated in any other extant Greek romance, and for the rest of the narrative the two lovers glide untouched and untempted above comically lengthy sequences of importunate suitors, trial by fire, and even torture by a lascivious queen. It is not an accidental deviation from the Perseus and Andromeda story that in the end Theagenes proves his worthiness to marry Chariclea not by rescuing her directly but by wrestling a bull to the ground, thereby preserving himself apart from the Persean equation of monster with husband.

Eric Aversa notes that it is possible to read the entire plot of *Aethiopika* retrospectively as an elaborate justification for the Ethiopians' banning of human sacrifice at the end, and if we follow Aversa in considering sacrifice in René Girard's terms we can see even more fully chastity's function in Heliodorus's narrative.[8] When Chariclea returns to Ethiopia with Theagenes as a prisoner of war, King Hydaspes (who does not recognize his daughter, never having seen her before) orders the couple to be sacrificed as the "first fruits" of his victory—in Girard's terms, as ritual substitutes whose murder is designed to put an end to both extra- and intracommunity violence. But after their identity is revealed, the couple is declared by the Ethiopian public to be an unacceptable sacrifice because as real, particular children of the throne they are no longer "pure," no longer merely representative, either of the enemy or, more significantly, of the Ethiopian community itself. Since he has been "the father of the people abrode," the crowd tells Hydaspes, he should now "be father in your own house at home also," which is to say, claim as literal the function he has been fulfilling symbolically.[9]

The problem with human sacrifice, we learn here, is the fictional and unsustainable symbolic logic by which one person represents another. In the ordinary situation of an encounter between a viewer and a work of art, such logic risks devolving into appropriation; in the sacred situation of sacrifice, we are now also told, the truly pure victim fails by definition to sustain her representativeness and becomes particular. As she was for Persinna at her birth, Chariclea now is not a metaphor but the thing itself, carrying no significance beyond her separateness from everyone else. It is only on these terms, perhaps, that Heliodorus can imagine what becomes in *Aethiopika* the paradox of mixture. Chariclea and Theagenes can be permitted to wed, bringing Greece to Ethiopia, because marriage is really just a pose, because like Chariclea and Theagenes the romance's many opposing terms need not really engage with one another. Furthermore, by slyly revealing himself in the last lines of the romance to be Ethiopian, a man who has "fetched his petigree from the Sunne," Heliodorus performs a triumphant recuperation of Persinna's narrative, claiming for himself a perspective that has trained itself on Greek things (specifically, on Greek things claiming themselves as cultural ancestors) but at the same time has preserved for him a purely Ethiopian integrity.[10] Or, in the terms of the Calasiris anecdote we might say that Heliodorus has pronounced Odysseus's name, recognized him formally, and nevertheless written himself a separate story. It is not that mixture has been made admissible by being formalized, but rather that chastity has truly trumped it by offering a model of integrity preserving independence even in the face of the other. We may find this naïve, and perhaps the romance means to present it as a fantasy, given Heliodorus's acknowledgement of the relentless drive, common to almost all of the characters except Chariclea and Theagenes and, remarkably, Chariclea's father,[11] toward possession and appropriation. But we are also asked to recognize its ethical force, as a method of achieving identity that tries to avoid implication in the complex dynamic of subjugating and being subjugated that always accompanies any encounter, whether real or through representation, between self and other.

2. Incest and Chastity

In *Aethiopika,* then, Heliodorus asserted integrity as an alternative to the sexual and cultural appropriations that his romance makes metaphors for each other. Much later, as I suggested, Ariosto's version of the Andromeda story would devote itself to demystifying idealism, showing how acquisitive desire underlies love or pity and renders it always already compromised. This later reading of pity as corrupt or at the very least inefficacious was consistent with (and perhaps itself an element of) the new humanism, and it became standard in early modern English romance (for instance, in Shakespeare's *The Winter's Tale,* where the Clown's and Shepherd's inability or unwillingness to intervene in the scenes of suffering that so horrify them in Act 3 sets up Autolycus's bemused realization that the good he does is despite himself—an idea that might be said to be the reigning irony in all of Shakespeare's providence-driven romances). Wroth and Barclay belonged to this early modern tradition, but in taking up the problem of politic self-interest they also contested it, and *Aethiopika*'s insistence on chastity, I will show, was one of their primary models for resistance.[12]

Wroth's main route back to Heliodorus was through her valorization of constancy, which in post-Reformation England often functioned as a softer substitute for chastity. Constancy frequently takes an object, as it does, say, for Pamphilia or for Barclay's princess Argenis, and so can be formulated as a will toward something, in opposition to chastity's logic of withholding—a distinction that in this period was generally understood to prove an ethical advantage for constancy. Milton offered a classic statement of the distinction in *Areopagitica*, declaring that "I cannot praise a fugitive and cloister'd vertue, unexercis'd & unbreath'd, that never sallies out and sees her adversary, but slinks out of the race."[13] Stoic constancy was often blamed for being a withdrawal, but the constant woman was presumed to enjoy an advantage over the constant man because she did not have as much to withdraw from; in fact, her erotic constancy in some cases increased her ties to the public realm, by functioning as quasi-private support for a man who was in the public eye. Female chastity in early modern England, in contrast, was often condemned as a perverse, selfish, and fruitless withdrawal from social obligation, for example, by Theseus in the opening of *A Midsummer Night's Dream*, or by implication by Isabella in turning away from her condemned brother for the sake of her own virtue in *Measure for Measure*. For this reason, chastity in the Renaissance, for those who sought to preserve it as a feminine virtue, tended to slide into constancy, the classic example being Spenser's Britomart, Knight of Chastity, whose adventures are all aimed toward the clearing of a symbolic space for union with Artegall.

In Wroth, however, Pamphilia's constancy moves back in the other direction, toward retirement and singularity. Despite Wroth's reservations about autonomy, Pamphilia's absolute devotion to her own passion makes her oddly self-sufficient, not like a multiplicitous stalk of wheat but like a single flower, "one in truth, and being as come from one roote, or graine of matchlesse worth" (317). She spends a great deal of time in seclusion, is almost obsessively pri
emotions, and when she does wander, like Heliodorus's
gives herself up to contingency rather than, in the manne
Britomart or Wroth's own Nerena, purposefully seizing
Whereas the romance presents Urania's dissent, her end
moderation and change, as rational and compassionate,

heroism clearly consists in her preservation of herself inviolate from the temptation to turn away from her passion, hopeless though it may be. If we read Pamphilia's constancy in the light of contemporary thought about morality and ethics, as I argued in chapter 1, the obvious contextual influence upon her characterization was Stoicism, but nevertheless Wroth's notion of constancy was not as close to its contemporaries as to Chariclea's mode of chastity, which similarly did not preclude love but nevertheless emphasized singularity and autonomy. Indeed we might almost read Pamphilia as an elaboration of Chariclea, Wroth's attempt to explain in psychological terms how such a seeming paradox as passionate chastity, already modeled within the generic tradition of romance, might in fact make moral sense.

Pamphilia's construal of constancy, then, was a move away from the more common Renaissance tendency to turn chastity into a social virtue. Against a mindset demonstrated by Shakespeare's Theseus, whose obviously masculinist desire would keep women bound by their subordinating relationships to men, Wroth asserts the power of feminine singularity.[14] But *Urania* also carried Heliodoran chastity forward in another, even more unusual form—one more consistent with Renaissance norms in admitting relation, but also far less consistent, in that the kind of relation it endorsed was endogamous pairing. Like Wroth herself, whose primary erotic attachment was to the first cousin with whom she had been raised as a child, not only Pamphilia but several other of *Urania*'s female characters pursue intrafamilial relationships with their roots in childhood.[15]

James Nohrnberg has observed that in the context of Renaissance thought incest was a form of "intentional chastity," a father's or brother's attempt to keep out of circulation the sexuality of a daughter or sister that would otherwise take its place as a commodity in the larger world outside the family, not just by withholding her but by preempting any exogamous attachment she might otherwise form through an endogamous union he enforced himself.[16] Though on the surface incest might seem an excess of sexuality suddenly extended into places it does not belong, in this period it also functioned as a cancellation of sexuality construed as a social drive, an effort to deny or restrict sexuality's fundamental directedness outward toward another. Thus, as a metaphoric desire during this period incest conflicted directly with the idea behind the word "commonwealth," that wealth belonged in common circulation, which is why it was so often used in Renaissance drama as a figure for tyranny—in Shakespeare's romances, for instance, or in John Ford's *'Tis Pity She's a Whore* (published 1633) or John Webster's *The Duchess of Malfi* (1613?). Webster's tyrannical Duke

Ferdinand is almost hysterically preoccupied with the possibility that his sister might bestow herself in marriage upon an outsider, and he is also, not merely coincidentally, guilty of such commands to his courtiers as to "be my touchwood, take fire when I give fire; that is, laugh when I laugh."[17] Ferdinand's problem, as Frank Whigham astutely argues, is that he wants to shrink the rest of the world and expand himself until he becomes a "peerless class of one," a drive he tries to realize in relation to everyone in the play except perhaps his brother.[18] In a classic Renaissance paradox, his impulse to tyranny is actually an expression of his social and political weakness, a sign that he cannot withstand challenges from others.

Both tyranny and Norhnberg's "intentional chastity" are qualitatively the same kind of sin as Isabella's in *Measure for Measure*, to the extent that Isabella can be called a sinner—the indulgence of the self at the absolute expense of the other (though to be fair, the conditions for Isabella's sin are set up by others just as self-indulgent, perhaps even more so, than she). This is the meaning we ought to attribute (and not just in hindsight) to Basilius's sin in *Arcadia* too, though in a somewhat more comic vein. Through his uncomprehending fear of the oracle's warning that his daughters will be subject to an "uncouth love, which nature hateth most," the fatuous duke ironically brings just this love to pass in not one way but two—effecting his own symbolic act of incest by withdrawing the eminently marriageable Pamela and Philoclea to Arcadia, and thus all but necessitating that they be stolen from him.[19] Basilius, of course, is not a brother but a father, a difference without much significance to the conceptual link between incest and tyranny in Renaissance drama but one that early modern thought about incest did take note of in other ways. Incest in the sixteenth and seventeenth centuries, following both Leviticus and Justinian's *Institutes*, was believed to violate natural law, but the establishment of the prohibited degrees of incest, following Justinian, was left to civil law; and it was widely known that such distinctions could sometimes be a matter of politics or other concerns extraneous to natural morality. (Thomas Cranmer's declaration of the indispensability of the Levitical prohibitions against marrying the wife of one's dead brother so that Henry VIII could annul his marriage to Catherine of Aragon and marry Anne Boleyn instead was a widely cited example.)[20] This recognition of the blurry line dividing incestuous unions from permissible ones was complemented by an apprehension that sibling incest might in some sense be natural. Father-daughter incest in Renaissance England seemed to violate the life-cycle—the father had had his chance, and should cede place to the younger man—but most commentators from Augustine on agreed that sibling incest was wrong not necessarily in itself but in a larger social context, the strongest argument against it being that it blocked the benefits of exogamy, halting the spread of influence and wealth that occurs through in-law relationships.[21] Against this concern it was sometimes noted that Adam and Eve were siblings of a sort, and Montaigne's difficulty with marriage between a brother and a sister was not the incompatibility between sexual and familial love but rather the power of their combination, a "surcrease" of love that "may easily transport the husband beyond the bounds of reason."[22]

The problem with sibling incest in this view was not that it was unnatural but that it was too natural, pushing against cultural restrictions on erotic passion and threatening to supplant the societal ends of marriage. Yet from the evidence, Montaigne's specter of an overly loving husband was not as alarming to Wroth as it was to Montaigne, and we might thus speculate that early modern women, who were not as often as men the direct beneficiaries of the exogamous circulation of wealth nor as often the agents in making arrangements for it, were not as worried about its restriction. In any case, it seems safe to say that outside the political arena, sibling incest was not felt to violate the natural order to the degree that father-daughter incest did. In Wroth's *Urania* incest is largely depoliticized, by the romance's focus on siblings and its mostly dead or dying fathers. But in turning away from the political problem *Urania* was not just dodging some of the more troublesome aspects of endogamous relationship. Rather, Wroth's romance proposes endogamy as a real and tenable alternative to the corruption of the marriage market, in a way that strongly recalls Heliodoran chastity's defiance of mixture and engagement.

The most significant example of Wroth's argument for endogamy occurs within Pamphilia's relationship with Amphilanthus, but Wroth offers much more explicitly illustrative examples elsewhere, the most pointed appearing late in the romance, at the beginning of the fourth and last book, when the once unhappily but now more stably married couple Parselius and Dalinea take a day trip to a "greate Desart." Dalinea is fishing when she is lured by an old woman to a "place thicke, and scratching, ful of bushes and thornes," in the middle of which is a stone with a ring, and underneath that a stairway to a gallery, then a garden, and finally a hall with an altar at its center, on top of it a book containing (as also in *Urania*'s second enchantment) a family history (518). Dalinea takes up the book to read at the very moment Parselius and an old man appear from the other direction, and the old man recounts out loud what Dalinea is reading, the narrative of a crucial endogamous event in Dalinea's lineage. Dalinea's paternal great-uncle Distantes fathered a daughter by his wife, who died in childbirth, and at almost exactly the same time a son by the wife of another man. In order to see his mistress more freely the great-uncle asked her to bring up the daughter, and "these children continually nourished, fed, and conversing together, did breed, feede, and discourse affections by this meanes, growing like trees incensible yet to perfection" (520). This apparently inevitable passion, independent of any exercise of human will, inspired a secret vow of marriage, but then Distantes precipitated a crisis by revealing his own plans for a match for the daughter. The mother of the son confessed to the children that they shared a father before dying of her own guilt, and the pair fled to the desert to die there, united by love and despair. Later Distantes found their bodies and made this place a monument to them, asking that their history be put in a book and reserved for a queen "loving as well, as much deserving, but more happily enjoying to her comfort" (526).

Sibling incest in this story is hardly a tenable alternative to other kinds of passion, nor is it entirely condoned. Although the tragic resolution may seem to side with the lovers' passion, the main function of the mother's revelation is to offer moral reform, bringing the siblings "gaine" by "making them know the ill they had runne into, and the sinne they had committed" (521). The narrator also tries to forestall the inevitable parallel between her characters and the more lascivious lovers in Ovid's tales of incest, noting that although the son may seem to flee to the desert "like Caunus from Biblis," "the comparison holds not clearly, because these Lovers were chaste and pure after the secret was disclos'd" (525).[23] Yet despite these reservations, Wroth's narrative also celebrates incestuous love, which is commemorated in the tomb Parselius and Dalinea pledge to maintain and even figuratively consummated by the journey the tomb requires of its visitors. When Distantes built the monument, says the old man to Parselius and Dalinea, he had the option of constructing the entrance along the side of the mountain, where there was "light in aboundance," but instead he chose, "strange as their lives," to build it straight through the rock, "as if to pierce the Center, as that part in their hearts had beene sealed" (525–26). Through their passion the lovers closed off their bodies from customary commerce with the outside world, and at the end of their lives they had to close them to one another, but now the iconographical architecture of the tomb allows the visitor to "pierce" the seal around their hearts, to insert herself, as a figurative consummator, into the structure that commemorates their desire.

In the wrong hands perhaps this would be a violation, but the old man sees Dalinea's arrival as a fulfillment: she "loves" and "deserves" as much as her dead cousins, but she is "more happily enjoying to her comfort." And as Dalinea's luck in love completes the trajectory of the siblings' love, so their innocence and faith certifies hers and Parselius's, offering a confirmation that Parselius and Dalinea, because of their checkered marital history, need more than does any other couple in the romance.[24] In celebrating the siblings' doomed relationship through their stewardship of the tomb they prove their own good faith, laying claim to the paradoxical combination of innocence and passion that incest in this story enables.

One of the models for Wroth's sibling lovers is *Arcadia*'s most idealized couple, Argalus and Parthenia, who battle great odds to marry. At Argalus's death Parthenia puts on men's armor and sacrifices herself in battle, and afterward the lovers' dedication to one another is memorialized by an elaborate tomb on which is engraved, "As all the rest, so now the stone / That tombs the two is justly one" (*NA* 530). Both Sidney's and Wroth's lovers champion free and uncoerced love against the norm of arranged marriage, and neither pair seems able to survive very long in the world in any form but as a commemorated ideal. On the other hand, the reason Argalus and Parthenia's love is heroic is because they have struggled against such great opposition and never wavered in their constancy. They have achieved their union in the public world of men, not the domestic one of women, an accomplishment Parthenia marks by insisting on dying in the public realm of battle as if she were a man. The blonde hair that cascades out of her helmet at the moment of her death recalls quite precisely Britomart's unmasking in *The Faerie Queene* (3.20), emphasizing Parthenia's public role as defender of marital constancy and indeed the importance of such constancy in the public realm. *Urania*'s lovers, by contrast, never have the chance to be heroic because they never leave home. Their love is not achieved, not in any way an issue of moral choice, and the pathos they evoke comes entirely from the conflict between their childlike innocence and the dictates of civil and, to some extent, natural law. Wroth clearly set out to revise the heroic code of Sidney's romance, specifically its emphasis on moral choice and responsibility, and to consider instead the plight of characters whose social role is emphatically to be without agency. Insofar as her characters exist (as men, for the time being; as women, permanently) in a realm where agency does not quite have meaning, one of the most fascinating aspects of Wroth's treatment of endogamy is how differently it values this lack of agency—as a difficult, even tragic, limitation, but also as conducive to a certain kind of purity and beauty.

3. Between Endogamy and Marriage: The Fantasy of Agency

In *Urania* incestuous passion between siblings remains transgressive enough to be celebrated only hypothetically, after it has ceased to be a real possibility, but Wroth's story of Distantes' children also serves a normalizing function within the romance as a whole, offering a quasi-moral and aesthetic argument for a kind of erotic passion that in another, less shocking guise—namely, between first cousins—*Urania* could advocate and freely depict as realized. In Jacobean England sexual relationships between first cousins were not understood to be on a moral par with sibling incest, but they were certainly endogamous and therefore open to the usual charge against incest, its failure to spread "social charitie" through in-law ties. Before the Reformation, the Catholic Church had forbidden intermarriage to the fourth degree of consanguineal or affinal relationship—that is, up to second cousins by blood or marriage. Statutes under Henry VIII declared marriage between first cousins legal, but during James's reign Rome and Continental Protestant Churches still considered it within the prohibited degrees.[25] Wroth's own sexual relationship with her first cousin William Herbert, which produced two children, was not only endogamous but extramarital, tipping the scales altogether against virtue. The stories in *Urania* that shadow this aspect of Wroth's life, however, are not apologetic; on the contrary, they go so far as to portray endogamous romance as the only kind in which aristocratic women can be real beneficiaries.

One of the most exceptional of these stories in *Urania*, for its happy ending, is that of a noblewoman whom Amphilanthus meets while she is angling for fish. Since her childhood, she tells the emperor, she has been in love with the son of her father's sister, who was always "much in my fathers house" (291; as usual, the Wroth/Pamphilia pattern), and for years she was "busied like a Spider" trying to "worke my end," to bring her father's wishes and her own into line and marry not only for money but also for love (293). After several setbacks, however, she gave up and submitted to a "businesse" proposed to her father (292), that she match with a young man whom she did not know personally but who had a large estate. Meanwhile she continued her relationship with her true love, and as a result they have now obtained "all pleasures we can wish, content, and love, and happines in that" (294). The reason this lady is able to maintain her ideal endogamous love within the practical, social arrangement of marriage is because her husband is willing to accept the truth that exogamous emotional bonds bear only an imitative, derivative relation to originary endogamous affection. At first, she admits to Amphilanthus, "Humors [her husband] had of jealosie, which I could not blame him for," but then he "came to know, or better, to bee cleane deceived," and after that "wee grew good friends, and like kinde mates, have lived these last three yeares" (295). The husband has agreed to look away from his wife's adulterous passion, but also, the lady suggests with her complex pun on "kinde," from the fact that he and she are only "like" people who are of the same "kinde," or family. They may act as if they were "kinde"—act, that is, kindly—but because they do not share an authentic endogamous bond this kindness must be only ironic imitation, and the husband's acknowledgment of this irony creates a space for the wife to sustain her true love. Though for reasons of domestic harmony it was often expedient to pretend otherwise, marriage, this episode suggests, was really a matter of estates and settlements, of deals between fathers and exogamous suitors. Love, in contrast, belonged to intrafamilial relationships that women had some part in establishing and that were commonly formed well before their male relatives put them on the marriage market. Relationships thus outside of the ordinary "traffic in women," in Gayle Rubin's famous phrase, did not necessarily have to pose a qualitative challenge to the economy of aristocratic marriage.[26]

Although the fisher-lady's happy ending is exceptional enough in *Urania* to make the peaceful coexistence of ordinary marital relations and endogamous erotic attachment seem little more than a fantasy, Wroth was clear-eyed about the conditions that made such a fantasy essential for women. Endogamous relationships contained the problem of women's agency by restricting dramatically the field of potential partners and naturalizing their attachments. In exogamous negotiations, in contrast, which required choice, women might find themselves condemned for trying to act as their own agents when the code of virtuous behavior required that their agency not extend past constancy, and also for being the very commodities that their passivity consigned them to. *Urania* illustrates this double bind most vividly through a quasi-feminist revision of the classic pastoral love triangle, a standoff between two men over one woman that Amphilanthus's friend Ollorandus is asked to resolve when he happens upon them in a forest. For a while the men shared the woman's affections, but now the woman's father has told her it is time to marry, and she declares herself unable to choose between them. As the first suitor reveals, her inability is not really surprising, since the second suitor is the best friend of the first and fell in love at his friend's invitation, with the deliberate intention of imitating, even sharing, the first suitor's passion. When the first suitor fell in love, he recalls, he "could not be contented with my happinesse, being nothing me thought, if onely by my selfe enjoyed," and so he related all to the second, who soon "beheld us so well contented, as he did wish himselfe the like, and I thinke the same fortune" (450). Ollorandus is hesitant to "meddle" lest he "divide the perfect love" between the two young men (449). Nevertheless he is about to blindfold the woman and have her choose randomly when the men arrive at what their history has set up as the obvious solution, deciding that "they would as before passionatly loving, equally leave her"—the second remarking, as they depart, that "he was the cause of my affection, and my love-tye continues as firme to him as ever" (452–3). Wroth here makes what is essentially Girard's point about mimetic desire, that men desire women not as objects in themselves but because other men already desire them.[27] The woman might be supposed to be well rid of such suitors, and at the very end she does adopt a "changers boldnesse" in front of the amused Ollorandus, declaring that she will not miss either man and that "the fault lyes on your sexe," but she is also left to "cover her selfe with her owne shame" in front of an audience that has gathered to watch the judgment (453). If before she seemed to have the advantage, the "freedome," as she says, to enjoy both suitors, now she has been taught that she was never really an agent, only a contested prize, and that as a prize she has a merely temporary value, one easily transferred to another object. The extrafamilial social world, her story suggests, is constituted by social bonds between men, and as the story issues a warning about the hazards of exogamy for women it announces that when women threaten these bonds, even if only by their presence, they must be reminded that they are extraneous and expendable.

As *Urania* explores the moral and social consequences of exogamous ideology for women, it illustrates some of the protective benefits offered by early endogamous attachment, especially in Wroth's extended narrative about the princess Antissia's erotic fortunes. Antissia, as her name signifies, is Pamphilia's negative double, a figure in whom rivalry with Pamphilia (first for Amphilanthus's affections, later for the title of poet) becomes almost a pathology. The source of Antissia's rivalry is an early history that robbed her of her self-possession, rendering her desire free of all natural and virtuous constraints. As a young girl she became the victim of a classic exogamous arrangement gone wrong: sent from home to live with the family of the prince to whom she had been promised in marriage, first she was betrayed by her guardian, who planned to abscond with the wealth she was bringing to her prospective parents-in-law; then abducted by pirates, who sold her to an Italian merchant; and then in the merchant's house she was kidnapped again, this time by two courtiers intending to rape her. Fittingly they murdered each other trying to decide who would go first, and eventually she was returned home, but by this point her fiancé had fallen in love with someone else and she was left without a social network, belonging neither to the family she was supposed to join nor to the one she left too early. Antissia's story, devolving from childhood betrothal through cash transactions to rape, is a demystification of aristocratic arranged marriage, a reduction of the practice to its structural essence. As she herself exclaims at one point during her journey, she has been "made merchandize" (38), a fate that makes the courtiers' attempt to rape her seem all but inevitable.

By a logic quite close to that which governs the cultural understanding of rape in the Renaissance, Antissia is morally sullied by her victimization, mirroring the faults of her oppressors. Acting as if infected by the corruption of the marketplace, she becomes by her very nature a rival, competing continually for goals that (as for the suitors in Ollorandus's love triangle, but far less lightheartedly) are not nearly as important to her as the feelings she holds for her competitors. Unable to curb her passions, Antissia asks impertinent questions, declares her love for Amphilanthus indiscriminately and without any assurance that he loves her back, and writes embarrassingly disordered poetry. All of this behavior, of course, is in direct contrast to that of Pamphilia, who is everything Antissia is not: tactful, perfectly discreet, and authoritative in her relationships with others and as a poet. In this respect Pamphilia's advantage both springs from and is expressed by means of her endogamous attachment to Amphilanthus. The cousins have enjoyed "long conversation as from our youthes," Pamphilia declares when Antissia jealously accuses her of trying to secure Amphilanthus's affections for herself, and Antissia even remarks that Pamphilia and Amphilanthus resemble each other (95). As a result of their history of intimacy their affection can go unspoken, a liberty signifying to the vociferous Antissia all that she must remain excluded from.

Antissia's isolation is, in this sense, not just social but moral: by removing her from the private context of endogamous relationships,

Antissia's premature entrance onto the marketnot only stripped her of an important social advantage but disfigured her character, rendering her incapable of keeping her passions to herself. In this she bears striking similarities to Nerena, the absolutist queen I discussed in the last chapter, who is likewise incapable of temperance and self-control and leaves the boundaries of her own island to take on a "Knight-like search" for Steriamus. Whether by design or bad luck, both women leave home when they should not, and both manifest as a result the same moral shortcomings. Thus endogamy, in Wroth's view, is a defense against the damage inflicted on women by the extrafamilial social world, a way to resist the corrupting influences on the will of the marital marketplace and to maintain the boundedness of self-possession.

If we can map endogamous passion as a form of intentional chastity in the Renaissance, then Wroth, we might say, through her use of Heliodorus, reconfigured such chastity as a virtue—not an arrogant withdrawal from social responsibility but a defense against what from an aristocratic woman's point of view were necessarily the corruptions that accompanied marriage. In Heliodorus, I argued, such defensiveness was also a challenge, not just a division of spheres. Even as it disdained open rivalry, *Aethiopika* was addressing Greek culture on its own terms, claiming real parity for its "race of the sun." Similarly, in Wroth endogamy served not just as a private alternative to public structures of authority but also as an engagement of them on their own ground. That this outlandish idea was indeed one of endogamy's available significances in early modern culture should be clear to us from a reading of Shakespeare's 1604 *Measure for Measure*, which by linking chastity and endogamy as modes not only of moral but also of something close to civil or political autonomy revealed them to be comparable only to slander in the threat they posed to authority.[28] According to the plot the Duke presides over in order to shore up his own fading authority, Isabella is first asked to choose between love for her brother, Claudio, which she might express by yielding herself to rape by Angelo (an act Isabella herself calls "a kind of incest"),[29] and love for her own virtue, embodied in her resolve to keep herself chaste. Her choice is in fact a false dilemma, because the two turn out to be not really opposed. And the proof of this lesson resides in Isabella's ability to have both at once. In his preservation of Claudio's life and by the device of the bed trick, the Duke demonstrates narratively the symbolic compatibility of chastity and endogamous affection. Then, in the final scenes of the play he also subjects Isabella to dual forms of discipline, the psychological experience of Claudio's death and the subordination of her entirely warranted feelings of disgust and anger toward Angelo. Clearly the Duke is trying to purge his subject of a certain righteous pride, expressed equally, it turns out, by her erotic indifference to men and her allegiance to her brother. And all of this is preparing the ground, as it were, for the coup de grâce, for Isabella's direct subjection, through exogamous marriage, to the very embodiment of political authority. The Duke's plot for Isabella reveals that to his eyes, at least, extramarital sex is only a metaphor for what really ails Vienna. The unconfined sexuality represented by prostitution defies the law; Isabella's devotion to chastity and to her brother threatens the Duke's rule much more directly by putting another authority in his place.

Exogamy, Shakespeare's Duke suggests, was the ultimate method of shoring up civil authority, because it redefined what were potentially the two most powerful social alternatives to the state—the family and the church—as instead only inducements to morally contemptible self-love. Ultimately, with respect to authority what look like alternatives are no alternatives at all; structurally the Duke wants the world to be perfectly monocentric. What he intuits, from his position of power, is the solution *Aethiopika* represented from the opposite perspective as its problem: Ethiopia seemed everywhere penetrated and compromised by Greece, the two unavoidably implicated in one another, and in response to Greece's apparently overwhelming influence Heliodorus wished to establish as a tenable notion the idea of Ethiopia's otherness. And just as *Aethiopika* hypothetically corrected for the apparent interpenetration of cultures suggested in Persinna's conception of Chariclea by insisting on Ethiopia's separation from Greece, *Urania* argued in seventeenth-century England that the family was not a metaphor for court culture but a separate institution, and with *Aethiopika* it was able to construe separation as a source of strength. *Urania* conducted this argument not just thematically but formally: almost all of its characters, erotically entangled or not, were fictional representatives of Wroth's own family, as Wroth framed the whole romance as a response to and continuation of her uncle's *Arcadia*. In this sense Wroth's entire literary project seems an effort to define coterie fiction and roman à clef, those forms so central to romance's nature, as versions of endogamy. Often we tend to think of coterie fiction and roman à clef as restricted, "smaller" versions of more fully fictional and public forms of narrative, but in Wroth's hands they served as formal, ideological contestations of the more nascent value of free and wide-ranging circulation, warning that entry onto the literary market might render an author complicitous with the very structures of authority she sought to criticize.

4. Barclay's *Argenis:* The Cultural Plot of Rivalry

If *Aethiopika* used chastity straightforwardly as a metaphorical corrective for the cultural appropriation of the subordinate by the dominant, *Urania*'s development of endogamy as a version of chastity, similarly promoting a kind of subjective integrity for those not usually recognized in the public realm as anything but objects of negotiation, perhaps owed more to this classic Heliodoran tradition than to conventional seventeenth-century ideology. *A Midsummer Night's Dream*'s Hippolyta, *Measure for Measure*'s Isabella (though it is unclear whether she receives the lesson), and Marvell's Isabel Thwaites in "Upon Appleton House" all were taught to know their heterosexual, exogamous destiny, while such a paradigmatic figure as Cervantes's Don Quixote, neither English nor Protestant but determined to adapt the metaphorical chastity of romance as a way to opt out of ordinary self-interested social relations, was declared by his author to be functionally insane. But insofar as Wroth's endogamous woman lovers at least sometimes succeeded in using their intrafamilial erotic affiliations as a way to avoid the social symbolic order, Wroth had constructed them to withstand an ideology that all too often blamed women for lacking the very integrity it would take away. In the second half of this chapter I want to turn to a romance that on the surface looks quite different from *Urania* and would seem to treat Heliodoran idealism much more ambivalently, but nonetheless developed a theory of friendship surprisingly similar to Wroth's endogamous attachment.

John Barclay's *Argenis* was first published in Latin, in 1621, and almost immediately translated into English, first by Ben Jonson, who entered his translation in the Stationers' Register in 1622 but apparently lost it before publication in the fire that destroyed his library, and then by Kingsmill Long in 1625 and again by Robert Le Grys in 1628.[30] *Argenis* was a product of the same court milieu that gave rise to *Urania*, and it has a stronger claim to belong to the literature of England than of anywhere else.[31] Though Barclay was educated mainly in France, his father, the noted Scottish scholar of jurisprudence William Barclay, brought him from France to James I's court in 1605 in hopes of patronage, and the younger Barclay stayed on as a polemicist and occasional diplomat until 1616.[32] The published English keys (there were probably several more in manuscript[33]) that circulated with *Argenis* mentioned England only rarely and, when they did, tended to confine themselves to Elizabeth's reign, but the romance quite obviously portrays aspects of the Jacobean court. Indeed, the description of King Meleander, Argenis's father and the monarch whose weakness provokes the entire plot, who is too fond of hunting, overly given to peace because of the lack of military challenges early in his reign, and too disposed to young male favorites, was a conventional portrait of James. Through his mouthpiece Nicopompus, Meleander's resident court poet, Barclay called his *Argenis* a "new kind of writing" (132), an unprecedented mixture of statecraft manual with gripping fictional narrative. Throughout the romance he advertises both his position on the inside of court intrigues and his own politic wisdom, so as to offer his readers not only a faithful and canny account of real politics but a practical guide for participating in them.

As we might expect, such a work was not ostensibly sympathetic to Heliodoran forms of idealism. With its cast of court characters always already enmeshed in social and political relationships, their task usually to figure out how to negotiate for their own ends rather than succumbing to manipulation by others, *Argenis* seems descended from Sidney rather than Heliodorus.[34] Much more so than *Urania*, *Argenis* was written as a practical guide to a social and political world already given. But even as it revisited through a sophisticated perspective what it cast as the more naïve aspects of Heliodoran romance, *Argenis* preserved something close to Heliodoran idealism in its configuration of identificatory friendship between young men. This dual impulse, toward at once a demystificatory realism about the politic laws governing sociality and an idealism about same-sex love and friendship, set up a tension between self-interest and relationship to others that was to become one of the reigning concerns of the generation of romance after Barclay, and more than anything else it established *Argenis*'s place as one of the first modern, (nearly) English inaugurators of MacKenzie's seventeenth-century romance tradition.

If *Argenis* sought to be part political treatise and part effective narrative, we might at the risk of schematism map the strategic split between its politic and idealistic sides onto these two separate generic aspects of its identity. Greek romance was clearly the chief model for the narrative part of *Argenis*'s project: the central subject of the romance is the relation between Meleander's and Argenis's Sicily and the African country Mauritania, birthplace of the prince Archombrotus, and its great revelation is that Archombrotus is the son of the king of Sicily, a mirror image of Heliodorus's own plot secret (wherein an African prince turns out to be European, instead of a Greek-looking princess learning that she is in fact African). Barclay employs Heliodoran suspense and paradox as Wroth does not, and in a manner much more consistent and centralized than Sidney's exploitation of ancient romance conventions in the *New Arcadia*. Moreover, in the integration and coherence of its narrative structure *Argenis* remains much closer to *Aethiopika* than to either *Arcadia* or *Urania*. Notably, Barclay also chose to allude directly to Heliodorus in the mechanics of his narration, for instance in the complaint of one unsatisfied listener to a long inset story that he "despised" the teller "that had with such a circumlocution drest up so faire a Stage, upon which at last nothing should be acted" (319). This moment is explicitly parallel to one in *Aethiopika*'s third book when the receiver of another inset story complains that it was as if the teller had "but opened the Theatre, and straight shut it up againe" (Underdowne, 79).[35] In the light of such debts, Barclay's decision to combine in his title an anagram for *regina* (Latin for "queen"—compare Machiavelli's *Il Principe*) with the Greek-sounding suffix *–is* almost certainly signaled his intention to convey his Latin treatise through the medium of Greek fiction.

Thematically, *Argenis*'s most pointed and significant diversion from *Aethiopika* is in the introduction of the very politic problem of rivalry into its plot. Barclay's romance is the story of a series of rivals for the princess Argenis's hand and throne, culminating in a single dominant love triangle-cum-political rivalry that almost leads to civil and international war until Barclay provides narrative principles by which the spoils may be divided. *Aethiopika*, in contrast, is markedly dismissive of rivalry as a threat and uninterested in it as a problem.[36] As we might expect from his depiction of chastity as an unapproachable singularity, Heliodorus's strategy with respect to rivalry was to cast it as the impulse of the weak, or else to suggest that it was for a prize not really worth the fight. There is one potential rivalry in *Aethiopika* that can be taken as an exception, in that it is not subject to either of these defusing tactics, and Heliodorus's indifference to its problematic nature must have seemed from a politic perspective such as Barclay's to be difficult to interpret as anything but a glaring narrative lapse. Meroebus, who is the heroine Chariclea's cousin, has in the absence of a direct heir been groomed for years by Hydaspes as his successor to the Ethiopian throne, so that when Chariclea is welcomed back into the Ethiopian court Hydaspes proposes that she marry him. This union would resolve Chariclea's history of waywardness through endogamy, returning her to the central unit of the

Ethiopian royal family and thus displacing doubts about her legitimacy while at the same time binding Meroebus even more tightly to the Ethiopian throne. When Heliodorus instead legitimates Theagenes' status as Greek prince and lover of Chariclea, Meroebus, as the endogamous and Ethiopia-solidifying solution, vanishes entirely from the narrative. In short, as Meroebus melts back, as it were, into the family, his temporary distinction as a suitor, unlike Theagenes', is revealed to have functioned purely as a plot device, an antidramatic narrative possibility that would have failed to test Ethiopian integrity by way of the cross-cultural challenge Theagenes presents.

Still, Meroebus's unwritten perspective suggests the suppressed problem of rivalry. If we take Meroebus not simply as Hydaspes' temporary structural stopgap but as an agent in his own right—as seventeenth-century court culture, in its preoccupation with the problem of competition, might well have been inclined to do—then Heliodorus's absolute lack of concern with Meroebus's feelings upon being disinherited, or with any resultant familial or political instability, must have seemed a dangerously loose thread. Indeed, the suppressed problem of rivalry might be read as the conceptual instigator of Barclay's central project in *Argenis,* which is to insist on the fundamental importance to his romance of the relationship between competitors. To establish his own version of the Meroebus situation, Barclay begins not with prospective heterosexual union nor with the love triangle complicating it but with two competitors in relation all by themselves. In the romance's first sentence Archombrotus arrives in disguise on the shore of Sicily, Meleander's kingdom, where he has been sent by his mother, the sole monarch of Mauritania, ostensibly to absorb the manners and customs of Europe before assuming rule. At once he is enlisted by the noblewoman Timoclea to defend Poliarchus (also in disguise, so no one will know he is the heir to the French throne) from an ambush, and although he arrives too late to help, this is no barrier to the intense bond that forms immediately between the two princes. When they first see each other it is as if each young man has unexpectedly caught sight of himself in a mirror, and they stop short in a kind of identificatory trance: they "paused in a mutuall contemplation one of another," says the narrator,

> each wondring at that in his companion, with which himselfe also ravished him with admiration. Their age, beautie, garbe, and inexpressable sprightlines of their eyes; their yeeres equall, and though in a different face, one maiestie. With so great beautie to find such valour ioyned, was almost a miracle. Neither did *Timoclea* any lesse worship fortune, that by so strange a way of meeting had coupled so rare a paire. (3)

The narrator is not quite clear here whether he finds the greater "miracle" to be the exceptionality of each of the individual princes or the way one reflects and repeats the other, and the ambiguous syntax of "with which himselfe also ravished him" suggests between the princes themselves both reciprocity (as each wonders at that in his companion which in himself his companion also wonders at) and also, somewhat less firmly but nonetheless suggestively, identification (as each wonders at that in his companion which he also wondered at in himself, in part, one assumes, because he saw it in his companion at the same time).

While these double princes are very un-Heliodoran, Barclay might have found a precedent for them in the *New Arcadia,* in which the love between Pyrocles and Musidorus provided the pretext for the initial action. But Barclay's opening scene also establishes a profound difference from Sidney. Pyrocles and Musidorus, like Wroth's worthiest lovers, are cousins and were brought up together; Poliarchus and Archombrotus not only have no family connections but also have grown up in different countries (Archombrotus is even a Moor, although Barclay is careful to note that his features are European), which leaves their marvelous likeness with no explanation. Sidney had also gone to pains, as I have already suggested, to differentiate and balance his princes.[37] Poliarchus and Archombrotus, by contrast, have nothing beyond their origins to distinguish them. Indeed, in one of *Argenis*'s earliest episodes a crowd of Sicilians mistakes Archombrotus for Poliarchus (who is officially wanted by Sicily at the moment for sedition) and at Meleander's orders hauls him into court for reward. This is a representation on a different level of the same apprehension of likeness to which we were privy earlier, this time for the purpose of base gain rather than aesthetic and ethical appreciation.

Whereas Sidney distinguished Pyrocles and Musidorus from one another so that they would not have to be rivals, Barclay clearly chose to make his pair of princes indistinguishable so that they would compete. Some time after their initial meeting, long before either knows the "real" (social and political) identity of the other, Archombrotus reflects that he is not "the sole man, whose birth and estate is not to be valued by this maske of dissembling, which I have put on," and considers the idea that Poliarchus too may be a prince in disguise. Immediately the practice of identification becomes problematic: if Poliarchus is a prince, Archombrotus reasons, there may then be a "secret neernesse" between Poliarchus and Argenis, and predictably this leads Archombrotus to insert himself in Poliarchus's place (90).[38] Eventually, concludes the narrator, "[a]s much as he [Archombrotus] liked and loved *Argenis*, so much was abated and growne cold the friendship, which had before linked him to *Poliarchus*. At the first, envy, afterward the sicknesse of emulation growing upon him" (90). This outcome, as I have suggested, would hardly be difficult for a Renaissance reader to anticipate; Sidney seems to have had the possibility of it always in the back of his mind, and Leontes' story of what happens to his childhood friendship with Polixenes in *The Winter's Tale* provides another, canonical precedent. Minus woman as the prize that turns likeness into competition, even Fredric Jameson's functional definition of European vernacular romance as a response to the problem of likeness turns on a surprisingly similar logic.

In his argument that twelfth-century male aristocrats, not perceiving any distinction between themselves and the others around them, displaced difference onto the realm of the supernatural, Jameson assumes a basic cultural idea, that the distinction between self and other is a fundamental social requirement. Likeness is presymbolic, prior to the social order; a world governed by likeness has no thought structures for making sense of the otherness that always asserts itself as a basic reality, whether conceptual (as in Jameson, that notion of evil for which we are always trying to find a material vessel) or experiential (as in Shakespeare and Sidney, the feminine that is always violating the paradise of masculine likeness). By this argument, to the extent that it has not already been acknowledged as fantasy, the valorization of absolute likeness necessarily results in crisis, an immediate rush toward triangulation and differentiation that from the perspective of likeness as a lost ideal seems dangerous and chaotic. Sometimes the rush can be forestalled by an act of balanced distinguishing such as Sidney's, or by the projection of what is different onto an imaginary realm, as twelfth-century romance attempts by Jameson's account, but often it seems to threaten a form of competition intense enough to annihilate one or the other of its parties. Barclay's choice to erase Sidneian distinction between his princes is thus by its nature a reproblematizing move, inciting instability where before romance had preempted it with balance.

In this view, it is important that Barclay's princes, like Wroth's endogamous lovers, first encounter each other out of time, in a kind of utopian pre-time in which fast boundaries between self and other do not have to obtain. In the course of describing this meeting the narrator tells us that Timoclea vowed to erect a commemorative "Table," and he then includes in the text the verses she ostensibly appended to her picture many years later. Already, this break in the narrative frame suggests, the princes' extraordinary meeting is far in the past.

Unlike Chariclea's nonencounters with others and Wroth's almost-encounters between lovers who are already family, Archombrotus's and Poliarchus's happy meeting with versions of themselves is already nostalgic, a fantasy of self-sufficient immunity to ordinary social pressures. In the real time that commences immediately afterward, their likeness provides quite the opposite of protection; in fact, it leads to the chaos of rivalry that Sidney had forestalled in his romance, a chaos that Barclay can address only by belatedly carving out distinct identities for the princes according to which they can divide up the spoils for which they have found themselves compelled to compete. If we wonder why Barclay chose to open a problem that both Heliodorus and Sidney made a point of not taking up, we might speculate that he meant to be demystificatory, to work against what Jameson defines as romance's generic imperative, so as to reveal through the unstable middle of his narrative, sandwiched between Edenic fantasy and idealizing Sidneian balance, the real dangers likeness can pose.

There is also, however, another narrative for likeness embedded in *Argenis*, one directly opposed to this notion that likeness is a nostalgic fantasy with pernicious consequences for actual, real-time social relationships. Barclay's princes are young men, not Shakespearean boys, and they find each other in the middle of another narrative that at least temporally is already constituted, the love affair between Poliarchus and Argenis—both details that make it more difficult than it is in, say, *The Winter's Tale* to sustain the notion of likeness as an Edenic fantasy. And indeed, at the end of the romance, when the rivalry between Poliarchus and Archombrotus is on the brink of destroying social and political order, Barclay recuperates likeness, giving us a solution that legitimates and even celebrates the identification between the two young men rather than distinguishing them. Furiously angry at one another, each with a large retinue and each awaited by a domestic faction, the two princes are converging on Sicily to compete for Argenis's hand when at the last minute it is revealed, via some documents that Archombrotus's supposed mother, Hyansibe, queen of Mauritania, sent with him to Meleander, that Archombrotus is in fact Meleander's son and Argenis's half-brother, by Hyanisbe's long-dead sister. Without a pause the very relieved Meleander exclaims to the two princes, "You both did love *Argenis;* and both of you now shall have her," and at once "the young men renewed betweene them the mutuall dearnenesse, which long since they had in happy houre contracted" (472). What is most surprising about this conclusion, what we find slightly comical and also discomfiting, is the notion that Argenis will be shared property, "had" by both men. The competition could have been forestalled simply by the revelation that as brother Archombrotus could not be husband, but instead Barclay chooses to emphasize the sense in which brother and husband are versions of the same thing, suggesting that the "mutuall dearenesse" is once again a function not only of an absence of strife but of a substantive likeness and consequent identification.

Argenis ends, then, with a restoration of the love through likeness with which the Poliarchus-Archombrotus narrative and the romance itself began. It might be argued that in Barclay's terms this is only the simplest of fantasies, an argument by assertion for a return to the predifferentiated state of sociality that *Argenis* has already shown to be impossible. To suppose that a husband and a brother might "have" a woman in the same way, might indeed be different manifestations of the same figure, is to suppose the restoration of a mythical, endogamous time before the subject steps out into the public realm of trade and competition. But while Wroth's proper social role as a woman was to avoid that public realm, Barclay has made it his very subject in *Argenis*. It is too simple, I think, to conclude here that Barclay's interest in the politic complications of relationship to others is simply at odds with his drive toward conventional romance resolution, separate though those projects sometimes seem. Through his plot Barclay offers likeness as a cure for competition rather than simply a fantastic retreat from it, with a persistence that asks us to think further about the relation between likeness and politic ideology.

5. Toward Emulation

In differentiating his princes from the start—almost, as it were, naturally—Sidney's aim was clearly to forestall not competition per se but competition for the benefits to which the princes would eventually be heir. Distinction as such obtains its value as a principle governing the distribution of goods. The presumption behind this idea is that the relation between the subject and the objects it wishes to own is prior to or more powerful than the relation between subjects, and that until a clear and uncontested right of individual possession is established there can be no genuine (i.e., sustainable) social ties.

Relationship to others in this Hobbesian model proceeds by analogy: since the relation between the self and its possessions is primary, insofar as one apprehends the other it is as another subject with a similarly uncontested relation to its possessions. I am related to my fellow not directly, through any feeling *for* him, but instead because I feel as he does, because I feel for something else in the same way

(I presume) that he does. But likeness as a positive fantasy, rather than as a Jamesonian sign of emergency, says something different: by this logic one is drawn directly to another by the qualities of his person, the fact that they resemble so closely one's own. The idea that accompanies this kind of connection—it is not quite clear whether as a prerequisite or a result—is that the tie between subject and object, the individual and what he possesses, is loosened or undone.

This is why likeness as an idea so often accompanied in Renaissance thought the hypothesis of a kind of relationship separate from any system or practice of ownership. In *The Winter's Tale*, to give one example, Hermione interprets her own entrance into Polixenes's narrative of perfectly identificatory masculine friendship as another version of woman's creation in the Genesis story, implying that as in Eden what disrupts man's version of paradise is the introduction of woman as sinner.[39] But it would be more accurate to say that what destroys Polixenes's childhood Eden is woman's absolutely unambiguous status as object.[40] With respect to woman both men are forced entirely into the position of subject, and now they can constitute their relationship only through this third term that they both wish to possess. If the third term is singular (one woman) they must be rivals, as they turn out to be in Sicilia, and if it is multiple, if there are enough goods to go around—the differences among which, in turn, will bring to light distinctions between the otherwise-rivals sufficient to govern their distribution—then they can each imagine the other by analogy with the self, as friends who possess similar objects in similar ways.

Establishing a multitude of goods and enough distinction to simplify division would be one way to address the viselike connection between the self and what it wants to call entirely its own, by accommodating it. Then likeness might be safely redeemed as a principle of affinity, a reason for affective ties between self-sufficient entities. The other way to address the individual's drive toward possession, of course, would be to contest it, by asserting that it is not as powerful as it seems, and this was Barclay's own solution. At the moment in *Argenis* when Poliarchus and Archombrotus realize that they already share Argenis, they have in effect realized what likeness really means, understanding that as a basis for relationship it trumps, rather than complicates, the possession of property. Archombrotus was wrong to think that his likeness to Poliarchus dictated his need to take what belonged to his friend; in fact he never needed to, because what was Poliarchus's was also already his. Once each has been liberated from his mistakenly possessive urge to secure Argenis for himself, the two men can recall and dwell again in their more authentic connection, recognizing each other directly rather than through their common tie to something else. Contra Sidney, Barclay is asserting that relation to others temporally and perhaps logically precedes our relation to property. Sociality based in emulation does not require that the self first secure its right to what it wants to call its own. Indeed love based on likeness has the potential to defuse the subject's desire for the object, rendering such politic givens as greed and ambition virtually nonexistent. Barclay's contestation of the usual assumptions about the self and its possessions is perhaps most evident in the fact that his heroes end up sharing precisely what Renaissance ideology deemed least amenable to joint possession: wives and political sovereignty. Richard Brathwaite, ever reliable as a mouthpiece for political commonplaces, notes in his 1659 *Panthalia; or the Royal Romance* that "Crowns, and Nuptial Beds" above all "admit no competitors," a metaphor that at once naturalizes the drive toward exclusive political authority by analogizing it to sexual jealousy and also politicizes possessive masculine sexual desire.[41] In the conclusion to *Argenis* Barclay is arguing, if only implicitly, that wives and crowns are not ultimately sacrosanct after all, that in fact the bond instigated by men's likeness to one another might preempt their attachment to these primary possessions.

It is possible, as I have already suggested, to read the kind of intense likeness that characterizes the relationship between Poliarchus and Archombrotus primarily as a sort of cultural back-fantasy, constructed only retrospectively: if competition for scarce resources inspired the necessity for distinction in order to rationalize distribution, then likeness looks like a lost ideal, a characteristic of a time before the reign of law, rather than simply an absence of differentiation. But likeness in itself, as we see in *Argenis,* also describes an energy between subjects independent of triangulation—an energy for which Barclay had precedent in the Renaissance notion of *emulation*. Several different men, we recall, want to take Argenis from Meleander, but Archombrotus alone arrives at this desire through what Barclay calls "the sicknesse of emulation," which leads him first to imagine Poliarchus in his own place (Poliarchus might be, as he is, a disguised prince) and then to imagine himself in Poliarchus's (in order to take on Poliarchus's role as lover of Argenis). Archombrotus makes a mistake in believing that his emulation must lead to an annihilative form of competition; it is the envy shown by the ambitious courtier Lycogenes and the tyrannical king Radirobanes, on the contrary, that inevitably leads to the elimination of one or the other competitor. By this logic Barclay distinguishes envy, which is simply wanting what the other has, from emulation, which escapes the triangulative origins of envy and involves a much more radical, ambivalent desire: the emulator wants to take on not the other's possessions but his very identity, which is not quite aggression nor homage but something in between, or perhaps both at once.

Emulation was originally a rhetorical term and retained a rhetorical meaning in the Renaissance, although even in classical poetics the rhetorical term *aemulatio* already pointed toward character and relationship, specifically, the attitude a speaker manifests toward a source. Emulation in both classical and Renaissance rhetorical theory was a species of *imitatio*. Especially in the Renaissance it tended to connote a hypothesized psychological relation between an imitator and a predecessor or between their two texts' rhetorical postures, one of simultaneous admiration in the modern sense, even reverence, and also of aggression. One of the metaphors used often for imitation in the context of this ambivalent stance, going back at least to Lucretius and Quintilian, was that of following in someone else's footsteps: as the emulator traced the path of his model, in order to do the model homage and to educate himself, he did so always with the potential motive of overgoing the model, subsuming the earlier path into a new one or extending it onto new ground. In his study of emulation as a rhetorical mode G. W. Pigman recognizes this very ambivalence in the emulator's motives, speculating that emulation never became a technical term in rhetorical theory because from its earliest uses in the classical period it carried such an "ambiguous moral significance."[42] Since emulation always "calls attention to itself and deliberately challenges comparison with its model" (26), Pigman argues, we should understand it primarily as an "eristic" mode, governed by conflict and strife (3ff.). Renaissance rhetoricians were not consistent, however, in using the term only or primarily in this way, and it seems likely that its attraction for Renaissance thinkers lay at least partly in its real ambiguity, not just in its usefulness at connoting competition and aggression but also in its ability to capture the truly dual nature of identification. At any rate, the Renaissance fascination with this duality was quite likely one reason why emulation came so often in the seventeenth century to describe social relations, which were not governed by temporal difference to the extent that literary imitation was conventionally understood to be. The ambiguity in emulation seemed most compelling—most threatening and most productive, and also most mutual—when model and imitator were positioned face to face, forced to confront at every moment the manifold implications of their likeness.

Social emulation in this sense described relation at its most intense, with the imitator at once overtaking the model and submitting to being cast by the model as mere copy, both parties continually oscillating between subject and object as they simultaneously vied for and conceded dominance. If we think back to Archombrotus's "sicknesse of emulation," we can see how Barclay's conclusion does not dispense with but extends and fulfills emulation, which rightly construed is actually the cure for the imbalance it would seem to have instigated. Since the real function of the ostensible love object in emulatory love is to provide an occasion for the two subjects to emulate each other, Barclay argues that in effect the subjects already share the object, and in recognizing this basic fact of contention the lovers further stabilize their rivalry, formally acknowledging the likeness between them as a permanent tension, rather than a spur toward some resolution—necessarily arbitrary, given their similarity—by which one of them might "win." Emulation, then, in functioning as mimetic desire becomes completely self-conscious, and for this reason the emulative subject need not pretend that possession of the object is his goal because he knows that what he really wants is connection with his rival. Carried to its logical conclusion, mimetic desire argues for a form of relationship much like the model of allegory I described in Chapter 1, a continual oscillation between identity and difference, by which in this case the subject tries both to merge with his rival and to show himself larger or better.

Such an allegorical model for relationship recalls Heliodoran chastity, in the sense that it renders its participants impervious to desire both for and by outsiders, safe in an enclosed, self-sufficient unit. However, the focus on doubleness rather than singularity in Barclay also differentiates his model from *Aethiopika*'s paradigm of chastity, protecting the subject from the kind of appropriative arrogance displayed even by so innocent a figure as Heliodorus's Persinna. It is the nature of the singular self, *Argenis* suggests, not to recognize others, to achieve its subjectivity by turning something else into object. This self belongs to an economy driven by envy, in which the identity of the other is synonymous with the goods he owns or represents and the subject's main motivation is to commandeer them for himself. Such an economy, and such a foundation for subjectivity, are profoundly unstable, because the subject has no defense against the moment when he himself will be rendered an object by someone more powerful. Far safer, Barclay supposes, to enter into relation with another subject—but the only other the self seems able to recognize truly as subject in *Argenis* is barely other, indeed is so similar that he seems an alternate version of the self. Beset on both sides, by the threat of otherness and of singularity, *Argenis*'s somewhat paradoxical solution is to exploit the tiny space of extraordinary likeness. As in the biographies of themselves with which Urania and Veralinda are presented in *Urania*'s second enchantment, in emulatory likeness Barclay's subject sees a mirror image that is at once self and not-self, thereby disciplining his tendency toward tyrannically objectifying the other while at the same time assuring himself that he too is always more than an object.

Emulation in *Argenis*, we can conclude, was a fantasy defense against the same overweening ambition and aggression evident in *Urania*, the kinds of social and moral threats that in the Jacobean period were typically identified with Tacitean thought. Insofar as emulation stabilized rivalry between peers, by defining it as reciprocal and endlessly repetitive, it also argued—or was used to argue—more generally against the acquisitive subject, who could perceive the world only as a series of possessions to be secured for himself. Part of what made Barclay's defense fantastic, of course, was that it described a drastically restricted social world; emulation, like chastity, worked hypothetically because it was exceptional, signaling to its participants not only that each might be uniquely similar to the other but that there were few other pairs in the world who could approach the perfection of this match. Nowhere in *Argenis* did Barclay explicitly acknowledge the aristocratic assumptions behind this idea, seeming to take for granted that all real rivalry was encompassed within a very small political theater. And yet Barclay did indulge a specific element of emulatory fantasy in *Argenis*, that fantastic quality which is marked by its fundamentally nonnarrative function. I am referring to that moment during Poliarchus and Archombrotus's first meeting in which Timoclea vows to erect a "Table" to their memory so that their first apprehension of their extraordinary likeness can be transmitted to future ages. In the same way that Venus freezes her beloved Adonis, already gored to death in real time, in perpetual dalliance with her in the middle of Book 3 of *The Faerie Queene*, much as Perdita in *The Winter's Tale*'s wishes she could turn Florizel into a living corpse, so Timoclea knows that the heroes' emulation would come closest to perfection in a monument unmarred by time or change. What Timoclea's insight teaches us is that emulation is a stasis-in-movement, its goal to suspend narrative event.

The implicit contention of emulation, then, is that which it is time's very function to deny, that there is no reason why one person must necessarily replace another. In emphasizing the rivalry specifically between peers, Barclay proceeded in *Argenis* as if this might be true. Still, unlike *Urania* Barclay's romance was fundamentally a succession narrative, a story not about death-in-life but about death as an instigator of change. Any succession narrative acknowledges, if only in its rudimentary structure, the necessity for substitution, not of one rival for the other but of young successor for dying king. According to this context Poliarchus and Archombrotus must appear just as aggressive toward the king they would supplant as they ever threatened to be toward each other, and in this respect Barclay opted for a politically realist swerve away from *Arcadia,* employing his doubled princes to separate love from rule and, surprisingly, to divide up monarchical power so as to curb what he would present as a natural, even inevitable tendency toward tyranny.

6. SUCCESSION

In his essay on Oedipus, Vladimir Propp deploys Freud's famous reading of intrafamilial rivalry as an interpretive key to Western monarchical succession narratives, arguing that all of them depend on rivalry and are accomplished through violence, which they all also take as their task to rationalize or sublimate. In the earliest succession stories, Propp concludes, the inevitable struggle between predecessor and successor was signified through the contest between a king and a would-be son-in-law in love with the king's daughter, who eventually managed to kill the aging king and thereby secure both daughter and throne. Charting in the broadest historical terms a shift to narratives of hereditary succession, from sons-in-law to sons, Propp invokes Oedipus as a linchpin, arguing that hereditary succession rather than superseding the logic of exogamous succession fulfills it, even as it also submerges or deintentionalizes the violence that nevertheless remains, in the most basic sense, at center stage. In ways that are now commonly held up as limits to such formalist insights, Propp's view of narrative patterns was schematic. Nonetheless, his literary reading of Oedipus as poised between two models of succession seems suggestive for thinking about Barclay, and his quasi-Freudian thesis that family bonds do not dissipate succession violence but only reframe it uncannily echoes one of the central lessons of much Renaissance romance, which for all its insistence on family lineage and the political legitimacy it ensured remained decidedly anxious about succession.

In *Urania,* as I have argued, Wroth focused on relationships between endogamous contemporaries so as to turn away not only from the marriage market but also from the complications of intergenerational succession. *Urania* signaled this in its very first episode, which depicts an elderly king who gracefully cedes his authority to the next generation, dies, and is mourned, all in a single paragraph. This was clearly a response to *Arcadia,* in which Sidney had emphasized the aggression of the exogamous successor by parodying it, eventually concluding his romance with an allegory in which the hero is "forced" by an importunate princess to accede to a throne for which he never expresses any desire. Still, on the whole, Renaissance narratives about endogamous succession were more likely to dwell on the resistance of the father. So, for example, in his *Method for the Easy Comprehension of History,* Jean Bodin tells the story of a king who learns that his son the prince is literally dying of love for the king's beautiful new wife and is persuaded by the royal doctor and counselor to give her to him, thereby saving his son's life and preserving the royal line. This same story is repeated almost exactly in Percy Herbert's *Certaine Conceptions, or Considerations . . . upon the Strange change of Peoples Dispositions and Actions in these latter Times* (1652). Herbert (also the author of the romance *The Princess Cloria*), after describing the father's ceding of his wife as an example of "perfect friendship" winning out over "appetites" and "private interest," represents the father's renunciation of his power and youth both as an extraordinary sacrifice and as a restoration of the natural order (the father has taken a wife much too young for him; the son is "sick" from having his patrimony withheld). By this sacrificial emphasis Herbert was indicating, and also efficiently resolving, the conflict inherent in all hereditary succession between the father's legitimate authority and the necessity imposed by time for the transfer of power.[43] Still more common was the version of this narrative familiar from fairy tales, in which after the prince's mother dies the king takes a new wife who turns out to have only her own interests at heart, not those of the kingdom as signified by her stepson, and so must be overcome by the prince, who then appropriates the throne from his exhausted, humiliated father.[44] By intensifying the king's hostility and displacing it onto the stepmother, this version of the story provided the son with a less ambiguous target and a clear justification for assuming his hereditary role as quickly as possible.

Both these narratives appear to have been designed to reveal even as they also managed the king's inevitable resistance to being supplanted and the son's impatience to assume sovereignty. Whether exogamous or endogamous, a succession narrative fights against the sovereign's natural desire to maintain power and thus casts the successor as aggressor, intentionally or not. Viewed in this light, *Arcadia*'s concluding fable allegorized the obscured will not just of an exogamous political interloper but of all successors, who manifest what is potentially a threateningly acquisitive desire merely by stepping into their new role. Most succession narratives emphasized family feeling to get over the stumbling block of aggression: the son-in-law's love for the princess; the prince's respect and love for his father; and in Bodin's odd example, the king's solicitude for his son. According to the last of these situations familial love was supposed to conquer an inappropriate will to power, but in the first two political ambition was simply recast as love, which served to distract attention from the ambition's violence without in any way curbing it.

That this was love's function in such a situation, of course, was the central point of Sidney's demystifying succession fable. Sidney reminds us that love is an allegory for violence through the princess's unexecuted threat that if her exogamous beloved will not take the throne she will accuse him of rape. In *Argenis,* Barclay brought the aggression of the succession narrative forward through the mechanics of the rivalry plot: as the emulatory bond between the princes cancels or weakens the bond between each prince and the object he seeks, the bond between prince and object comes into sharper focus in the succession narrative, in which the temporal difference between Meleander and each of his would-be successors makes reciprocal emulatory identification impossible. In this way we are made to see the successor not as a participant in a social network but as a solitary and ambitious agent; and in the conclusion to its succession narrative *Argenis* confronts this agent far more directly and effectively than does any of the plots I have yet described.

Though with respect to each other Barclay's princes share Argenis, with respect to Meleander they come to possess her in quite different ways, and Barclay even divides between them the qualities that establish the worthiness of the ideal successor, as if after drawing our attention to the successor's aggression he meant to some extent to conquer it. Burning with jealousy toward the absent Poliarchus, Archombrotus does manage to dispatch the plot's first challenger for Meleander's throne, the Sicilian rebel Lycogenes, thus earning in advance his place as royal son. But more often he is not in the right place at the right time, as is forecast by the initial episode of the romance, in which Timoclea calls on him to help Poliarchus against several bandits and he arrives to find that Poliarchus, with superhuman valor, has already triumphed alone. Poliarchus foils Lycogenes' attempt to abduct Argenis and kill Meleander before Archombrotus appears on the scene, and even rescues the little cabinet with the proof of Archombrotus's birth from the hands of pirates, thereby winning the eternal gratitude of Archombrotus's foster-mother, Hyanisbe, and ensuring Archombrotus's accession to Meleander's throne. All this makes the division of spoils at the end—not the metaphoric sharing of Argenis, but the actual distribution of goods—look rather strange. The relatively ineffectual Archombrotus gets the throne, and the heroic Poliarchus gets only the princess, who brings as dowry merely the lands Poliarchus already conquered for Hyanisbe (which now, via Archombrotus, Hyanisbe's heir, belong to Meleander). In brief, Poliarchus receives via Argenis nothing he should not already have won through his own heroic and generous actions. Thus Barclay permits exogamous succession, but he makes it stand outside of the motives of ambition and acquisition, as though the rivalry story and succession narrative had nothing to do with each other. Meanwhile, despite Archombrotus's lack of heroic valor endogamy is its own reward, and it is hard to decide whether Barclay has meant to characterize its inertia ironically.

There are several ways we might read this ending. The author of the "Clavis" appended to Le Grys's translation, apparently anxious to see Poliarchus as the real hero of the romance, tried to normalize the plot, disregarding the separation Barclay inserted between princess and throne to conclude that by the terms of the main allegory Poliarchus was Henry of Navarre, Argenis the French throne he added through marriage to his birthright, and Archombrotus (alone among the principal characters) perhaps merely a "supposed One," inserted "onely to embellish the fiction" (487).[45] More likely Barclay means for us to read Poliarchus's entrance into Sicily and into Argenis's inner sanctum in disguise, against her father's explicit wishes, as aggressive, in which case the conclusion is perhaps meant to contain or even rebuke his exogamous ambition. Poliarchus may get Argenis, now that she is no longer worth anything, but he receives no thanks beyond what he has earned with his own actions for his protection of Meleander. Or, a more oblique reading might suggest that we should interpret Poliarchus's love for Argenis as a way of delivering to Meleander, a weak king from the start, the benefits of exogamous energy without the costs he is ill able to support. By this logic Poliarchus's actions may offer a threat to Meleander's sovereignty, but at the same time his accession to the throne may also be warranted by Meleander's and Achombrotus's weakness, and the conclusion's separation of accession from obvious material gain thus works to purify Poliarchus's accession and emphasize the benefits to all parties. But this solution, of course, is still too dangerous to endorse.

Barclay's Poliarchus narrative, in which an exogamous successor is more vigorously heroic and effectual than his endogamous counterpart, provides a warning against the modern tendency to read similar stories in midcentury romance entirely as local political allegories; to some extent, Barclay demonstrates, they were also part of generic convention. Nor, in the earlier period, was this particular succession narrative confined to romance, as a brief look at Francis Beaumont's and John Fletcher's almost contemporary play *A King and No King* (1619) will suggest. In this play the apparent prince Arbaces is cured of his tyrannical aggression by the revelation that he is not the son of the former king after all but of his own adviser, which means that he may now marry the king's real daughter and take the throne as son-in-law. Loving the king's daughter may be, for the exogamous successor he turns out to be, an ambitious act, but apparently it is far less of a threat to the kingdom than an assumption that one is the king's son. Hereditary succession in this play is aligned with incestuous desire, tyranny, and a general inability to apprehend the boundaries that separate both the monarch and the self from others, all of which are signs of endogamy unnaturally extended; and we should read Arbaces' explicit subordination of himself to his father at the end ("Tread on my neck I freely offer it," he says to his adviser and now father Gobrias, in recompense for his many crimes) as a necessary disciplining of the rampant aggression that hereditary succession requires of a son. Since the play has conveniently split father from throne, Arbaces is able to declare his submission to the one without giving up the other, in effect purifying himself symbolically of aggression, and like Sidney's reluctant suitor he is then allowed to accede to the throne via love. If a brother's marriage to his own sister, as Montaigne says, encourages his natural (and weak) passion for women to burst all its customary cultural bounds, in this play a son's succession to his father's throne works almost exactly analogously, giving free rein to the inherently tyrannical ambition we all share, and exogamy offers a curb to the latter just as it does to the former.

In *Argenis* Meleander manifests at least two of Arbaces' weaknesses, an inclination toward incestuous withholding and extraordinarily rude treatment of a foreign prince, and Barclay's assertion through Poliarchus of the principle of exogamous succession is similarly meant at least in part to correct for the kind of tyrannical overreaching such weaknesses represent. At the same time, *Argenis* also makes the counterargument that endogamy disciplines the ambition displayed by the would-be exogamous successor. In essence Barclay divides the ideal successor in two, the hero and lover separate from the son, with the aim that each should curb the passions and supply the defects of the other. Whereas Beaumont and Fletcher had come quite close in *A King and No King* to arguing symbolically against hereditary succession, the same cannot be said of Barclay. Nonetheless it is striking how different the version of sociality presented by Barclay's conclusion to *Argenis*'s succession narrative is from that in the romance's configuration of emulatory passion. Emulation as a form of balance is realized imaginatively in *Argenis* by replacing history with a sort of narrative oscillation. Poliarchus and Archombrotus manage their ambition with respect to each other by radically restricting their social world, enclosing themselves in a space where there is nothing but subject, or two subjects. If this can be read as a protest against objectifying modes of relationship, it does not offer much of an alternative, since it mounts its protest only by withdrawing from sociality altogether. Barclay's conclusion to his succession narrative, by contrast, balances one agent against another, establishing differentiation rather than erasing it, so that ambition is addressed through relation to others rather than by withdrawal from them—an opposite solution, begetting a very different legacy for midcentury romance.

7. The Readers of Romance

Earlier in this chapter and in the previous one I argued that Wroth's *Urania* took up questions of virtue and sociality not only thematically, through its narratives of relationships among its characters, but also formally, through its parallel consideration of the relationships among writer, text, and readers, and that ultimately it construed its roman à clef form as the paradigm for a virtuous mode of relationship both to the self and to others. Though in *Argenis* Barclay did not reflect on his romance form quite as persistently or as rigorously, he also drew a parallel between romance's thematic depictions of relationship and its construction of the relationships among writer, readers, and text, particularly between the text and its projected readers, and in closing this chapter I want to consider some of the implications of this parallel. In an important metafictional conversation about a quarter of the way through *Argenis,* Barclay gives notice that identification serves as the mechanism not only for friendship but for all the moral benefit incurred by reading his romance. Describing for his courtly audience how he wants his "Fable like a Historie" to work, Barclay's mouthpiece, Nicopompus, suggests that first his readers "will love me, as they doe the showes of the Theater or the Tilt-yard," but then "while they reade, while as not concerned in it, they shall be angry, or favor, they shall meete with themselves, & as in a Looking-glasse, shall see the face and merit of their owne fame" (131). In other words, Barclay projects for his readers only two kinds of relation to his text: either they will find themselves foreign to it, "as not concerned" in its merely diverting fiction, or they will realize that what they read about is identical with themselves. Obviously Barclay has in mind his own roman à clef form when he argues for this model of reading as self-recognition, referring not merely to those aspects of self that mimetic narrative is traditionally supposed to reflect, but also to something so particular that the sudden encounter with it in a fiction ostensibly about other people will produce a shock that provides the impetus for his program of moral reform.

At the same time, Barclay has generalized his identificatory model of reading, calling not just on the princes and courtiers who are the subjects of his political allegory but on ordinary and ostensibly anonymous readers to see themselves reflected in his pages. If Hamlet with his *Mousetrap* plot revises a tradition going back to classical drama, by which tragedy means to show the tyrant his true face and thus goad him to reform, Barclay's wonderfully politic revision is to imagine all his readers as little tyrants—everyday, ordinary tyrants who will not expect to be addressed by the "showes of the Theater or the Tilt-yard" (those, they know, are for monarchs) but will be caught up short by the their own faces reflected in the more modern mirror of prose romance.[46] One of Barclay's main goals in writing *Argenis* was to exemplify the idea that romance can be a morally serious and even reformative genre, and the notion of readerly identification that is at the heart of roman à clef's formal aspirations became a way to stimulate his readers' self-reflection and activate their consciences. Obviously this model of the relation between reader and text shared an affinity with Barclay's identificatory model for friendship, in which each participant potentially apprehends the other as a version of himself just different enough to forestall complete identification while at the same time motivating a perpetual moral desire to merge. The implicit logic is this: as emulatory friends are allegorical versions of each other, so the text itself is an allegory for the reader, offering her a slightly estranged version of herself that by blocking easy identification spurs her toward moral improvement. Extending the metaphor to other kinds of relationship in *Argenis,* we might call hereditary, exogamous succession too, in its wishfully ideal form, an allegorical idea in this identificatory sense, in that it tries to use the identity between father and son ("the King is dead; long live the King") to camouflage the temporal difference that, in de Man's view, always makes allegorical identity impossible. Barclay, I have argued, though he was apparently happy to situate friendship between peers in an ideal realm outside of time and narrative, could not allow succession to approach such an ideal, and so although in the social vacuum of emulatory friendship Poliarchus and Archombrotus may each seem the perfect equivalent of the other, in relation to Meleander they are only partial matches, and as successors also to each other only analogues, son and son-in-law.

In closing this chapter, I want to suggest that such an analogous model of relationship, if we follow the logic by which *Argenis* associated emulatory friendship with allegory, might find its representational equivalent in verisimilitude. Just as emulatory friendship and ideal endogamous succession mirrored in the social realm the identificatory relation between people that allegory supposes between its literal and conceptual senses, and in roman à clef between the real and the representation, so relation based on analogy might mirror the sort of approximate relation between reality and representation described by verisimilitude. Where allegory defines truth as identity, and admits difference only because it is required to do so by the belatedness of representation, verisimilitude takes as sufficient the quality of being "like" the original or other, of being analogically related (the fictional character acts *as if* he were real, I *as if* I were you) rather than the same. Such a sense that likeness alone is sufficient, that the representation does not have to strive to be "true" (identical to the real, or to history) might open the door to a notion of fiction as its own realm—just what the Le Grys Clavis to *Argenis* picked up on in conceding that Archombrotus might be merely a "supposed One." In interpreting Archombrotus as mere embellishment, the Clavis-writer underestimated his importance to the ideological structure of Barclay's resolution, but he did perceive something else crucial to the resolution, that in dividing Meleander's successor into two Barclay left historical allegory for verisimilar fiction. Archombrotus's and Poliarchus's dual presence may have been necessary, as I argued, to curb the kind of passions that in early modern political ideology led to tyrannical weakness in the ruler and morally inadmissible arrogance in the subject, but both could not at once be "real," which is to say, correspondent to history. It probably seemed to Barclay, as I have been suggesting, that he had no choice but to leave the realm of identificatory allegory if he wanted to take up the problem of succession. Perhaps too, we can speculate, he glimpsed that his recourse to the principles of verisimilar fiction to address some of the ethical difficulties inherent in the transfer of power might have an ethical function, estranging his readers, in their acknowledgment and acceptance of their own necessarily approximate nature, from their Chariclea-like impulse to be absolute.

Urania and *Argenis*, then, made the oppositions between endogamous, intrafamilial sexual unions and commerce-driven, triangulated marriage alliances, and between atemporal emulatory friendship and time-bound succession, respectively, analogues (not, in their terms, allegories) for the opposition between identificatory allegory and analogizing, approximating verisimilitude. As love for a cousin or sibling was to marriage, or identificatory friendship to succession politics, so allegory was to verisimilitude; or, equivalently, as emulatory love was to allegory, so succession was to verisimilitude. This set of analogies has several implications for our histories of prose fiction and of allegory in the seventeenth century. In *Urania* and *Argenis*, first, it is clear that at least for romance's purposes allegory was a mode of identification, not analogy. It is a critical commonplace to say that realist or verisimilar fiction is superior to allegorical fiction, but often it is also difficult to see the difference between the allegorical and the verisimilar, the distinction that would make the mimetic analogue for reality not also an allegory for it. In their particular historical moment, Barclay and Wroth drew a rigorous distinction: in its longing to merge what was separate, allegory pushed as hard as it could against the difference it also had to acknowledge, always working toward the ideal of a perfectly self-contained, perfectly reciprocal relationship between self and other or among its various senses, while verisimilitude took as much less problematic and indeed relied upon difference, as the premise legitimating its entire representational project. Allegory's fantasy was emulatory love, the slightly estranged self-image, the ideal reflection that spurs the subject toward truth and virtue; verisimilitude, in contrast, broke the reign of identification, as both a representational and an interpretative principle. The contemporary critic Thomas Luxon, as I noted in the conclusion to the last chapter, claims in his defense of midcentury religious radicals that allegory was "incessantly about the business of othering" in the seventeenth century (26), hence its use as a discipline by those who wanted to deny the radicals the authority of their identification with the historical and textual Christ. But romance's construal of allegory in this period suggests that, on the contrary, allegory also might have served as the radicals' ally, as both means and authorization to identify. As allegory in romance celebrated the emulatory pair, so it asked readers to narrow the difference between reality and representation as much as they could, and to bring themselves into line with what they read in order to make representation truly an alternative for, not just a copy of, the real.

Wroth's and Barclay's conception of allegory as a mode of identification substantially complicates Michael McKeon's argument that the novel, in its claim to be *like* history, supplanted the confusion and naïveté of roman à clef's claim actually to *be* history. Roman à clef's ambition to be history, Wroth and Barclay help us see, was actually a claim to be allegory, and it made this claim not because it was confused about the relationship between fiction and history nor simply because of allegory's historical prestige, but because it was working out, through its self-conscious deployment of allegorical form, complex questions of how its readers should approach both representation and one another. From our own literary historical perspective, bearing in mind the eventual (though perhaps never complete) triumph of novelistic verisimilitude, allegory in Wroth's and Barclay's sense may seem in the seventeenth century to have been already formally on the cusp of obsolescence. From the point of view of Jacobean romance, however, allegory was both the instigator of and the route to exploring a whole set of political and ethical questions about identity and difference, questions that during the rest of the century, as I will show in the next two chapters, remained the animating concerns of romance.

Chapter 3

The Trials of Love: Interest and Social Bonds in Midcentury Romance

As synecdoche, and sometimes scapegoat, for fiction in general, romance in early modern England was regularly denounced for its service to fancy over reason and its corresponding appeal to women and other undisciplined readers, all criticisms that literary history has taught us to expect. But in the middle of the seventeenth century romance was also subject to another, more specific charge that has since fallen from our view: that it promulgated and even celebrated a belief in self-interest as the governing motive of social behavior. Thus when James Harrington, in *Oceana* (1656), wanted to condemn Elizabeth I for pandering to her own and her subjects' short-term self-interest rather than supporting the long-term common interest, he accused her of construing her rule as romance: Elizabeth, he wrote, sold out the future stability of her kingdom by "converting her reign through the perpetual love tricks that passed between her and her people into a kind of romance," aggrandizing her personal power rather than submitting to the checks on monarchical power enforced by a properly balanced government.[1] And thus Robert Boyle justified his attempt at reforming romance in *The Martyrdom of Theodora, and Didymus* (probably written in the late 1640s or 1650s) as necessitated by the fact that the entire genre was fundamentally tainted by self-love: tempted by romance during his youth into what he [illegible] "raving," a sort of ecstasy of self-regarding passion, he stru[illegible] *Theodora* to establish an alternative ethos of "disinterest," to [illegible] both youthful readers and the romances they loved toward reason and the common good.[2]

Boyle understood the typical romance as an overflow of passion, a psychologically dangerous form of self-indulgence, while Harrington saw the genre instead as cynical political exploitation of those unequipped to perceive the real workings of politics, but both philosophers made a connection between long-standing complaints that romance gave free rein to passion and more contemporary anxieties about self-interest. This association of romantic love with self-interest and the sense that romance was above all the genre that effected it were not new; that romance's love plot was one road toward the realization of self-interest, as I argued in Chapter 1, and that this was the genre's most significant lesson, was the point of *Arcadia*'s concluding fable. What was new, in the 1650s, was the open acknowledgement of this fact: Sidney's "love trick," to enlist Harrington's apt phrase, had been demystified, opened to public criticism.

Part of the reason for this shift in romance to an explicit acknowledgement of Arcadian insights was that the problem of self-interest in midcentury romance belonged to an intellectual context significantly different from that of Elizabeth's or James's reign. After about 1640, Tacitean ideology was increasingly subsumed within and diffused by the newly fashionable concept of interest, explicitly named as such in England by Henri, duc de Rohan's widely read treatise on the interest of princes and states. At midcentury interest was an unstable concept with an enormous variety of meanings and implications not always compatible with one another. Often erotic desire was called "interested," insofar as it aimed at the fulfillment of self rather than other; and a wide range of discourses, from sermons to moralistic literature to political polemic, described passionate ambition as a manifestation of interest, whether it was for traditional heroic glory or more contemporary political influence. At the same time interest was also often portrayed as a discipline for passion, weakening it by recasting it in the light of rational, prudential calculation. For some writers interest referred to what it was in the nature of an entity to do, what described its identity, and at other times English thinkers followed Rohan in seeing interest as an essentially social concept, referring to that which a self wants in relation to the others around it. Within midcentury romance interest was represented at various moments in all these ways, but it was consistently interpreted as a social issue, provoking not only self-discipline, as it had earlier in Barclay and Wroth, but also an investigation of one's relationship to others. In fact, in the late 1650s and 1660s the exploration of interest helped spur in romance what at least from the perspective of the Arcadian tradition was a distinctly new conception of virtue, measured not so much by the subject's subordination to traditional modes of authority as by her willingness to put the interests of another next to or even before her own.

I will turn in a moment to a discussion of the midcentury interest discourse in which romance played such a central part, but first I want to offer, as a sort of exemplum for this shift to a social, relational notion of virtue, a brief comparison between *Argenis* and *Urania* and a later text, one that is emphatically not a fiction of any kind but shares to a surprising extent Barclay's and Wroth's view of the fraught relationship between self-interest and reading—Hobbes's 1651 *Leviathan*. In *Argenis,* we recall, Barclay had argued that the explicit purpose of his roman à clef form was to reform his audience, by bringing them into abrupt allegorical identification with what they read. Because his audience "will beleeve that I trifle," declares Nicopompus/Barclay,

> I shall have them all . . . While they reade, while as not concerned in it, they shall be angry, or favor, they shall meete with themselves, & as in a Looking-glasse, shall see the face and merit of their owne fame. Perhaps, they will bee ashamed to play any longer that part upon the Stage of this World, which they shall perceive in my Fable to have beene duely set out for them.[3]

Barclay seduces his readers, by the ostensible fictionality of his narrative, into forgetting themselves, and then suddenly shocks them into self-awareness by presenting them with their own images. Implied in this tactic is the sense that the suddenness and intensity with which his readers identify with such images will preclude, or at least postpone, their natural tendency to distance themselves from moral accusation, thereby conducing to the shame that stimulates reform. Barclay's roman à clef, as I have suggested, differed from Wroth's in its focus on the relationship between text and reader instead of text and writer, but it was also strikingly like Wroth's in its conception of the moral ills roman à clef was designed to address. In this passage from *Argenis,* as in *Urania*'s second enchantment, the subject is diagnosed as tending naturally toward a sort of stupid self-satisfaction, and the function of the self-image is to jolt her into a more virtue-conducing realization of her own insufficiency.

Thirty years later in *Leviathan* Hobbes characterized the dangers of using one's imagination in terms that Barclay and Wroth would have found entirely familiar, warning his own representative reader-sub-

away from prideful and ignorant self-satisfaction. In section 1.2, "Of Imagination," Hobbes famously defines imagination as "*decaying sense,*" the faculty of mind that retains the lingering image of some object earlier apprehended by the senses. He divides it into two kinds: "*simple,*" when the mind imagines a "whole object, as it was presented to the sense" initially; and "*compounded,*" when the mind combines objects that the senses perceived distinct. As examples of compounded imagination Hobbes offers first the straightforward conception of a centaur, then the instance "when a man compoundeth the image of his own person, with the image of the actions of an other man; as when a man imagins himselfe a *Hercules,* or an *Alexander.*" The latter, which is "properly but a Fiction of the mind," "happeneth often to them that are much taken with reading of Romants."[4] Though Hobbes presents these examples as analogies for one another, in fact they are significantly distinct. In both the product of the imagination is something unreal, but in the latter Hobbes seems to have diverged somewhat from his model: if the centaur is the mind's mixture of two real entities, the man who thinks he is Hercules has transformed something that does exist into something that never was, has allowed what was already imaginary (or so removed in space and time, as is the case of the historical Alexander, that in the present it might as well be imaginary) entirely to subsume the real. And not only that, but in the second example the deluded imaginer veers into moral danger, trying to transcend his ordinary limitations by reconceiving himself as larger or braver or more powerful than he really is. Like the ladies of Wroth's second enchantment, Hobbes's imaginative romance-reader overidentifies with the image before him in order to forget his real self, rather than using the image as Barclay recommends, as a spur to correct the faults in that self. This misuse of fiction wastes an opportunity, but in itself it is also a mark of hubris, of the reader's readiness to embrace an unwarranted pride.

As Hobbes echoed Wroth and Barclay in his diagnosis of the typical subject as especially vulnerable to prideful and fatuous self-love, he also followed them in advocating as a remedy the subject's self-consciousness. Thus, he offered in his introduction to *Leviathan,* as a guiding principle for reading his own book and also, more generally, [illegible] understanding the words of other people in all kinds of social [illegible]xts, the adage "*Nosce teipsum,*" (mis)translated by Hobbes as [illegible]*hy self*" (10). If Hobbes's subject, whom he presents explic- [illegible]taphorical reader of the world around him, is not to be [illegible] too much trust, or by too much diffidence"—that is, [illegible] too fully to what he reads, to succumb to what we might also describe, in the terms of my previous two chapters, as overidentification and its inevitable result, that paradoxical Wrothian combination of pride and loss of self—he must constantly "compar[e] with [his] own" the actions of others with which he is presented. Not to do so, says Hobbes with a nod not only to the structure but to the very terms of roman à clef, is "to decypher without a key" (10). In this respect, Hobbes's model seems similar to both Wroth's and Barclay's: the deliberate insertion of the self into what one reads is the "key" that grounds one's interpretation of the other, preventing it from turning into a fatuous or flattering exercise in self-delusion.

But the condemnation of overidentification on moral grounds intersects in *Leviathan* with another kind of argument against it, not present in Wroth or Barclay: Hobbes worries about pride not only because it is an evil in itself but also, as his anxiety about "trust" and "diffidence" suggests, because from an ostensibly more pragmatic standpoint it renders the reader dangerously subject to the will of others. "[W]hosoever looketh into himself" while reading (of) others, remembering to keep his own real identity firmly before him, "shall thereby read and know, what are the thoughts, and Passions of all other men" (10). In other words, the real benefit of keeping one's own self always present to consciousness, Hobbes suggests, is to become a cannier reader of other people. And this is an ability the subject cannot afford to be without if he is to "discover" what Hobbes calls, with strong politic resonance, others' "designe[s]" (10). For Hobbes, politic ideology evokes not anxiety about the moral status of the subject's agency, as in Wroth, but rather apprehension of the subject's social insecurity. The point of reading the self and thereby the other is to remind the self of that insecurity and by doing so to correct for it, to give the subject the knowledge to take preemptive or corrective defensive action. If the logic of roman à clef for Wroth and Barclay was primarily an idealizing tool, a way to purify agency of politic contamination, reading the self for Hobbes, I want to suggest, became instead part of a practical strategy for negotiating the inevitably politic realm of social relations.

This contrastive relation between Hobbes and his predecessors gets more complicated when Hobbes notes that the adage "Nosce teipsum" is often "now used, to countenance, either the barbarous state of men in power, towards their inferiors; or to encourage men of low degree, to a sawcie behaviour towards their betters" (10). The moral argument reappearing by implication, Hobbes worries that the exhortation to think of oneself may be mistakenly interpreted (as in romance-reading) as an inducement to pride, another avenue toward forgetting one's proper place and role. In this context the defensiveness implied in reading oneself to ascertain others' designs becomes not only a canny politic tactic but also a moral corrective, a spur toward recalling one's essential humility. Reading oneself as its own end leads to aggression; reading oneself as a tactic in the effort to protect oneself from others' aggression not only puts the self on the correct side morally but also, by construing self-knowledge as merely instrumental, probably protects against self-love. Hobbes weaves into one strand here both of the major kinds of politic anxiety I have described so far in this book, Wroth's and Barclay's worry about the hubris of human agency and also the politic fear of competition. For Hobbes, oddly, politic competition offers an ethical corrective for the very problem politic ideology diagnoses, defining others' aggression as the moral cure for one's own. To remember one's perilous social position is to render aggression impossible; in a self-consciously politic world, Hobbes suggests, there will be no Alexander or Hercules.

For Hobbes as for Barclay and Wroth, then, the kind of naïve and prideful self-love associated with an unsophisticated reading of fiction was to be corrected by a better kind of self-involvement, a slightly alienated self-consciousness that conduced to humility. To "read oneself" in this sense had by midcentury apparently become conventional moral medicine, and as such it was available throughout this period as a justification for allegorical romance. In Hobbes, however, self-awareness was not only a moral virtue in my terms but also a social one: its primary function was to foster a right relation to others, neither overly subordinate nor self-aggrandizing at others' expense. Thus for my purpose here *Leviathan* can be said to denote a basic shift in thought, one by which interest took its place in a crowded social world rather than as an attribute of the self in conceptual isolation, and consequently also became primarily a problem for ethics in my sense, having to do with the way people do and should get along with one another. Hobbes's subject was presumed to be already launched in a social world populated by multitudes of others each with their own interests, against which Wroth's and Barclay's turn to chastity seemed to offer little defense; in the context of *Leviathan*, Barclay's retreat to a twinned emulatory unit could be only nostalgic fantasy, little better than a delusion that one was Alexander.

For Hobbes, the other impinged on the self, in a way too insistent and immediate to be addressed by the kinds of traditional recourses to which romance laid claim in the early part of the seventeenth century. And this view of the self in relation to the social world, this insistence on the indelible presence of the other and the threat he or she inherently presented to the interests of the self, was characteristic both of much of the discourse around interest at midcentury and more particularly of the romances that played such a central role in it. Perceived by critics and practitioners alike to be bound to the problem of self-interest, from the 1640s until the early 1660s, when it went abruptly out of fashion, prose romance became one forum for a thorough and wide-ranging exploration of what I want to call the specifically ethical problems that coalesced around interest—now, no longer primarily whether self-interest could or should be admitted, nor its implications for such traditional virtues as constancy or humility, but rather what bearing it had on the fact that people exist in relation to others. In the 1650s, I will show in this chapter, romance's response was a skillful exploitation of the traditional structures and concerns of fiction in order to foster a sympathy that could at least hypothetically counter individual acquisitiveness, and to propose a kind of relationship free from interest's necessity.

1. The New Discourse of Interest

By the 1650s it was generally recognized, as the Lancashire minister Charles Herle remarked in his 1655 treatise *Wisdomes Tripos*, that the word interest had "of late much come into use among us," and for the English term, as I have said, there was at least one concrete point of origin, Rohan's treatise *De l'intérêt des princes & des estats de la Chrestienne*, published in Paris in 1634 (under Rohan's name for the first time in 1638) and then in an English translation by Henry Hunt in Paris in 1640 and in London in 1641 and 1663.[5] Rohan's argument that states should be understood as entities each possessing their own interests, and that these interests should dictate their actions in the theater of international politics, was a mainly predictable and, in France, not a unique outgrowth of European reason of state theory, but the treatise's pithiness, the translation's timing, and Rohan's fame in England as a Huguenot general (and also as godfather to the infant Charles I) combined to make his name a frequent anchor for interest discourse in England in the decades following 1640.[6] Most widely cited, as I suggested in the introduction, were his rhetorical elevation of interest as an authority even above princes ("The Princes Commaund the *People*, and the *Interest* Commaunds The *Princes*" [1]) and his declaration that, in Hunt's translation, "the interest alone can never faile" (1)—or, in the words of the more commonly circulated English maxim, "interest never lies." "The *Prince* may deceive himselfe," Rohan argued, "his *Counsell* may be corrupted," but his interest properly understood will always be a reliable guide to action, and if his subjects are assiduous students of interest discourse they too may come to understand his political imperatives just as clearly. One of the great virtues of Rohan's treatise for English readers was that it seemed to lay open the mysteries of state—indeed, to argue that properly understood they had never been mysteries at all—and at the same time to sustain their stature, in fact to elevate it among those inclined to complain about politic secrecy. It bears emphasizing that although interest eventually became a cornerstone of bourgeois individualist and capitalist economic theory, the term entered English thought by means of an aristocratic ideology, one primarily concerned not with commerce but with international politics.[7]

Despite Rohan's emphasis on relations among states and princes, in the following decade interest in England quickly became a discourse of domestic politics employed across the domestic spectrum. Levellers used Rohan to insist that the old notion of reason of state as a set of *arcana imperii* closely guarded by the monarch ought to give way to a new transparency in politics, and argued as well that the true common interest was to be discerned not by calculating benefit to the monarch but by aggregating all individual interests. A less radical republican theorist such as Harrington vested the public interest in the landed nobility, while at the same time famously identifying a "mankind interest" that might assure political sociability and cooperation. And although Royalists might be thought to have had little use for the notion of interest, and did entirely reject any notion of the common interest separate from that of the king's person, by around 1647 even Charles himself found it necessary to begin declaring his concern no longer for the common good but for "the satisfaction of all interests."[8] This generalized and widespread incursion of interest into politics probably marked a growing sense of politics as factional, proceeding by negotiations between groups self-defined as distinct, but there also seems to be a scholarly consensus that the political language of interest in the 1640s and 1650s was not very profound, that interest in these decades, as J. A. W. Gunn puts it, was primarily a slogan, a way to gesture vaguely toward individual or factional desires without really threatening political unity.[9]

In his account of interest discourse at midcentury Gunn notes the prevalence of such sentiments as John Bramhall's in his 1658 *The Catching of Leviathan*, that where Hobbesian "principles prevail, adieu honour and honesty and fidelity and loyalty: all must give place to self-interest,"[10] and finds it frustratingly inexplicable that even in the face of these worries about what he calls "individualism," political discourse did not manifest more awareness of the conflict interest theory seemed to open up between self-interest and the good of the group. I would suggest that the apparent inconsistency proceeds at least somewhat from the fact that at midcentury interest was part of two relatively distinct discourses, one that was explicitly political and another, more diffuse but also with a stronger memory of its origins in politic ideology, having to do more generally with social motivation and behavior. If reason of state, as Gunn proposes, was to some extent subsumed in the 1640s by the notion of the public interest,[11] in the decades after Sidney Tacitism also followed another trajectory, shifting from a political ideology to one more widely social. We can see an exemplary instance of this diffusion in Richard Brathwaite's 1640 romance *The Two Lancashire Lovers,* a domestic fiction about a girl determined to marry her tutor against her parents' wishes. At the opening of one of the final chapters, after the heroine has faked a fever to convey to her parents the sincerity of her emotional anguish over her forbidden lover, the narrator declares, "Who knows not how to dissemble, he knows not how to live."[12] This is a revision, of course, of the familiar Tacitean sentence "Qui nescit dissimulare, nescit regnare," or "he who doesn't know how to dissimulate doesn't know how to rule," the same sentence George Puttenham quoted half a century earlier in *The Arte of English Poesie* in his famous description of allegory as the tool the canny courtier cannot be without. Possibly a bit of comedy is meant to attach to the incongruity here between statecraft discourse and the plight of the romance's lovelorn heroine, but overall Brathwaite seems to have meant his Tacitism to be taken straight, as a flattering nod to the reader who considered herself savvy in the ways of politics both civil and domestic. Either way this rewriting of a politic maxim as a commonplace about "living" was a sign that Tacitism had achieved a kind of universality, the cliché's dual status of seeming at once obvious and yet profound.

Brathwaite's recasting of *Urania*'s evil dissembling queen as a exemplarily ordinary young woman marked a shift quite representative of Tacitism at midcentury. Less typical was the almost cheerful unconcern with which Brathwaite acknowledged dissimulation's ubiquity. Most commentators complained that the normalization of Tacitean ideology had brought everyday social relations to the brink of crisis: Francis Finch in his 1654 treatise *Friendship* lamented the many "over-politick" fathers who taught their children the "pernicious Axiomes of Dissimulation" (the word "axiom," like maxim, suggesting the idea's origin in statecraft discourse and politic history), and in the first part of his 1655 *Wisdomes Tripos,* a reluctant guide to "Worldly Policy" before he turned to holier matters, Charles Herle declared that a belief both in dissimulation's value and in its prevalence had become so widespread that the ordinary conversationalist characteristically found himself required to "smell and *travaile* by an imaginary plot or designe in every jest, and complement." In a familiar complaint, he blamed both dissimulation and self-love, the other fundamental politic sin, for leading to a "knocking off and disbanding of *Society.*"[13] In his enormously popular collection of essays *Resolves,* issued twelve times between about 1628 and 1709, Owen Feltham observed of dissimulation (in yet another echo of the "Qui nescit" sentence) that "if *Man* had noe faln [fallen], he should never need have us'd it: and as he is now," at his apogee of sinfulness, "I think no *Man* can live without it."[14] And Percy Herbert, in his 1650 *Certaine Conceptions, or Considerations . . . upon the Strange change of Peoples Dispositions and Actions in these latter Times,* named as "the first general corruption" of this particularly "unfortunate age" "Dissimulation; unto which as I may say people are so inclined, that it is unpossible almost in any communication to know what another meanes."[15] Dissimulation, Herbert concluded, was "a custome now adaies so much in fashion, that I have observed it sometimes affected, without any intention at all of compassing benefits; but as it were onely to be esteemed wiser then other persons in worldly affaires" (143). If for Puttenham in *The Arte of English Poesie* dissimulation was a rhetorical tactic, albeit a crucial one, in Herbert it had become a social reflex. Presumably by this view its practitioners were not all evil, as they were, say, in Wroth, but in a way this new normalization of dissimulation was for Herbert even worse, because it negated any possibility for sincerity and authenticity in social relations.

Most of the scholarly attention to interest in the mid-seventeenth century, as I have indicated, has focused on the concept's political meanings, and consequently historians have tended to overlook most of the midcentury anxiety about interest, locating the self-critical phase of interest discourse later in the history of English thought. So, for instance, it has recently been argued that the duc de Rohan's ideas about interest were first applied to "the psychology of individuals" in late 1660s and 1670s France, and that English thought on disinterest as an ethical virtue in the 1690s was mainly a translation of the French.[16] But within this context of continuing social anxiety about politic ideology that I have just described, interest was already perceived in the 1640s as a social problem, and it was within this context that romance primarily located its own exploration of interest. Before I return to this dynamic in romance, I want first to sketch some of the different and sometimes even contradictory meanings and associations that attached to interest outside of the specifically political arena.

2. Interest and its Discontents

Charles Herle was tapping into an established tradition of thought when he aired in his moral philosophical treatise *Wisdomes Tripos* one of the most influential definitions of interest, that "'tis of the enterest of a stone to endeavour its way to the earth, of a drop to pursue its way to the Ocean. . . . If a man know what is his true *Interest*," Herle analogized, directly paraphrasing Rohan, "he is undoubtedly true to it" (169–70). This metaphor of the stone making its way to the earth had a complicated history of association with interest as an idea: in *Of the Laws of Ecclesiastical Polity* (1593), arguing (not, yet, of course, within the terminology of interest) for our apprehension of a common good as well as of self-advantage, Richard Hooker had claimed that governing even "agents naturall" incapable of acting voluntarily were laws both "direct[ing] them in the meanes whereby they tende to their owne perfection," and also "bind[ing] them each to serve unto others good, and all to preferre the good of the whole before whatsoever their owne particular." As an example of the second he described the instance when "things naturall . . . forget their ordinary naturall woont, that which is heavie mounting sometime upwardes of it [*sic*] owne accord . . . to releive the present distresse of nature in common."[17] Hobbes would retort, in the first postulate of his *Philosophical Rudiments Concerning Government and Society* (his English translation of *De Cive*), that every man shuns death "by a certain impulsion of nature, no less than that whereby a stone moves downward,"[18] subtly implying that only Hooker's first law was worthy of being named as such, while on the other side Harrington would call on Hooker's vision of heavy flying objects as one of the few essential antecedents for his notion of "mankind interest," an "interest of mankind or of the whole" as distinct from individual or private interest (171).[19] Herle's allusion to the metaphor, of course, is more Hobbesian than Harringtonian, as he stresses the stone's tendency to fall as its truly significant attribute.

In his definition of interest as a force analogous to gravity, Herle, as did Rohan, seemed to promise his interested agent liberation from the rigors of practical deliberation. If the behavior it was most fitting for an actor to engage in, what the agent must want if he or she was not deluded, was simply a function or expression of his or her nature, then the agent might imagine himself without will or choice. To "know thyself," in the humanist dictum, was to know in every situation what one must do, and consequently not only motivations but actions themselves should become transparent, their every step seeming predetermined or inevitable. Obviously this would take a practical burden off the actor; it would also offer exemption from the kind of moral considerations usually associated with practical deliberation, which is the very point Albert Hirschman makes in his classic study *The Passions and the Interests: Political Arguments for Capitalism before its Triumph.* An essential part of interest's function as a concept, says Hirschman, was to posit motivation as entirely open to apprehension, creating an impression of transparency that made it seem "almost as though," Hirschman adds with some irony, the agent were "a wholly virtuous person."[20] In the anxiously competitive society of middle and late seventeenth-century England, such transparency effectively functioned as virtue's substitute. To the agent it held out assurance that if she did what it most belonged to her nature to do, then the reproach of others could not have any bearing on her, nor could she be required to feel remorse; to the observer it indicated that trusting the agent was not unduly risky. As Marchamont Nedham declared in his 1659 *Interest will not Lie,* in the company of a person with an understanding of interest's workings, another could not lie even if he meant to: "If you can apprehend wherein a man's interest . . . doth consist, you may surely know, if the man be prudent, whereabout to have him, that is, how to judge of his designe."[21] If we recall the opening argument of Hobbes's *Leviathan* that to know (or, in his translation of "nosce teipsum," to read) oneself is to be able to read others, and thus to be also able to profit from rather than succumb to their "designs," then it seems clear that for Nedham, as for so many of his contemporaries, interest was the conceptual bridge making possible the move from self-knowledge to the knowledge of the other advocated by Hobbes. Simply put, interest was to be the analogous principle by which others became as legible to us as we were to ourselves.

The problem with this conception of interest (as theorists have complained since the seventeenth century) was that it tended toward tautology. The theory of interest, James Macaulay remarked in an oft-quoted attack on the work of James Mill in 1829, "means only that men, if they can, will do as they choose . . . it is . . . idle to attribute any importance to a proposition which, when interpreted, means only that a man had rather do what he had rather do."[22] In Hirschman's view, interest was rescued from tautology in the seventeenth and eighteenth centuries through its affiliation with rational calculation and prudence, which served as the "content" of an otherwise mainly empty idea.[23] Rational calculation, it might be objected, would seem superfluous to interest in Herle's sense (how much more is there to say, after all, about a stone's inclination to move toward the earth than that it exists?), but modern proponents of interest as an interpretive principle have acknowledged that interest is this simple only at the most general level. In any particular situation actor and interpreter must fit interest to the circumstances, and thus transparency would seem to mean not so much self-evident-ness as susceptibility to the process of rational understanding. Still, the question remains why self-interest should be associated with reason rather than some other method of coming to knowledge—why, that is, self-interest is so often understood as an inherently reasonable principle and why it should be felt to inspire reasonable thought—and indeed the intellectual historian Pierre Force has recently remarked that he can see no necessary logical connection between self-centeredness and rational calculation.[24] The early modern assumption was apparently that self-interest was so universal and so dominant as to function incontrovertibly as a first principle, crowding out any other principles that might compete along the way and thus allowing both agent and interpreter a closed and linear thinking process. Not only was his or her own interest by definition what it was best for the agent to follow, but by this logic the agent who followed it could not be distracted or swayed, and against prevailing views of passion as groundless and inconstant, self-interest seemed a mainly reasonable alternative.

As Force's objection might lead us to expect, interest at midcentury was also defined, contradictorily, as a passion. In politic ideology the drive toward self-advantage was understood as a form of desire, in opposition to the more rationally construed providential good, and romance followed this logic in presenting erotic desire as the ultimate form of self-interest in its single-minded drive to conquer and secure the beloved in order to produce pleasure for the self. Similarly, ungoverned ambition in romance and elsewhere, since it aimed at the aggrandizement of the self's power, was often allied with interestedness and with passion. Hirschman argues for rationalizing the apparent contradiction in interest's affiliation with both sides of the reason/passion dichotomy by understanding interest in the seventeenth century as a mediator between them, offering self-love "upgraded and contained by reason" and reason "given direction and force by that passion."[25] This formulation would seem to be borne out by Rohan, for one, who described interest as an antidote not to passion and desire but rather to "violent passions" and "inordinate desires" (38–9). Hirschman also argues, famously, for the theory of the "countervailing passion," tracing the view in the late seventeenth century that passions were best held in check by other passions and suggesting that interest was construed as a passion in this period precisely for the reason that it could be marshaled to govern and supersede more dangerously destabilizing passions.[26] The great virtue of interest as mediator or as tempering force, as I will show in readings of Roger Boyle's *Parthenissa* and Percy Herbert's *Cloria,* was that it made possible a view of the will as both forceful and self-moderating. On the other hand, such a sanguine view of interest was hardly universal or even consistently held, as is made clear by the story with which Herbert opens *Certaine Conceptions,* about a dispute between two brothers, each of whom holds so passionately to the hypothetical proposition of his own megalomaniac self-interest (one, looking up at the sky, imagines populating it with an enormous flock of sheep; and when the other says he too deserves a piece, the first counters that he claimed it first) that they fall to blows escalating into double murder. In this ridiculous extension of the Cain and Abel story, competitive self-interest becomes tragically, if also absurdly, ungovernable, a passion that refuses to submit even to the most basic reasoning.

Herbert's narrative brings into view a corollary of the concept of interest in the mid-seventeenth century, that insofar as people were governed or guided by self-interest they were necessarily in conflict. Hobbes accounted for this idea in *Leviathan* by arguing that if self-interest (which he understood as a passion) were given free rein, there would always be some people in whom it would turn to overweening ambition and who would thus attempt to tyrannize over others. There seems no necessary cultural or philosophical reason why self-interest even if it is a passion must crowd out all other impulses, especially in an economy not characterized by scarcity, and recently it has been argued that self-interest and conflict are linked only by the prior postulate of a fundamentally asocial self.[27] Nevertheless the two ideas were almost always paired at mid-seventeenth century, and to make sense of this we might consider politic ideology in its early manifestations, when to follow one's own interest was by definition to violate the good of others insofar as that good rested in God's plan. It is also probably not a coincidence that mercantilism in the seventeenth century consistently portrayed trade as a zero-sum game, nor perhaps that the Long Parliament witnessed a shift from an emphasis on consensus to adversary politics.[28] Within the "culture of credit," to borrow Craig Muldrew's term, the rapid growth of commercialism from the 1550s on meant that there was an intensified emphasis on the fragility of and competition inherent in interpersonal relationship.[29] And in the drive toward self-advantage that was one facet of the ideology of early modern commercialism, interest may have come by association also to imply conflict.

Some modern theorists of self-interest have suggested (pace Hirschman) that as tautology the concept of interest held no meaning except insofar as it functioned to counter an opposite idea.[30] One such opposite, I argued, was the notion of a commonweal governed ultimately by providential order, that ideal brought into particular relief by politic ideology in the late sixteenth century; another, which we can perceive in the debates over interest in midcentury romance, was the sense that human beings were as oriented toward concern with the welfare of others as toward self-interest—even perhaps toward an investment in the interests of others for their own sake. Partly as a consequence of the reigning influence of Hobbes on studies of this period, this idea has received little critical attention, but it does have an early modern philosophical anchor, in the work of the Dutch political philosopher Hugo Grotius, which two contemporary scholars have called "the modern *locus classicus* of the concept of sociality."[31] Grotius's work was never alluded to directly in midcentury romance, but it provided a rare and significant precedent for the genre's turn toward ethical concern.

Grotius's thought was known in England mainly from the *De Jure Belli ac Pacis* (*Of the Law of War and Peace*, 1625), published in London in an English translation by Clement Barksdale in 1654 and probably circulated in manuscript in other translations before that. His *De Jure Praedae Commentarius* (*Commentary on the Law of Prize and Booty*), solicited in 1604 by the United Provinces as a defense of their authorization for their trading companies to seize Portuguese vessels, was not published in its entirety until 1868, though Grotius did publish the twelfth chapter, "Mare Liberum," in 1608, and it is likely that the work also circulated in manuscript.[32] Grotius's fame in moral philosophy proceeds in part from his suggestion that the impulse toward association with one's peers for the sake of association itself was at least as basic in the human being as the drive toward self-advantage. Modern scholarship is caught in a debate over whether "suggestion" is too strong or too weak a word: Richard Tuck, for one, argues strongly that self-interest is the logical starting point of Grotius's ethical theory, the fundamental natural right, but other scholars find that what Robert Shaver calls the "law of love" in Grotius dictates an equally primary emphasis on consideration for the other, and that Grotius is the early modern inaugurator of an anti-Hobbesian tradition in which the question "Why should I pursue my self interest?" is not necessarily presumed to have a more obvious answer than "Why should I sacrifice it?"[33] The disagreement stems from a few key passages in Grotius, especially the assertion in *De Jure Praedae* quoted on both sides of the question, that "love, whose primary force and action are directed to self-interest, is the first principle of the whole natural order. Consequently, Horace should not be censured for saying, in imitation of the Academics, that expediency might perhaps be called the mother of justice and equity" (9). Such an idea, that love is reducible to self-interest and that this self-interest is the foundation of both the natural and the political orders, would seem entirely consistent with Hobbes's thought, but Grotius also offers shortly afterward the un-Hobbesian idea that sociality proceeds not from care for one's own advantage but from a "regard for the welfare of [one's] fellow beings" instilled directly by God (11); that this care for others is the starting point of all justice concerned with the good of others; and that those Academics Horace imitates who argue that natural and civil justice are both based on "personal advantage" are in fact wrong (13).

In *De Jure Belli,* similarly, Grotius refutes the ancient Greek Skeptic Carneades' notions that self-profit is the primary motivation of human behavior and that utility is the mother of justice and equity with the counter ideas that "among [the] things that are proper to Man, is the Appetite of Society"—an appetite instilled, again, directly by God—and that the real mother of justice and equity is "humane nature it self, which would carry us to a desire of mutual society, though we wanted nothing" (*3v). Utility, Grotius adds, provides merely the "occasion" for society, not the real motive (*6v). And this leads Shaver to suggest that when Grotius says in *De Jure Praedae* that self-interest is the "first principle" he means this only temporally, not logically (35); I might add that Grotius's immediately subsequent willingness to allow Horace's idea about expediency is not necessarily an endorsement of it, especially in light of the fact that he is about to refute Horace's sources. Clearly, Grotius does argue that love's "primary force and action" are for the good of the self, not the other, which is why he must concede at the end of *De Jure Praedae* that he knows the order of his argument has suggested that one's own good takes precedence over another's. At the very least it seems fair to say that the conflict epitomized by Tuck and Shaver reflects an ambivalence within Grotius's work (one that Grotius himself, in a suggestive allusion to Carneades, may have meant to draw attention to[34]).

Grotius, I think we should conclude, was reluctant to advance the notion of care for others far enough to put it in conflict with self-interest, intending instead to show that the two could coexist in relative comfort. For my purposes here, it is important to emphasize that Grotius's work helped to make possible at midcentury, perhaps precisely by this effort to show the comfortable coexistence of interest and care for others, the rehabilitation of such terms as "politic" and "policy," tarred as they had been by their politic association with love for the self rather than care for the common good. This rehabilitation was evident in a little book that appeared in London in 1654, the same year as the publication of *De Jure Belli* in English, called *Politick Maxims and Observations, written by the most learned Hugo Grotius, Translated for the care and benefit of the English States-man by H.C.S.T.B.*[35] This work, a collection of Grotian ideas intertwined with commentary, complained that "Politique Reason" had once been synonymous with "Equity," which "respects the Publique Good and Truth," but had since devolved into merely "Reason of State," "nothing else but a devise of Tyrants" that "looks upon [onely] [*sic*] the private and seeming good of the Power in being."[36] The author invoked Grotius's authority to call for reform and to protest other ideas associated specifically with interest, for example, the "Doctrine of fatall Necessity" (74) and the faith among devotees of politic reason that if they take proper account of it then "by their owne Wisdome they can Fathome, and foresee all things" (34). On the conflict between Hobbes and Grotius the author of this volume compromised, suggesting that people must form communities both for the Hobbesian reason that man originally could not stand alone and was "compell'd by Necessity to betake himselfe to the support of others" (1) and also for the more Grotian reason that "Man [was] borne to hold Society with All Men" (2), the signs of the latter being both his natural propensity to language and his "uncorrupted [i.e., prelapsarian] Affection" (4). As a compendium and interpretation of Grotius's ideas, this volume was interestingly contradictory: even as the title enlisted Grotius on the side of "politick" wisdom, the text inside used him to counter such conventionally politic and Machiavellian ideas as reason of state and self-interest, arguing at least half-heartedly for love as the impetus for society. What it tells us is that Grotius was understood to be, or at least susceptible to being advertised as, a modern, sophisticated commentator on politics, but that he could also be recruited to temper and to some extent refute what Tuck calls the first principle of the new humanism codified by Hobbes, self-preservation as the foundation for sociality.[37]

If Grotius's argument for natural affection had an obvious influence on Harrington's notion of a "mankind interest" as distinct from the interest of the self, it also made more thinkable elsewhere a model of relationship and of society as proceeding from something other than self-advantage. So in *Wisdomes Tripos,* Charles Herle insisted that if we can understand "Policy" rightly as simply (echoing the Grotius volume) "transaction in a society of men" (1), then we must acknowledge that there are two distinct kinds of love. One, which advertises itself as for another but is really for the self, "envies this *soul* any larger room then that of a mans own narrow hide-bound skin . . . 'tis the very Hedg-hog of Conversation, that rouls and laps it self within its own soft downe, and turns out brizzels to all the world besides" (21). The other is "communicative, transactive, and diffusive" love, the love belonging to authentic policy rather than the perverted notion of it that now dominates social life (20). "[T]o love another as ones self," says Herle in a pointed rejoinder to Hobbes, "may be a good *level,* but to make it ones *mark* too, and love another but for ones self (which is a main maxim in this kind of Policy) 'tis to make a mans self, not only the Epitome of the world, but the whole Volume" (22–3). Herle makes a distinction that the biblical injunction perhaps leaves unclear (a distinction even less clear in the related injunction to "do unto others as you would have them do unto you"), between love for another as an extension of love for the self and love for self and for other in merely analogical relation. Self-love for Herle may be a guide to love for the other, a "level" to show us in another context what we are aiming for, but in the social realm it is not an origin and must not be an end. As Herle intimated, and as romance would make even clearer, at midcentury the idea of self-interest brought into relief as its opposite not the providentially governed commonwealth of early politic ideology, nor the kind of abstract obligation to serve the greater good elucidated by the epic value of pietas, nor even the notion of pity as an urge to partake imaginatively in another's suffering. Instead the debate over interest generated as its counterargument the potentially more radical idea that in society people were constituted by what Herle calls interpersonal "transaction" with one another—that in a social context, as the Royalist theorist William Sedgwick hopefully proposed, interest might come to signify not acquisitive desire but rather "*inter esse* . . . to be in, or amongst each other."[38]

In closing this section I want to reiterate that it is a mistake to see the increasing concern with interest at midcentury solely as a move toward a rationalistic, extra-ethical view of human relations. A few decades ago it was common to tell the story of a shift, culminating in

in 1640s and 1650s France, particularly the work of La Calprenède, drew a distinction between what it called "*l'amour d'élection*," love by choice, usually associated with marriage, and "*l'amour d'inclination*," love by something close to passion, assigning *l'amour d'inclination* the moral honors. A few decades earlier Honoré d'Urfé's phenomenally popular pastoral romance *L'Astrée*, published in installments in the 1610s and 1620s (and translated into English almost as quickly as it appeared in French), had pleaded for the exercise of reason in love, suggesting that because women were not as subject as men to passion, they might raise the moral level of masculine erotic love by insisting that it be governed by deliberation and rational choice. But as pastoral romance was supplanted by the *roman heroique* in France this formula reversed itself, and by the middle of the century French romance unambivalently privileged passionate love as more sincere and authentic than love willing to subject itself to calculation.[42] French romance's effort to cordon off love from other, more ordinarily self-interested kinds of interpersonal alliance seems to us now recognizably modern, and it throws into relief the extent to which, in objecting to erotic desire as self-interested, English romance was perhaps less in line with conventional wisdom than we might have thought.

Within *Eliana* Euripides' contention that erotic love is necessarily self-interested is also disputed—obliquely, by the later narrative of the hero Lonoxia's efforts to love Atalanta disinterestedly (which I will discuss in the next chapter), and more directly, by Euripides' new friend Argelois, lover of the titular heroine Eliana. Love "undetermined is *Lust, Lust* determined to one, *Love*," Argelois ventures, trying to mitigate Euripides' sharp distinction between true love and love yoked to desire (113). For one, Argelois objects, desire keeps us humble—to want to be without it, to deny our implication in sinfulness, is to commit the hubris of wanting to be as the gods (114, 171). Without desire, he claims, we would also "love all alike" (114), our own lack of self-interest apparently rendering us unable to make distinctions among others. Argelois tends to be practical whereas Euripides argues by principle, and his main solution to the problem of self-interest in love is to temper it. In his own view he is not a Stoic, advocating that "all passions and affections are wholly to be mortified, wholly slain and extinguished"; passions, he reasons in Aristotelian fashion, are not problematic in themselves but only in our excessive submission to them (114). If we "regulate" our "desires of attaining" (114), "bound them regularly" (171), then "they are not evill but may be used" (171).

Argelois is postulating here a familiar relation between reason and passion, by which reason, a power that "the Gods in justice leaves [us]" because without it we would be pathetically weak, does not expunge but simply subordinates our self-interested and acquisitive desire. He agrees with Euripides that in theory no love is truly virtuous unless one does not "desir[e] the use of the object" at all, but given the rarity of such ideal disinterestedness, he decides that we might as well "use" love, that we should be grateful for its effects rather than worry about its motivations (172). Euripides, unimpressed, suspects the complicity of such opinions themselves in self-interest, taunting Argelois with the accusation that it is his passion, not his reason, that offers this defense of love, and indeed immediately after this conversation Argelois finds himself unable to temper his passions despite all his good intentions (175). *Eliana* seems in this conversation to float the idea that self-interest might be a means rather than an end, a governable, harnessable force, only to sink it.

Eliana's reconfiguration of traditional ideas about love in interested terms, and its ultimate concession to passion-as-interest as both morally reprehensible and all-powerful, prove to be quite representative for romance at midcentury, and in a generic sense, especially, innovative. But philosophically these moves are conventional, more an act of renaming than new thinking. Much more unusual is the treatment of love and interest in a romance now almost entirely forgotten, one that at first glance might be expected to be more rather than less conventional, *Herba Parietis* (1650) by Thomas Bayly.[43] Bayly was a Royalist clergyman, son of Lewis Bayly, bishop of Bangor, author of *The Practice of Piety* (1612), one of the century's most popular works of practical and devotional piety.[44] The younger Bayly was briefly imprisoned in Newgate in 1649 or early 1650, probably for publishing *The Royal Charter Granted unto Kings by God Himself* after the execution of Charles I, and he probably converted to Catholicism around 1654 before dying in the late 1650s. The romance's title page translates the title as "The Wall-Flower, As it grew out of the Stone-Chamber belonging to the Metropolitan Prison of *London,* called Newgate," advertising the work as "a History which is Partly True, Partly Romantick, and Morally Divine, Whereby a Marriage between Reality and Fancy is solemnized by Divinity." Bayly meant his romance to reveal, through its stories of "*vertuous and honest Love, . . . like so many Sparkes of the* Divine," "*all that* Divinity *of Our* Savior," and he sought therefore to find a way to address the problem of acquisitive desire between his many pairs of lovers.[45]

One of the ways *Herba Parietis* does this is by its marked effort to render love as transitive, and thereby inclusive, rather than exclusive, an attribute that seems to diffuse and weaken self-interest. At the romance's opening, for instance, the Carthaginian prince Lorenzo has just transferred his passion from Amarissa to Honoria and now offers Amarissa to Honoria's brother Bertaldo, declaring that "I will not onely grant thee this, but assure thee, were I a woman my selfe, thou shouldst have me." When Honoria protests, disturbed by the revelation of Lorenzo's faithlessness to Amarissa, Lorenzo replies to her, "*And rather then thou shouldst build a discontent on such foundations, he* [Bertaldo] *shall be Prince of* Carthage, *and I will be* Bertaldo." After some grumbling to Lorenzo, Amarissa consents to the new plan, at which point Honoria promises her, "*Love him* [Bertaldo], *and you shall not lose your first love; for* Lorenzo *being my selfe, and I yours,* Bertaldo *and* Amarissa *shall so agree in a* third *person, that* foure *shall be happy all at* once" (10–11). The dizzying language of identity transfer here, which recurs several times in the romance, seems designed not to shadow alternative, illicit forms of desire, for instance Lorenzo's for Bertaldo or Amarissa's for Honoria, so much as to establish love as communal rather than exclusive. Even the resistant Amarissa has the right idea in wanting to obtain revenge by joining Lorenzo in loving a third person ("I am sorry I am not a Man; for then would I love Honoria better then your selfe, and so be even with you"), a predilection that sets her up for consent to Honoria's scheme. Urania's anxiety over her change in Wroth's romance would not obtain here because she could love Perissus and Parselius at once, along with the fourth lover whom Bayly's romance unstintingly supplies to every triangle it sets up. If Argelois's disapproval of "loving all alike" pertains at all in this scenario, it is apparently not important enough to disrupt the vision of a group "happy all at once," the "desires of attaining," in Argelois's phrase, relieved of their sting by the lovers' willingness to share. We should recall here Sedgwick's definition of interest as "inter esse . . . to be in, or amongst each other," which in this case is borne out so lavishly that there is no space left for any narrower conceptions of interest.

Bayly's other, ostensibly more conventional route to earthly virtue is to dispense entirely with sexual passion—a common enough response to interest in romance when it is troped by the figure of the hermit, but Bayly more radically attempts to pull it off from inside the context of erotic love. Lorenzo's military commander Corderius was once a merchant but resigned this identity because of its interestedness and thus "*found* himself at *last* by *beginning* to be a *loser*" (72). In Bayly's inset narrative Corderius approaches the virtuous lady Fortunata, Machiavelli's strumpet recast as chaste and kind, with a marriage proposal, but he refuses to tell her his name, nationality, or "what meanes I have to Maintaine you," asking her "but these two questions, First, Can you Love? Secondly, Can that Love have any Influence upon my person?" (74). Fortunata agrees to marry him, and on the wedding night he reveals his estate, then recounts that as a young man he suffered shipwreck and promised the gods, while clinging to the mast, that if he survived he would stay a virgin for life. Since then, he says, "Divine providence" has made him its instrument, casting him as "Father to the Fatherlesse, a Husband to many a Widow" (83). Fortunata, delighted by his virtue, reiterates her commitment to the marriage, and the two then occupy themselves for the rest of the romance in doing good for others. This episode allegorizes the ethical triumph of providence, and perhaps the genre of romance as well, over self-interest: at the moment of ultimate contingency represented by shipwreck, Corderius realizes that he can gain some control over his fate by renouncing the effort to attain his own ends, which paradoxically turns fortune from his ruler into his helpmeet.

The logic by which erotic desire represents self-interest is entirely conventional for romance, but Bayly's attempt to present an alternative rather than simply to lament human nature is unusual. And more unusual still is Corderius's second question to Fortunata at the moment of his proposal, "Can [your] Love have any Influence upon my person?" Midcentury romance, I have been arguing, inherited a long tradition of worrying constantly about the moral status of the lover but almost never about the ethical efficacy of love on another. Self-interest, correspondingly, was generally problematic in romance because it compromised the lover's own virtue, not because it kept him from "influencing" another in a positive moral sense. It would be even more surprising if Corderius asked whether his own love could have any influence on Fortunata's person, because this would mark a much more decisive turn away from self-interest and also because it would recognize the woman in a love relationship, in particular, as partner rather than object. Within the context of seventeenth-century romance, nonetheless, and indeed more generally of interest discourse, Corderius's perception of love as a force capable of actually impinging on another would seem to be quite exceptional—an exceptionality that points, by contrast, to a kind of associative narrowing of attention that seemed more usually to accompany the idea of self-interest in the seventeenth century. The possibility that one's love might impinge on another does not violate self-interest—in fact, it might be very much in one's own interest to influence another by love—and so there seems no necessary reason why some consideration of love's influence on the beloved should not accompany an exploration of relationship that takes self-interest as its founding assumption. But self-interest tended nevertheless to crowd out moral attention to anything but the self's internal state, as if one's own desire not only motivated and governed one's actions but also epitomized the whole world. Perhaps we should conclude that it is only when love is made exempt from its usual implication in self-interest that it can be conceived of as at all a matter of relation rather than simply a proving ground for individual virtue—that is, that romance in this period could not begin to make the turn from morality to ethics until it stepped out from under the notion of self-interest as inexorable and all-consuming.

4. FRIENDSHIP

Herba Parietis was unusual in its effort to purify heterosexual erotic love from the taint of self-interest, and even Bayly could not quite take the idea seriously in its most extreme version, marking off his episode of disinterested love from the main text with the subtitle "*the fantasticall* Wooing, *Humoursome* Wedding, *and Platonick love of Corderius and Fortunata*" (72). More conventional was the attempt to redeem love through friendship, for which romance inherited models as ancient as the *Aeneid*. The pathos of Virgil's story of Nisus and Euryalus, of course, depended culturally on the young men's willingness to sacrifice their lives for each other, thus providing proof of true disinterestedness even at the heart of Aeneas's great acquisitive venture. Perhaps because in seventeenth-century romance eros was so firmly identified with interest, the genre at midcentury usually substituted erotic love for life as the good to be sacrificed and then triangulated the relationship between its rival heroes, asking one of them to prove his love for his friend by handing over to him a woman for whom he had great passion. But although this narrative scenario recurred in many variations, for instance in *Eliana*'s account of the relationship between Argelois and his friend Dardanus or in the Perolla-Flamminius plot in *Parthenissa,* unlike its classical model it was almost never carried through, one of the lovers realizing at the last minute that his love was not really sincere after all. Like Grotius and indeed interest discourse in general, romances of this period seemed reluctant to push disinterested love all the way to the sacrifice of interest, or even to allow that such a sacrifice might ever really be necessary, and were usually content just to demonstrate that their noble protagonists had the hypothetical will to renounce their heteroerotic desires in favor of masculine friendship.[46]

Besides the sacrifice narrative, the other main aspect of the classical friendship model available to midcentury romance was the perfectly twinned pair so united as to be at one in their interest, a narrative trope for which *Argenis*, as I have shown, supplied ample precedent, but also one that we might expect to be rare by midcentury given interest discourse's emphasis on sociality. And indeed, although midcentury romance was well aware of the trope—*Eliana*'s idealist Argelois, for instance, gives a textbook description in his characterization of the true friend's desire to "become one" with the object of his affection, "to be incorporated with it, and not to take any thing from it, but to immerge it self in it" (172)—realized examples of it are decidedly unusual in this canon of texts. One of the few examples against the trend would seem to be the rapturously identificatory friendship between Demetrius and Alexandro in the anonymous *Theophania*, but even here friendship gestured more toward its implication in the self-interest of ordinary erotic love than toward its exemption from it. *Theophania*, one of the very few midcentury romances to be republished in a modern edition, has very tenuously been attributed to a Sir William Sales of whom nothing else is known, and it was first published in 1655, though it may have been written a decade earlier.[47] The romance as it stands in unfinished form contains a central pair of twinned friends, Alexandro (Prince Charles in *Theophania*'s political allegory) and Demetrius (Prince William of Orange), who as in *Argenis* is in love with his friend's sister, although this time the sibling relationship is known to everyone but Demetrius and there is no rivalry for the princess's love. At their first encounter the two young men are instantly transported by passion for one another, flying "into each other's arms with such a mutual concurrence of affection that they seemd to breath their souls into each other's bosoms" (130). This would seem an echo of what happens when *Argenis*'s Poliarchus and Archombrotus first laid eyes on one another and apprehended their uncanny affinity, but in fact Demetrius has already recognized in Alexandro's features the resemblance of his sister Mariana (Princess Mary), with whom he has previously fallen in love, and for a moment before he embraces Alexandro he seems to confuse the prince with his sister, beseeching him not to disdain someone who has long been devoted to his service and adding that "You strangely resemble, if you are not the same, a person whose least regards are capable to subdue and triumph over whole nations" (129). Evidently the identification between the princes has been preceded by an identification between brother and sister, at least in Demetrius's mind, and in loving Alexandro Demetrius actually loves, albeit unconsciously, according to his interest—a point the narrator emphasizes through Alexandro's broad (but to Demetrius, comically, entirely opaque) hints about how useful he might be in pleading Demetrius's case to his sister.[48]

In *Argenis* friendship could still trump heteroerotic desire, at least with careful narrative plotting, but in the world of midcentury romance friendship's only hope was thus that such desire would either enlist it or pass by without forcing a showdown. Self-interest, we can speculate, had become powerful enough as an idea that in most romance there was not much space for an alternative. And the problem with self-interest in the romances I have been discussing thus far was simply that it put the self first—in most cases a moral failure not any different from the one Wroth investigates in *Urania,* although in *Herba Parietis* we do begin to see signs of a shift toward ethics. In *Parthenissa* Roger Boyle brought to the fore a different objection to interested affection, that it followed necessity rather than being an expression of choice. This was not, of course, a new idea; the tension between providence (or, less optimistically, contingency) and human agency always implies a corollary tension between constraint and free will, as *Urania* made very clear in its exploration of the moral ramifications of agency. But Boyle made this classic problem the central subject of his romance, refiguring it within the terms of interest discourse by construing erotic love as a form of necessity and friendship as proceeding from free choice. Although he could no more find a way, in the ordinary interested world, for friendship to redeem the self-interested agent than could the authors of *Eliana* or *Theophania,* he used romance to hypothesize an imaginary, utopian world, in which we might at least be free to formulate intentions if not to act on them.

Probably the most influential of midcentury English romances, cited well into the eighteenth century as a quintessential example of the genre and read in its own time as particularly serious and sophisticated, *Parthenissa* was published in five installments throughout the 1650s and in full, if that term is fair, in 1676 (Boyle left several story lines hanging but the 1676 title page proclaims the romance "compleat").[49] Roger Boyle, first Earl of Orrery (1621–1679), elder brother of the now more famous Robert, grew up in Ireland in the household of his father, first Earl of Cork, and like Robert spent a formative span of his adolescence in France, where he first became acquainted, he tells us in the preface to the fifth part of *Parthenissa,* with romance.[50] Strongly

Protestant, after the 1641 Irish rising he was employed by Parliament as a military general and politician; at Charles I's execution he was expected to dissociate himself from Cromwell as his older brothers had, and there were rumors that he was raising an Irish army for Charles II, but instead he was persuaded, apparently by Cromwell himself, to serve the new regime, and in the 1650s, convinced as he had been throughout his career that the Irish Protestants were the only secure basis for English rule of the island, he became one of Richard Cromwell's closest confidants. At the Restoration he transferred his loyalties back to the Crown with few complications and was installed as one of the Lord Justices of Ireland, and for much of the next two decades, in the midst of his demanding political career, he turned his literary talents to drama. Throughout his life he moved in literary circles—Suckling and Davenant and later Cowley were friends, and in the 1660s he became an acquaintance of Katherine Philips and had some part in persuading her to complete her translation of *Cassandra*.[51]

Of all the midcentury English romances *Parthenissa* probably had the closest ties to its French counterparts, and Boyle frequently used the word "inclination" to describe ties of affection, though with a significant revision of its French sense. In French romance, as I said, "inclination" generally connoted a morally salutary heterosexual passion, a kind of natural affinity for another, in contrast to the more calculating "election," by which one chose a lover according to one's own interests. But Boyle used "inclination" almost exclusively to refer to the admiration and respect one man has for another he wants as his friend, distinguishing it from the desire a man had for a woman precisely by the space it left for choice and agency. Boyle's hero Artabanes feels a strong affinity for his chief heteroerotic rival Surena, and protests to him that he would like to excuse "the employing my Life and Liberty against the generous *Surena* for *Parthenissa*" by "employing them for him, where her service comes not in competition," concluding that for both of them "Passion makes [us] think it fit (at least pardonable) to act against [our] Inclination."[52] Later, just before the two men engage in hand-to-hand combat to determine who will marry Parthenissa, Artabanes declares, "though my Love be infinite, my Friendship is proportionate; and that if I give the former the precedency, the difference proceeds as much from my Fate, as my Inclination" (573). Male rivalry, like erotic love, is what romance wants, not Artabanes; as it is his human fate, psychologically, to be self-interested, so it is his generic "Fate" to desire Parthenissa and fight with Surena. Through Artabanes' "inclination" toward Surena, in contrast, Boyle opens up the possibility of a different kind of space, both fictional and psychological, in which relationships might be chosen rather than simply enacted.

If Surena is in some sense a more authentic object than Parthenissa for Artabanes' affections, he nevertheless seems an strange choice for such attachment. Among other sins he unjustly imprisons Parthenissa several times, disguises himself as someone else in order to abduct her, and mimics Sidney's evil Cecropia in staging a mock execution of Artabanes in order to trick the princess into repudiating her lover, actions that are widely condemned not only by Artabanes' intimates but by people with no ties to him. Oddly, Artabanes does not let any of this behavior disrupt his esteem for Surena but rather identifies himself all the more firmly with his rival, insisting that it must be "acknowledge[d] we are both innocent, or both excusable" (566). In the context of erotic passion, Artabanes seems to imply, there is no distinction to be made between his own choice to put his desire for Parthenissa before his friend's interest and Surena's mendacious tricks; self-interest in this romance is not only irresistible but in a moral sense perfectly univalent, open to any and all means. Paradoxically, the desire for friendship through which Artabanes concedes his implication in Surena's self-interested villainy is also Artabanes' one real gesture at liberation from interest's necessity.

Artabanes' inclination toward Surena is sincere, but within *Parthenissa* it remains merely hypothesis, what he would realize if only he were not governed by self-interest. In much of Boyle's narrative, romance as a genre seems allied with self-interest in opposing this hypothesis, its traditional plots bearing inexorably down in the form of what Artabanes calls "Fate," but in his dedicatory epistle for *Parthenissa*'s first book, to Lady Northumberland, Boyle makes the surprising move of locating romance on the other side, with friendship as a mode of defiance against necessity. Although Lady Northumberland, as Boyle declares in an elaborate Spenserian conceit, is the incomparable model for Parthenissa herself, had he not decided to fictionalize and actually succeeded, instead, in rendering her real self within his narrative he could not have "continu'd the Romance," since "thereby my Hero's friendships must have yielded to their Loves" (A2v). Friendship and fiction, Boyle suggests in this compliment, are mutually constitutive, friendship the hypothetical content of fiction's hypothetical form. Together they make possible a respite from necessity, figured here both as heterosexual desire and as the real. In its ideal form, for Boyle, this is romance's real function, as a forum for imagining ourselves as true agents, for whom relationship waits to be written rather than following an ancient script.

Boyle's thematic hostility to necessity and his conceptualization of romance as necessity's opponent help explain why the plot of *Parthenissa* seems so averse to any incorporation of tragedy, why despite Surena's flaws, for instance, Artabanes and indeed the romance itself persistently imagine an alternative fate for Surena rather than meting out judgment (whether human or divine) for his sins. This hostility also offers a way to begin thinking about *Parthenissa*'s difficult relation to history. If *Parthenissa* is allegory—and insofar as it straightforwardly represents, say, Lady Northumberland, in my terms it must be—it explicitly resists being allegory in the sense I attributed to Fletcher in chapter 1, in that it refuses to conceive of its characters as "daemons" whose fate is already marked out for them either by their allegorical significance (Surena as rival overcome by passion) or by their historical identity (Parthenissa as the historical Lady Northumberland). Notwithstanding his compliment to Lady Northumberland, romance for Boyle bears not so much an allegorical as an ironic relation to history. Indeed, if we put it next to history we can see that it is what history is not, in the sense both that it reaches toward what is imaginary or hypothetical rather than actual and also that it sets itself against that kind of narrative structure by which in retrospect events come to look inevitable rather than merely contingent.

As context for this near-compulsion in *Parthenissa* to escape the necessity both of historical event and of heteroerotic relationship, we might recall that Boyle was known in the 1650s and afterward for the elasticity of his loyalties, not just at the Restoration (when many managed a successful transfer of political affiliation—though Boyle did have a particularly close personal relationship with the Cromwell family) but especially at that moment in 1650 when he was somehow persuaded to put his talents to the service of the revolutionary regime.[53] Historical writing might not provide much legitimation for this kind of behavior—much justification, that is, for turning away from people to whom one had long been obligated in order to ally oneself with others to whom one had no conventional political bonds, and with whom one might imagine a harmonious future only if tradition would loosen its grip. But for Boyle, such justification was just the opportunity that fictional, hypothetical romance afforded. It is tempting to speculate that in *Parthenissa* Boyle was formulating an ethics for a social and political world in which past and future did not seem to have much relation to one another, and in which it was perhaps prudent to derive from this at least a guarded hope rather than simply guilt. In such a situation it was no longer necessity but rather hypothesis that had to be aligned with the politic, as Boyle wishfully released his readers from the bonds of history so that they could make the best for themselves of a new and quite different dispensation.

5. *Oceana* and the "Interest of Mankind," or Reading Politics by Way of Romance

In the last sections of this chapter I turn to two narratives that of all the romances in this book would seem to have the least claim to the label, Harrington's republican treatise *Oceana* and Robert Boyle's virgin-martyr story *Theodora*. Harrington and Boyle are both self-proclaimed outsiders, insisting strenuously on their hostility to romance, but perhaps precisely because they are outsiders, both still see in the genre the possibility of an idealized sympathy for others that most romance writers in the period took *Arcadia* to have ironized decades ago. And both try to marshal this sympathy as a counterweight to the self-interest by now more conventionally associated with romance, in order to serve their own moral-philosophical ends and also, in effect, to reform the genre by setting it against itself.

Although its lightly fictionalized, roman à clef version of English political history is rarely discussed within the context of seventeenth-century literature, as one of the canonical treatments of interest in political philosopy *Oceana* is well enough known not to need any introduction.[54] One of Harrington's chief concerns, and his central contribution to interest discourse, was to rescue the concept of interest by extending it not merely to the individual but also to the whole or the collective, in which form it might serve as the foundation for a just republic. Harrington concedes the Tacitean, Hobbesian idea that by definition "reason is nothing but interest," the calculation of self-advantage (171), but he does not then conclude that we must fall back on a Hobbesian sovereign; rather, what saves us from the tyrannical rule of private interest is "a common right, law of nature, or interest of the whole," which he also calls "the interest of mankind" (171) and describes as synonymous with "right reason" (172). To explain how civil government might be able to lead its members to consider this general interest, he offers the famous case of two girls with a cake, who even in their entire political naïveté (they are only girls) know intuitively that the way for each to be most confident of the fulfillment of her interest (the largest possible portion of cake) is for one to divide and the other to choose, a system that will always produce equal halves (172). Considering herself in isolation, each girl's goal would have been to acquire for herself the largest possible portion of cake; when she recognizes herself as incontrovertibly part of a group, her goal shrinks to a portion as close to half as she can get it. A commonwealth that includes representatively the "whole body of the people" (173) in its decision-making process, Harrington concludes, and that divides any given political decision among its members, will always construe self-interest in such a way that it will be identical to or at least compatible with the interest of each and every individual insofar as she is in relation to others, the sum of which, for Harrington, is equivalent to the shared "interest of mankind." Not surprisingly, Harrington inserted a quotation from Grotius's *De Jure Belli,* that occasionally not just human beings but even "creatures . . . abstain from their own profit" (171), directly after his first assertion of an "interest of the whole."[55]

The concept of interest, then, should not have posed the same threat for Harrington that it did for the romances I have discussed up till now, because properly construed, he believed, it did not oppose the good of the individual to the good of the group but showed how the two might prove compatible. Harrington apparently lacked complete confidence in this formulation, however, because private interest refuses to stay under control in *Oceana,* asserting itself again and again in the particularly pernicious form of "ambition and covetousness" (240). Harrington was famously dismissive in *Oceana,* as his twentieth-century editor J. G. A. Pocock notes, of wealth in any form other than land (59–61), and a good part of the reason for this was his anxiety that riches of other kinds led to destabilizing greed. Governments consisting of parliaments, Harrington declares, following Aristotle's *Politics,* have always founded themselves on husbandry as the "least subject unto innovation or turbulency"; they have a natural "aversion" to the ways of courts and understand that a commonwealth made up of city-dwellers "would doubtless be stormy, in regard that ambition would be every man's trade" (158). The "plough in the hands of the owner, . . . produceth the most innocent and steady genius of a commonwealth" (159), because it guards against any challenge to Harrington's interest of the whole by acquisitive desire run rampant.

One of the great distractions from thinking about interest in the way Harrington recommends, indeed one of our primary frameworks for formulating interest as ambition and greed, according to *Oceana,* is romance. Advocating an agrarian that would replace the corrupt system of primogeniture and thus ensure income for children after the first son, Harrington's hero, the Cromwell-figure Lord Archon, says that such a law would demonstrate a "pure and spotless love, the consequence whereof I will not give for all the romances"—in which, goes the implication, love is corrupted by desire and greed. As an alderman makes his daughter a countess with twenty thousand pounds, so a romance turns its character into a "considerable mistress" by marrying her to a prince: "these are characters of bastard love" because they are aimed at selling women to the highest bidders and reward one child (or really, rather, the man who buys her) at the expense of her siblings. But Lord Archon's agrarian, in contrast, will "exclude ambition and covetousness," and thereby according to Harrington's conceit legitimize the marriage bed and the race of the commonwealth (240). In this same vein, as a foil for the genuine republican government he advocates, Harrington revises canonical accounts of Elizabeth's reign to offer a lightly fictionalized account of Tudor history in which Queen Parthenia "wholly neglected the nobility" rather than correcting its decline, and "convert[ed] her reign through the perpetual love tricks that passed between her and her people into a kind of romance" (198).[56] Such short-sighted and self-indulgent behavior, designed merely to increase her personal popularity, led directly, in the terms of Harrington's version of history as bad romance, to the overstrengthening of the House of Commons, the clergy's defensive appeal to Charles I, and the fiasco of the Civil Wars. Romance in these examples is figured as an inauthentic narrative: it deceives us into believing that politics is driven by short-term self-advancement rather than the interest of the whole grounded in the settled wealth of the hereditary aristocracy, and correspondingly misleads us into understanding history as a series of short, disconnected episodes rather than a sweeping and coherent story. Somewhat ironically, given its reputation among such critics as Michael McKeon, romance in Harrington's terms is a fundamentally unconservative genre. It belongs to cities and courts, places of rapid and disorganized change where people misperceive individual and common interests to be at odds, and Harrington hopes that as we embrace his more genuine notion of interest the genre will cease to compel us.

Given this hostility to romance, it seems all the more odd that Harrington should include it in any way as part of *Oceana*. Although *Oceana* opens as a treatise, when Harrington insists that England requires a single, overwhelmingly heroic legislator he begins to fictionalize. Cromwell, as "the most victorious captain an
rable patriot Olphaus Megaletor" (206) (soon to be red
Archon), almost single-handedly legislates Harrington'
commonwealth into being and then engages in a series o
cal edifying discourses that are fictionally extended into

well past Harrington's own time. There is nothing to call this odd mix of utopian fiction with historical reference, in its seventeenth-century context, but romance; and indeed Harrington himself all but applies this label in his very odd conclusion to *Oceana*. Instead of recounting Lord Archon's death Harrington repeats the story of Timoleon of Corinth substantially as it appears in Plutarch, at the end of which he explains that "the life and death of my Lord Archon . . . is so exactly the same again [as Timoleon's story], that (seeing by men wholly ignorant of antiquity, I am accused of writing romance) I shall repeat nothing" (358). In the eyes of everyone else, Harrington all but concedes, his fictional projection of Cromwell's future will look like a romance, and to forestall this accusation he reverses the conventional practice of covering history with fiction and instead covers his fiction with history, conveying Lord Archon's fictional future by means of Timoleon's real past. Harrington seems almost to stage here the complicity of his own narrative in what he has just defined as the sins of romance, as if he wants to be sure that we see it. Why this imbrication of fiction, ancient history, and real life, if what Harrington really wants to write is a republican treatise? Why extend his narrative into a fictional future at all, and thereby open himself to implication in a genre he despises?[57]

If the combined cloak of history and fiction allowed Harrington to speak more pointedly to Cromwell than he could have otherwise, *Oceana*'s self-consciousness about its own fictionalizing nevertheless seems too carefully conveyed for the fiction to be only a mode of political tactfulness. One place to look for another explanation is the title page's epigraph from Horace, "Tantalus a labris sitiens fugientia captat / Flumina: quid rides? mutato nomine, de te / Fabula narratur" ("Tantalus seized at streams fleeing from his lips: why do you laugh? Under different names, it's of you the story is told") (155). Obviously Harrington's readers were being instructed to understand *Oceana* à la *Argenis* as a mirror for their own society—but the admonition must also have seemed a little strange, for *Oceana* recounted the creation of a utopia, not a story of endless torment, and the image conjured up of a callous spectator laughing at someone else's suffering could not have seemed appropriate as a description of Harrington's potential reader. Near the end, however, *Oceana* offers a sort of matching bookend to this image that goes some way toward making sense of its oddness. Just after Lord Archon delivers the concluding "Epitome of the Whole Commonwealth" to the Senate, he is offering a final warning against "ambition, that fulsome complexion of a statesman," when he is suddenly interrupted by "a violent passion of weeping and downright howling" from Philadelphus (brotherly love), secretary of the council (337). Philadelphus has just received a message from "his correspondent Boccalini, secretary of Parnassus" (337), subsequently read aloud by one of the legislators and included in the text, consisting of a long, loosely rendered quotation from Traiano Boccalini's *Ragguagli di Parnasso*. In Boccalini's Tacitean work Apollo presides as judge in Parnassus over a series of historical figures, and in the passage quoted he brings onto the stage Caesar and his progeny in order to display "what havoc [Caesar's] prodigious ambition, not satisfied with his own bloody ghost, had made upon his more innocent remains, even unto the total extinction of his family"—a "grave admonition in a dreadful tragedy," as Lord Archon sums it up for the company, against rule by self-interest (338). In case the epigraph was not illustrative enough, Philadelphus here models for us the right way both of reading messages from Parnassus, home of the Muses, and of correcting for Caesar's faults: rather than laugh in derision we are to submit to bursts of fellow feeling for our compatriots, fictional or real.

Like *Oceana*'s entirely agrarian economy, fiction thus works in Harrington as a lesson and also a sort of insurance against self-interest. The commonwealth rightly ordered establishes the framework for the exercise of right reason, but in case people are tempted to turn away from the common interest, fiction inspires sympathy, a benign, humane form of passion that causes one to forget self-interest rather than fanning its destructive flames, and thereby acts as one of the most effective counterweights to ambition. Victoria Kahn has recently argued that midcentury romance tries to establish a category of what she calls "aesthetic interest," an "imaginative identification" established especially via pity (between characters, and of reader for character) that serves to model relationship.[58] The romances she discusses (Herbert's *Cloria*, Brathwaite's *Panthalia*, and *Theophania*) seem to me, as I have suggested about *Theophania* in this chapter and will suggest about *Cloria* in the next, actually to weaken rather than elaborate sympathetic identification, but *Oceana* comes close to endorsing her thesis in explicit terms—albeit with a significant qualification. What is strange but also, in the light of roman à clef's popularity, conventional about Harrington's sympathy is that insofar as it is literary and therefore implicated in his roman à clef structure, it is not really for an other. It is always of us, after all, that the story is told. Romance in *Oceana*, we can conclude, teaches us to check our scorn for others and instead feel sympathy for them by offering us the other as someone with whom we should identify, as a reflection of the self.

Romance may have been dangerous in its tendency to encourage self-interest, but as in *Urania* and *Argenis*, in *Oceana* it obtained social utility as roman à clef. For Harrington roman à clef helped to deproblematize the interest of the whole by collapsing the distinction between self and other—an operation in the end not that different from the work performed by emulatory friendship in Barclay's *Argenis*, and one that as in Barclay worked directly against romance's more conventional, Sidneian tendency to present self-interest as an immutable social law. J. A. W. Gunn might well see this more optimistic use of romance in *Oceana* as evidence for his complaint that Harrington's leap from individual to common interest is not very rigorous, that *Oceana* refuses to consider the inevitable variations among individual interests that render simplistic any notion of the common interest as by metaphoric extension a simple aggregate.[59] But in his distrust of romance more conventionally construed Harrington showed himself aware of and even sympathetic to contemporary counterarguments, both the admonitory claim that self-interest was powerful and destructive and also the Hobbesian condemnation of romance for encouraging it—which means that it also will not work to argue, as has recently been attempted, that *Oceana* marked a new, specifically republican embrace of romance as a model for popular government.[60] Probably the most accurate assessment of *Oceana*'s use of romance is that it is self-contradictory—that Harrington scapegoated romance, as Hobbes also did, for promoting self-interested, acquisitive desire, while at the same time turning to romance for a paradigm of identificatory sympathy that by the 1650s the genre had largely left behind.

6. *THEODORA* AND DISINTERESTED PASSION

Robert Boyle, who occupied himself with moral philosophy for most of his early intellectual career, had strong reservations about the effort his elder brother Roger spent on what Robert took to be a frivolous romance,[61] and it might seem strange that he turned to romance himself in *Theodora* to retell a story he had found in an old martyrology. Boyle's stated aim was to attract the kind of young reader he had been himself, but he also intended, more fundamentally, to reform romance itself, to break its powerful association with self-interest and prove instead that it could persuade to virtue. His method was to turn to pietas, to argue through the structure of martyrology for devotion to a transcendent ideal, in the context of which he intended to show that love between persons made them capable of surrendering their own ends, so that love could become entirely instrumental. Almost despite itself, however, *Theodora* demonstrated along the way the vulnerability of the ideal of disinterestedness to be recaptured by its opposite, making one of the strongest claims in midcentury romance for an ethics based in the particular interests of the other.

Boyle's career as a moral philosopher is now about as little known as *Theodora,* which after serving as the source for the libretto of Handel's unpopular 1749 oratorio by the same name virtually fell out of the canon of his work. As a young man, and part of an intellectual circle that included John Hall and John Milton, Boyle took as his model the Protestant philosopher and theologian Johann Alsted, who was particularly interested in the potential for schools to deliver moral education; in his own moral essays Boyle figured himself as teacher and rhetorician, trying to show readers, in his words, "not only How they may be Vertuus, but also Why," to "direct" but also "Persuade" them to virtue.[62] The text we have as *The Martyrdom of Theodora, and Didymus,* which very much fits these aims, most likely dates from the decade and a half before the Restoration, although it was not published until 1687. In the preface, initially a letter to a friend that circulated at some point with the manuscript, Boyle explained that many years earlier he had found Theodora's story in a martyrology and expanded it into a narrative in two parts, but that the manuscript had passed from friend to friend in loose sheets and the first part had been lost. When it was first circulated it was "lucky enough" to be attributed to both of the two persons "counted the best writers of disguis'd Histories," one of them perhaps Robert's brother Roger if we go by the contemporary reputation of *Parthenissa.* Now decades later, Robert's reputation as a preeminent natural philosopher firmly established, some "eminent Persons . . . some of them the repute of great Judges of this kind of Composures" had persuaded him to publish at least the extant second part, which was more "Historical" and more "remote from being Romantick" than the first half had been because it relied more heavily on the original story in the martyrology, picking up only a few days before Theodora's and Didymus's execution.[63]

In this preface, Boyle first disavows writing a romance on the grounds that romance is merely fictitious, recalling that although he had originally resolved to turn Theodora's story into "a somewhat voluminous Romance" because he found it told so "succinctly and imperfectly" in the martyrology, "upon second thoughts" such a transformation of a "True Example" into a form known for being "fabulous" seemed "incongruous" (A3v–A4r). Yet a little later he concedes the label, insisting that though it is "a kind of Profaneness, to transform a piece of Martyrology into a Romance; yet I thought it allowable enough, where a Narrative was written so concisely, and left so unperfect" (A6r). *Theodora*'s main conceptual terms are conventional for romance of the period: not only does it share the genre's preoccupation with interest, "meer Ambition" (193) and "Self-love" (139), but Didymus's turn away from the "Fame and Honours" that belong to heroic ideology (17) was also a central motif in *Cloria*, as I will discuss in the next chapter.

More in keeping with romance than with martyrology, Boyle does not seem as concerned with Theodora's death at the hands of the Romans as with her relationship to Didymus, a soldier who loves her and spends a good portion of the story trying to convince her not to martyr herself before he eventually dies with her. Theodora's composure never wavers when she is made to suffer, an event Boyle handles summarily, and at her and Didymus's deaths the narrator even retreats to describing events for the first time with the qualifier "probably," as if he had less access, suddenly, to this aspect of the story by comparison to the rest, or as if the execution had turned out to be a nonessential part of the plot. By contrast, we get a very full account of Didymus's educational progress away from the heroic ideology associated with his profession as soldier and toward the kind of love Theodora requires of him. When the extant portion of the narrative opens Didymus has just come to rescue Theodora from the brothel to which the Romans have consigned her for refusing to repudiate her Christian faith, and she initially congratulates him for being "disinterested," because he has turned from soldierly glory to rescue a mere "persecuted and affronted Maid" (17). To hold her attention Didymus must then convince her that he is proof against other kinds of interest, taking on the "difficult task" of certifying to her "without prejudicing his Love" that although he does love her, "he did not serve her upon the score of That" (24–5). Didymus declares immunity from the form of interest we are most familiar with in romance, namely, erotic desire. He may appreciate Theodora's beauty, but he wants her to know that more important to him is her moral goodness, from which he has nothing to gain for himself. To this Theodora responds approvingly that by Didymus's actions she has been "not a little confirm'd in the opinion I have alwaies had, That Virtue may inspire as Noble and as Hazardous Enterprizes, as Passion can" (51)—an idea that might stand as an epigraph to the romance as a whole. At the end the narrator sums up the couple's story as an "admirable Contest" in which "Self-love, the most radical affection of human Nature, is sacrific'd to a Love, equally [in equal measure] chast and disinteres'ed" (139). Clearly Boyle wants his readers to understand that ethically the most significant sacrifice that can be made, by the terms of this revised martyr narrative, is not of life but of self-interest.

But why this imperative to sacrifice self-interest, in a narrative that in the end spends very little time addressing the divine love that ostensibly supplants it? Boyle provides some clues to an answer in the preface, where he reveals that he has written *Theodora* as much for himself as for his purported readers. At the outset he confesses that he was anxious about his complicity in romance, and could not "allow" himself to depict the "Bold and Romantick" manner of lovers in most romances, lest he become a lover himself (a1r). Instead, he says, along with the "shining Example" of perfect spiritual "Beauty" in Theodora he decided to present the "pathetick passion" of virtuous love in Didymus (a1v), and then a little later he backs away even from this relatively tame version of passion, protesting that his primary goal has been to prove "that One might have glittering *Idea*'s of Beauty, without being daz'ld by them" (a2r). The reader might assume that the "One" of which Boyle speaks here is Didymus, but Boyle then adds that "high Complements and passionate expressions, are no certain Marks of His being really *Smitten* (to speak in a Lovers Phrase) that can Imply them, since I retain'd my wonted freedom of mind, while I was Writing; and presented them by the mouth of Didymus, but what Fancy, not Passion indited" (a2r). There is an odd slippage here between the figure of Didymus and Boyle himself, who in the surprising turn to "I" in this sentence reveals himself at least in his own mind to be Theodora's truest lover, able to conjure at will her presence as "glittering Idea" while Didymus can only struggle against passionate attachment. Romance, Boyle suggests, is for him a kind of moral proving ground, where he can pit himself against the most alluring of temptations and show himself disinterested.

And the risk of passion, for Boyle, is that it will prove "dazzling," robbing him of "freedom of mind." While Boyle identifies with Didymus as an ideally disinterested lover, he identifies even more strongly with the heroic Theodora, whose insistence on choosing her own death rather than submitting to the Romans' ultimatum parallels Boyle's task of maintaining a rational distance from a narrative that would try to steal his autonomy. If this seems too melodramatic a reading of Boyle's problem in *Theodora,* we might consider the account in his autobiography of his extended trip to France as an adolescent, during which, he says, he was occupied "above all" with "the reading of romances." Afterward he remembers with a shudder that "these Fabulous and wandring Storys" put his mind into a habit of "raving," by which he seems to mean a kind of imaginative free association, irresistibly attractive but also terrifying in its hold over him, that could be tamed only by moral and spiritual discipline.[64] If disinterest is, as *Theodora* suggests, Boyle's goal, here its opposite is not exactly passionate attachment to others but rather a sort of imaginative randomness, associated by Boyle as by early modern culture in general with fancy as opposed to reason and with the undisciplined intellect. In this sense Boyle drew closer than any of the other writers I have considered to the Italian political theorists, in that the grand struggle in romance as he conceived it was between the exercise of the will (albeit, for Boyle, the will to virtue) and the force of contingency.

Given this history as well as the oddness Boyle acknowledges himself of "transform[ing] a piece of Martyrology into a Romance," and given too his obviously greater predilection as a writer for philosophical and scientific genres, we must wonder why Boyle felt called to reform romance, what it was about the genre that he wanted to carry forward. One answer is that he meant to mount a defense of women's intellectual and moral capabilities through a genre traditionally associated with them, to contest the masculine "Interest, or . . . Envy" that kept women from "Instruction" and "Knowledge" (a3v) as he announced in his preface.[65] Another is that as in *Oceana,* fiction in *Theodora* was supposed to provoke a form of sympathy—not for other people but rather for what Boyle names "glittering *Idea[s].*" With reference to Kahn's argument that midcentury romance tried to establish an ethos of "aesthetic interest," we might call Boyle's goal here "aesthetic disinterest"—an immunity to the kinds of passionate investment inspired directly by other people but a readiness nevertheless to be moved in an analogous way by ideas. Boyle was reaching, I think, toward an odd hybrid of romance and philosophy, trying to retain romance's famous emotive power while at the same time disavowing the routes through which it had been traditionally generated.

Boyle, then, located what he took to be the serious problem of interest not in the fact that people were inherently self-centered, nor in the politic competition that many assumed to be the inevitable outcome of this self-centeredness, but rather in people's tendency toward passion, which insofar as it was ungovernable by reason compromised the self's integrity and freedom. Figured as a dissociation from passion, disinterest unsubjected the persons it acted upon, which might well lead us to see disinterest not as interest's opposite but rather as its tactic—an idea that was in fact at the root of most critiques of disinterest construed this way, as a renunciation of emotional investment. One of the conceptual problems with Stoic disinterestedness, as Gordon Braden has explained, was that as soon as it was read within a social context it threatened to become a means toward an interested end rather than an embrace of an ideal apart. So, for instance, when a subject hypothetically renounced desire for an object that another had refused to bestow, it became very difficult even for the subject to know whether he or she had really left desire behind or was simply trying to rebuke or circumvent the withholding other.[66] This was a characteristic problem for seventeenth-century romance, one of the many objections, for example, that Wroth's Pamphilia had to forestall when she displaced her passion onto a deified love. For Boyle Theodora's impending martyrdom protects her from any accusation of self-interest in a simple sense, since she has offered up prospectively her most basic interest, living itself. But her martrydom is not proof against a more unusual kind of objection, one that directs itself—rather surprisingly, in a romance ostensibly so occupied with the integrity of the self vouchsafed by martyrdom—not toward her own moral state but rather toward the interests of the other she ostensibly loves.

After Theodora's rescue from the brothel she goes to stay with her friend Irene, who tells her that Didymus's extraordinary virtue merits Theodora's consent to marry him. Theodora makes the reasonable argument that her devotion to the church in these terrible times precludes increasing her "Commerce with the World" (71) and then startles Irene with the news that rather than marry Didymus she has resolved to sacrifice herself for him—or, at least, to stage her self-sacrifice so that it looks as if it is for him. The Romans, she explains, think the Christians act merely out of "Superstitious Frenzy," so if she gives herself up to the Romans out of "Gratitude" to Didymus, "which they, as well as we, look on as a Moral Vertue," it "may help to convince them, that our love to Vertue is general, and more disinterested, than they thought it" (85–6). In this extraordinary passage Theodora proposes a kind of allegorical performance of gratitude to Didymus in order to persuade her critics, somewhat ironically, of her capacity to love something beyond herself. If the Romans are able through their own set of values to understand her sacrifice of herself as an exhibition of her disinterested love for Didymus, then perhaps they will come by analogy to appreciate the political and ethical disinterestedness of her Christian beliefs.

In response Irene objects, even more extraordinarily, that gratitude should be a "relative thing"—that is, having to do with the relation between the two parties, its form determined by what would be acceptable to and welcomed by the person receiving it (86). In essence she asks Theodora, "But what about Didymus?" Irene's objection does not turn out to be narratively momentous, but conceptually, I want to insist, she makes a claim with great significance, that Didymus is not just the occasion for but the recipient of love, and as such his interests in themselves should constitute an end for Theodora. Like Corderius in Bayly's *Herba Parietis,* Irene considers as a criterion for love's worth its effect on the beloved, not only on the self, and by this standard she judges her friend wanting. Her objection pushes Theodora to harden her position until she seems quite outside the mainstream of romance opinion on the relation between love and interest: to Irene she retorts that she scorns friendship based on "Sympathy and Inclination," those ordinary human impulses so celebrated by Harrington and Roger Boyle (90), believing that people should be united only by their shared devotion to an ideal. Didymus provides her with a rhetorical occasion, little more; even his companionship as a fellow servant of God does not seem particularly compelling.

In the few minutes before Theodora and Didymus are led to the scaffold Boyle offers one more opportunity to see Theodora's position contested, when Didymus tries to console them both by telling her that he looks forward to conversing with her in heaven. Theodora responds that in heaven our "Notions will then be rais'd," and "other Affections, will be transfigur'd, as well as our Bodies" (156), to which Didymus replies, surprised, "Can you be so rigid as to think, that pure and vertuous affections cannot be admitted into Heaven?" Even the angels, he says, have their own interests: among them can be found not only the "Joy and Desire" of their common love for God but also "Care and Actings for opposite Ends" (159). Not so, says Theodora; in heaven the "accidents" of our individual differences will yield to the knowledge that we are "Children of the same Father" (157–8), and our "Rational Friendships" will derive from our being "Rivals in the Love of God" (160). Didymus and Theodora's disagreement on the subject of angels' self-interest points to the larger difference between them, that what for Theodora is the nonessential, simply accidental aspect of the person is for Didymus its core. Theodora has little difficulty in disavowing passionate attachment because she apprehends little to be attached to; for Irene and Didymus, in contrast, such disavowal of attachment must be a deliberate disregard of the other's very being.

I do not want to overemphasize the role Boyle's critique of disinterest takes within *Theodora;* Theodora herself gets the last death as well as, consistently, the last word. But the terms of the critique, as I have suggested, seem extremely significant within the context of mid-century romance, because they carry forward a logic already implicit in the discourse around interest. To the extent that Theodora's version of disinterest is faulty, we might say that it is not entirely genuine, as perhaps must be the case with all disinterestedness—and here we might cite its resemblance, in its solipsism, to the effects of self-interest. But it seems the case that in a different sense interestedness in *Theodora* is also a good, in that it teaches us to recognize in others their distinctness and particularity.

Overall, we might say, interest discourse in *Theodora* stimulated a newly emergent critique—not by precipitating a withdrawal from interest, but rather from within interest's own terms, by bringing the other into focus. Interest discourse helped *Theodora* to intimate that people, as objects of love, were not merely allegorical figures for a greater good but rather individual persons with particular interests, which at least in some kinds of relationship exerted a binding force on the self. If this claim does not perhaps seem all that radical to us, within its historical context, I have been arguing, we must concede that it was. In his portrayal of Irene and Didymus, Boyle asked his readers to question the classical notion of human love as instrument or analogue, on the grounds that it did not take enough account of the other. Unlike many other romances, *Theodora* did not try to flee interest altogether, nor did it assert the historically standard Harringtonian construct of the common interest nor even the Grotian ideal of natural sympathy. Instead, as if despite itself it reached toward the ethically more demanding idea that love between people had to be defined as that situation in which the interests of the particular other as distinct from the self functioned as the end of the self's actions. If we are to be ethical, Irene and Didymus tell Theodora, we must love the other not as or even in service to the way we love God, but rather in the way that the ideology of interest tells us we love ourselves.

Chapter 4

Interest, the Sovereign Hero, and the End of Romance

In this final chapter I turn to a consideration of interest's impact on midcentury romance's most basic narrative trajectory, the achievement of sovereignty.[1] In *Arcadia* and its seventeenth-century inheritors, of course, sovereignty was not a separate issue from love but rather an analogue for it—or better, the more fundamental expression of the same goal. For Roger Boyle's Artabanes as for Sidney's Pyrocles before him, to desire the princess was to desire the throne, and to achieve her was to accede to the throne as well. Despite the near identity between these goals, however, and despite the fact that as a rule midcentury romance was explicitly Royalist, sovereignty always seemed in these narratives to pose the more desperate ethical problem. In its heteroerotic forms love in romance was usually understood to be compromised by self-interest, but as a more generalized concept, I have shown, it also seemed to offer ground for resistance to interest's tendency to subsume all other explanations of motive—hence, for instance, *Parthenissa*'s development of masculine friendship, or *Theodora*'s celebration of love for God. Sovereignty, by contrast in both its more properly political and its moral-psychological senses, seemed at least in romance to be fundamentally about the consolidation and extension of individual interest; indeed, the successfully sovereignizing self was by definition the self realizing its interest. As a result, sovereignty in romance was much more fully in thrall to interest than was love.

In the 1650s Percy Herbert's Royalist *Cloria,* as I will show in the first part of this chapter, managed to sidestep this difficulty by proposing interest's tendency to stimulate social awareness as a principle for pragmatic reform, both of Royalist ideology and of romance itself. But the romances published after the Restoration, though outwardly just as loyal to Royalist ideology, found themselves unable to forge a compromise between romance's traditional idealizations and a notion of sovereignty now newly and explicitly owning its interested nature, and this failure had a profound effect on their form. In effect, as I argue in the latter parts of this chapter, their consistent refusal to achieve resolution offers a structural allegory of interest's force, a register of its ability, in only a few decades, to render *Arcadia*'s ironic compromises obsolete.

1. THE TYRANNICAL HERO

It is tempting to read the focus on sovereignty in the romances of the 1650s and early 1660s as owing chiefly to the execution of Charles I and the political turmoil of these and the preceding decades, and obviously there were connections between romance's sovereignty narratives and political events and ideologies of the period (some of which I will point out in this chapter). But even before the Civil Wars in the 1640s, sovereignty in politic English romance was a troubled and complicated idea. This is evident not only in Sidney's portrait of the weak and fatuous duke Basilius and in his inheritors, Barclay's and Wroth's weak kings, but also, from Sidney forward, in romance's concomitant irony about heroism. Traditionally, of course, the romance prince proved his fitness for rule by the heroic acts that won him the princess. In Sidney's ostensibly heroic revision of the *Old Arcadia,* however, the conventionally heroic attributes of the newly introduced prince Amphialus, his quickness to defend his honor and his passion for Philoclea, are shown up as hot-headed and ill advised, and his dismay at the unintended consequences of his own actions reveals him as at best foolishly tragic, a sort of Oedipal sinner despite himself.

This attitude toward heroism persisted in English romance over the next few decades, despite a very different ethos in the French fiction that according to conventional literary history has been supposed to be so influential on English romance. In 1630s France the pastoral romance was decisively supplanted by the *roman heroique,* whose heroes sought *gloire* above all, as a riposte both to the providence that drove Greek romance and its early modern pastoral inheritors in France (especially *L'Astrée*) and to the "prudence" and "politique" considerations that characterized new humanist ideology.[2] Even after 1649, however, English Royalist writers did not really imitate the *roman heroique* except piecemeal, for instance in the elements of

Parthenissa that I have already traced. And if the French *nouvelle* of the 1660s was, as Erica Harth has recently argued, a response to the new doctrine of absolutism in France, it is also possible to read its concern with the difficulty of ascertaining motivation and its urge to demystify politics as inheritances from its politic English predecessors (in this connection it is probably not mere coincidence that *Arcadia* enjoyed a surge of popularity in 1650s France).[3]

The reluctance of English romance to endorse heroism as a counterweight to politic ideology was probably in part the result of a pervasively nonidealist reading of *Arcadia* in England, but it also proceeded from a long-standing literary and more broadly cultural logic, one Rebecca Bushnell has definitively traced in tragedy and that is also central to romance, by which the hero and the tyrant are not quite distinguishable.[4] For a paradigmatic example from before the Civil Wars we can turn to Richard Brathwaite, whose vast seventeenth-century canon displays a consistent genius for epitomizing generic convention. In 1638 Brathwaite published the treatise *A Survey of History, or a Nursery for Gentry,* "an Intermixt Discourse upon Historicall and Poeticall Relations" at the intersection of which, for Brathwaite as before him for Barclay (whom he frequently cites), lay romance. History and poesy alike, says Brathwaite, show us that the heroic prince will always turn out to be another Alexander: there is

> "no Prince of so prosperous imployments, so successive proceedings, or generall forces, but either vanquished at home or abroad: abroad by forraigne powers, or at home by his owne illimited affections; instanced in that great and potent Prince of *Macedon,* who (though Prince of the whole world) could not play Prince of his little world, being slaved to distempered passions."[5]

One of the central implications of Brathwaite's observation is that the all-but-inevitable trajectory of heroism is tyranny. What makes the hero heroic is his enormous ambition, and yet this is also what causes him to fall prey to that paradoxical malady that from Plato onwards in Western political theory was understood to characterize the tyrant, an inability to subject his own overweening passions.[6] According to this dominant narrative the tyrant's passions signified not only his exceptional strength in relation to others but also, insofar as he was unable to govern these passions by reason and law, his moral weakness, a combination that helps explain both the attraction to the tyrant and the reserve about the hero in early modern culture. Politically this is a comforting story, in that it seems to guarantee at least a poetic justice for the tyrant's transgressions: to those who might find dismaying

Alexander's impulse to take over the entire world, or to the real slaves whose autonomy the prince would arrogate to himself, Brathwaite in effect says not to worry, that the hero-prince who is not vanquished by others will always eventually receive his comeuppance from his own passions and thus provide the moral we are presumed to seek.

This self-limiting quality of tyranny points to another crucial aspect of Brathwaite's paradigm, that this story of the heroic prince is always essentially a *psychomachia*. "Abroad" the prince encounters only "foreign powers," "at home" only himself. Like Heliodorus's chaste heroine Chariclea, Wroth's Pamphilia, or Barclay's emulatory twins Poliarchus and Archombrotus, the prince lives in a society of one, made peerless by his exceptionality. His own passions are his real enemy, and his struggle to govern himself the primary story, his inevitable failure at which is both harbinger and proof of his failure to gov ern others. In large part precisely because it is a psychomachia, as Freud perhaps most famously recognized, the ostensibly political story of a prince's struggle to achieve sovereignty is also always potentially a figure for another kind of narrative, a more generally applicable, moral-psychological story about sovereignty over the self. Freud gave us in his Oedipal narrative an enormously ingenious reading of the elements of psychomachia always already present in the basic Western European account of succession; other analogues available to early modern romance for the paradigm Brathwaite lays out here were the Aristotelian story of the moral subject's struggle for temperance, and also, for more adverse times, the story of the Stoic's suppression of his passions. We should be wary of universalizing our own post-Freudian tendency to read sovereignty as necessarily a psychological metaphor, but Wroth's account of her self-sovereignizing heroine Pamphilia in *Urania* is strong evidence that the figurative link between political and moral-psychological sovereignty was already in place in early modern romance. We might consider here, too, Catherine Gallagher's argument for the connection between Royalist ideology and the view of the self in writers such as Margaret Cavendish or Richard Lovelace as a sort of self-sovereignizing island.[7] Thus it is that in *Leviathan,* as I suggested in the last chapter, Hobbes's objection to romance rests precisely on the interplay the genre encourages between actual political and figurative psychological sovereignty, the temptation it offers its readers to imagine themselves little Alexanders when instead they should be buckling down under the political necessity of their own subjection.

In most of our modern conventional narratives for the achievement of sovereignty the concept has become entirely moral-psychological, for the most part disabling the two-way traffic between political and moral-psychological connotations for sovereignty that characterized early modern romance. But for a brief period in the middle of the seventeenth century, interest discourse instigated a different (and perhaps more truly destabilizing, if also short-lived) disruption in fiction's sovereignty narrative. As it struggled to come to terms with the concept of interest in the 1650s and early 1660s, romance offered the counterview that whether sovereignty was political or moral-psychological, the effort to achieve it was and had always been not just a psychomachia but also a social story, about others as well as the self. In the light of this insight it became one of romance's chief tasks in this period to show up the traditional, heroic models for sovereignty as inadequate. For one thing, as Herbert's *Cloria* insisted, and as we might expect from Rohan's early pragmatic emphasis on efficacy, the prince who concentrated on his own heroism failed to register that he was in fact in a large social theater with other interested agents, and that real political power proceeded from the skillful management of relationship. More surprisingly, and more radically, in the small body of original romances after the Restoration interest discourse inspired an ethical objection to sovereignty, as *Eliana, Aretina,* and *Pandion and Amphigenia* all argued in different ways that the old stories of sovereignty obscured the costs to others levied by the sovereignizing self.

2. INTEREST AS CRITIQUE IN *THE PRINCESS CLORIA*

Percy Herbert's monumental romance *The Princess Cloria* was published in parts throughout the 1650s under the title *Cloria and Narcissus* and then as a whole, once Charles II had been restored to the throne and the real Narcissus, Prince William of Orange, had died, as *The Princess Cloria* in 1661. Herbert, a Roman Catholic, was MP in the 1620s for Shaftesbury and then Wilton; he was imprisoned by the Long Parliament for allegedly stockpiling arms for the king, but later, because of his reservations about fighting next to Protestants even on the king's side, he disobeyed a royal command to fight in Essex's army and took refuge on the Continent. Like many English authors of romance at midcentury he spent time in France in the late 1640s. In 1652 his estates were forfeited and sold by Parliament, and beyond his authorship of *Cloria* little is known of his activities between that moment and his death in 1667. As an elaborate roman à clef, *Cloria* corresponds more closely to recent British and European history than any other romance of the period. It is also quite unusual, at least in the context of other romances, in its resolve to understand interest not as an ethical predicament but as a principle of reform.

Though explicitly Royalist, as announced by its subtitle "the Royal Romance," in its portraits of Charles I and his eldest son and heir *Cloria* offered one of midcentury romance's most pointed critiques of sovereignty. Herbert sets up a conceptual framework for these portraits in one of his first episodes, a contest between two versions of sovereignty in which both are revealed to be outdated and ineffective. Cassianus, who is the "Senate's" (i.e., the English Parliament's) candidate for the hand of Cloria (Charles I and Henrietta Maria's first daughter, Mary) is riding through the forest when he stumbles upon one of romance's most time-worn pastoral conventions, a dispute between two men over a woman unable to choose between them. As signaled by the name Herbert gives the lady, "Mantuina," this triangulated erotic standoff is also a political allegory, an account of the struggle between two branches of the Gonzaga family for the Mantuan succession in the late 1620s. But as so often in midcentury romance, Herbert uses both the generic convention and the political story merely as outlines to be filled with his own content, in this case a face-off between the sovereign as ambitious hero and as Stoic.

Out of keeping with pastoral convention, Fridius is "by extraction" truly a shepherd, not a prince in disguise, but he has enough money to buy himself a title, and he argues that he deserves the hand of the lady because "from a mean condition, I have created in my self a Princes soul . . . by which I have endeavoured to out-do my own fate." "'Tis ambition . . . that warms the Blood, and renders it Noble," he concludes, invoking the dual idiom of both heroic and politic ideology to justify his desire for social mobility (24). Navarinus, in contrast, is an aristocrat who has fallen on hard times, and he retorts that it is not wealth but virtue that renders a man truly noble. True virtue, he says, "consisted more in tempering of ambition, then violently aiming at Honours . . . Courage . . . never shews it self better, then in overcoming ones own passions," and "personal Poverty" is no disgrace but a "magnanimity, when it can be born with patience" (24). By this logic real sovereignty consists in the freedom from desire, achieved at length by the familiar Stoic struggle with the self—an argument that Herbert might have anticipated would be expected to seem particularly sympathetic to Royalist readers in the wake of Charles I's powerlessness during the final months of his life. Navarinus concludes as we would expect, with the essentialist Stoic declaration that was also, in the early 1650s, a Royalist battle-cry: "A King is a King . . . although he do not alwayes wear the Crown" (24).

At this point, with an indecision that emphasizes the historical crisis in sovereignty *Cloria* portrays here, Cassianus finds himself unable to endorse wholeheartedly either of these versions of sovereignty, and therefore he ostensibly splits the prize in two, awarding Fridius the political and Navarinus the erotic victory. Reflecting that "the one promised more hope, the other less fear; the one was endued with a Princes soul, which of necessity must put him on to dangerous and hazzardable attempts, the other more resembling a Lover was likeliest to continue the unity of affections without separation," Cassianus determines that "Fridius was fitter to be a Monarch, but Navarinus to become a husband," and so gives the "crown" to Fridius, the woman to Navarinus (24–5). The joke, of course, is that in this situation, as in the Mantuan succession crisis, crown and lady cannot be split, which means that Cassianus has not quite chosen either man as sovereign. And lest we think the judgment has gone mainly in favor of the Stoic Navarinus, afterwards Cassianus suddenly metamorphoses into Navarinus's comic double, forsaking the "Court ambition" and the "desire of glory" that drove his pursuit of Cloria to sell his jewels, cut his hair, keep company with a priest, and forget to think of the princess except "in such a dark way, as lights are accustomed to appear in a thick mist . . . when there was not desire enough in his intentions to give it nourishment" (43). Eventually, says the narrator, he is abruptly cured of this madness when Cloria herself, fleeing court, shows up in the woods, inspiring him to revert to his former, Fridian self and begin working with Parliament again to gain the princess's hand.

There is an obvious allegorical scheme at work here, in which the Fridius/Navarinus conflict epitomizes the conflict between Stoic constancy, as a traditional stand-in for Royalist legitimacy, and a stance somewhere between heroic and politic ambition. If by the terms of its adjudication the narrative seems to favor Royalist constancy, nevertheless the adjudicator himself, when he finds himself as well suddenly persuaded by Stoic ideology, is thereby rendered comically ineffective. According to the romance's overt political ideology Cassianus is supposed to be the representative of modern, interested politics against hereditary monarchy, and it is difficult to know how to interpret his absurd descent into Stoic pastoral idyll—punishment for having judged hypocritically (in choosing an option his career should have discredited) or perhaps even for his ambition. Either way it seems clear that in this early episode *Cloria* endorses neither Stoic constancy nor self-interested ambition as an adequate ideology for effective sovereignty.

Herbert's depictions of Charles I (Euarchus) and his elder son Charles (Arethusius) adhere quite closely to the dichotomous models for sovereignty represented by Fridius and Navarimus in this early episode. Euarchus, who by the time the romance begins is already in dire political straits and spends most of his last months in "deep examination of [his] inward thoughts" (170), hopes only for a pale version of Elysium populated by "such as were no injurers" (331). Herbert portrays his suffering as dignified, but he also explicitly raises the question as to whether we should interpret the king as naturally passive rather than, more kindly, as resolute in his suffering, as weak rather than temperate (e.g., 168, 174). In Euarchus's heir, concomitantly, Herbert portrays heroism as parody. Arethusius insists that the true prince should occupy himself with glory and conquest rather than the quotidian business of politics: fame, he declares, is "the life and being of a Prince," and it is achieved not by the "timorous subtilty" of Arethusius's grandfather James I, who by "pleasing [rather] than acting, and complying than contradicting," sought only to "defend his Government from invasion during his own life." Such politic tactics as "dissimulation" and "indirect dealing," he adds, are signs not of political canniness but of a lack of courage and resolution. A prince whose thoughts are not "heroical, and full of magnanimity," who shows a "timerous kinde of trembling" in domestic politics, is a terrible danger to his nation, "for how is it possible other States can fear to offend us abroad, if they finde our natures apt to be terrified at home?" (391–2). Arethusius resurrects the old militant Protestant complaint against James I in order to make the point that the prince's real theater of action, the realm where he can exercise his true natural heroism, is abroad, in the clash between nations. For him the lesson of the last fifteen years is that domestic politics are to be ignored, or transcended, except as a testing ground, an indication to foreign princes of how a king will handle himself in more important battles. Real success, he concludes, is proved by "eternal fame to continue in after ages" (392); the heroic prince finds his proper place in history, not in the transitory context of the local and the everyday.

We are taught what to make of such heroic principles by Arethusius's various interlocutors, who several times have to "wean" the prince from his opinions (e.g., 423), as if heroism were a childish attachment to the feminine. Arethusius's adviser Meliander repeatedly hushes him, counseling "reserved secresie" as behavior better fitting a prince (392), and his friend Parismenus counters that a prince's "victories and losses" do not really proceed from his will but are properly "accidents," products of contingency. The "impossible attempts" of the would-be hero, Parismenus concludes daringly, "ought rather to be esteemed a madness in the general, if not in some sort an impious lunacy of humanity, then any vertue or true fortitude at all in what person soever" (423). Though in some ways the fiery, histrionic prince would seem his father's opposite, in another, Herbert suggests through these interlocutors, the prince is his father's double: weak, self-indulgent, and similarly disengaged from the current political crisis.

The alternative to these two exhausted models for sovereignty in *Cloria,* as Victoria Kahn argues, is a prince who knows his own interest and understands the discreet, politic style of negotiation by which it is best achieved.[8] Herbert does not quite portray an interested sovereign in the romance (though Arethusius, as Kahn remarks, seems to have come some way toward that goal by the time of his accession[9]); rather, he conveys this goal through the advisers to the royal family, especially Cloria's nurse, Roxana, who is another version of Argenis's nurse Selenissa in Barclay. Roxana's status in *Cloria* indicates how far politic ideology has come since the 1620s: unlike Selenissa, she is not scapegoated but given pride of place for urging the consideration of interest. Following on *Urania*'s deep suspicion of constancy as a trope for narcissistic self-love, Roxana argues that the "extraordinary courage" of a Stoic response to persecution is mainly of "singular benefit," by which she means its power to preserve individual integrity (230). Much more useful for the canny sovereign is a "wise (though not a base) complyance," similar to the politic "darke conveniency" advocated by Arethusius's friend Parismenus (423), which will indicate the sovereign's willingness to negotiate with others and thereby prevent "further mischief and disreputation to our selves" (230–31). When Cloria exalts providence Roxana objects that sovereignty is exercised on earth, where constancy is not a transcendent ideal but political currency; if others default on their obligations, she argues, it is admissible to "blot out" one's own obligation (210), which obeyed too fervently signifies an infatuation with self similar to Arethusius's heroics.

Roxana's politic argument against self-love is brought to a reflexive level in the text when she teases Cloria with a barb that it is tempting to read as a direct allusion to Pamphilia's much-celebrated devotion to her own constancy in *Urania.* "In good sooth said the old woman, your conscience is so tender in matters of love, that I believe when you are married to your servant, you will make a doubt, whether he be the same man or no, and by that means call your affection in question . . . At these words the princess smil'd" (210). In Roxana's view, Cloria's real relationship is not with Narcissus himself but with her own scruples, which are so fascinating to her that they get in the way of everything else. This is not quite an ethical objection in the sense in which I have been using the term—Roxana is not really bothered for Narcissus's sake by Cloria's failure to see him clearly—but it does seem fair to call it moral. Constancy in Roxana's view, along with all of the romance's outmoded forms of sovereignty, tends toward solipsism, an attribute of the pettiest and most self-destructive of Brathwaitian tyrants.

If *Cloria* follows *Urania* more closely than does any other mid-century romance in making a link between solipsism and certain forms of idealism, its turn to interest as a counterweight is also more similar to Wroth's corrective strategies than it might at first seem. Interest's benefit in *Cloria* is to remind its sovereigns of others' presence, but not so that they might be prompted to ethical concern for others; rather, sovereign selves in *Cloria* as in *Urania* seem inevitably tempted toward an excessive self-preoccupation, and the apprehension of others, as Roxana says, avoids "further mischief and disreputation to [them]selves" by fostering a kind of morally useful shame, an apprehension of their excess that then inspires greater self-control. Herbert's reconception of interest as a discipline for self-indulgence rather than another name for it is a very modern revision, both politically and generically, and I do not want to underestimate the historical significance of the alliance *Cloria* makes between traditional ideology and the contemporary politic discourse of statecraft.[10] But in moral-philosophical terms interest in *Cloria* turns out to advance an entirely traditional moral goal, the same temperate self-governance that for centuries had been at the center of theories of the moral self.

And there is a moment when *Cloria* itself seems almost to admit this conservatism, during a strange episode in which Herbert airs a new kind of objection to self-interest—one that construes our obligations to others as an implicit rebuke to our concern for ourselves, and in doing so hints at an argument we might fairly call ethical. This episode follows directly, as if it were a gloss, on Roxana's advocation to Cloria and Ascanius of wise compliance. After a battle in which the Parliamentarian general Farezius overcomes the Royalist commander Leonides, Farezius, with ostensible magnanimity, offers terms of surrender that he presents as in Leonides' own interest, assuring him that upon surrender he and his forces may "freely [enjoy] those Priviledges that belong to the Senate party" (241). Leonides tells his men that they must scorn this offer of "absolute compliance," because under it "we shall be no more our own in will, but theirs in subjection." They must instead attempt, he exhorts, to "purchase an absolute freedom and security by our swords, whereby we may gain our own conditions, without the controul of other Masters but our King" (241–2).

Leonides is a mixture of Hobbesian and old-style heroic Royalist; for him, a government based on interest and self-advantage and proceeding by such politic tactics as strategic compliance would curtail the exercise of the individual will far more drastically than traditional subjection to a single monarch.

Just as soon as he has led us to see this conflict as a revised version of the Fridius/Navarinus contest between old-style constancy and modern, interested politics, however, Herbert changes the terms. The "Maxime" against harming women and children providing no protection against "ends and interest," Farezius ruthlessly kidnaps Leonides' young son and erects a scaffold in the center of the city to murder the child if Leonides will not submit to him (243–4); Leonides, for his part, decides to sacrifice his son rather than surrender. At this point Leonides' wife, Salona, enters the debate, outraged by both parties' absolute lack of concern for the boy and by their twin devotion to their own self-images. Just as Farezius's "Decrees for the most part were irrevocable, esteeming it a kinde of a sin against his Honour, to appear perswaded in matters of consequence," she rails, so she "knew her husband to be most wilfully constant in all the decorums, that belonged to those points of Honour he had once conceived in his thoughts" (244). "For your glory," she tells Leonides, you will "needs . . . shew your self the worst of tyrants" (246). For Salona the distinction between Parliamentarian and Royalist, interested politician and loyal subject, collapses in the face of their matching regard above all for their own "Honour." Both men are too constant, and even more egregiously, the object of their constancy is their own immutable integrity—a version of self-sovereignty, Salona concludes, that renders them tyrannical to those to whom they owe most responsibility and compassion.

Herbert would seem here to have set up a new dichotomy between self-love and care for others, but in conclusion the story shifts its terms one final time, with very ambiguous connotations. To Salona's condemnation Leonides first responds with the remarkable argument that in defending the life of her child his wife is not construing her interest correctly: fame, he tells her, not children, "is that must make us both live eternally," and anyway, "although now thou hast [our son] absolutely under thy own jurisdiction, yet it will not be long before others possess more of him then thy self" (246). His wife's affection for her the child, Leonides assumes, is a form of se[torn]
but not a very efficacious one, since he is sure shortly to s[torn]
from her. Salona is not persuaded, and when Leonides retur[torn]
soldiers it seems that her obstinacy has at last made some [torn]

with him, as he tells his men he cannot go ahead with his original plan to offer his son as an "innocent sacrifice." Even now, however, his reasoning remains based in self-interest: given that "the world" is now "more apt to desire, the effecting of those actions that are moral and compassionate, then to give praise and commendation to heroical accomplishments of strange natures," he has decided to rescue his son so that he will not be "looked upon like some horrid creature, contracting nothing but eyes of wonder and reproof" (247–48). Leonides has just registered, apparently, that he is living in a new political climate, one in which compassion is valued over heroics, and as a good politic strategist he decides that in his treatment of his son he had better pay lip service to this new reality.

Leonides' discovery of his self-interested reason does represent in part a conversion to Salona's position, or at least to a new understanding of contemporary social values and his obligation to them, but it is not, of course, a conversion to properly ethical concern. We might recall here Bernard Williams's critique of moral self-indulgence, his suspicion that virtuous acts are as often motivated by the self's desire to see itself in a virtuous light as by the virtue itself.[11] Perhaps Herbert directs us by Leonides' concern for his own reputation to perceive in him an ethical failure; or perhaps instead Herbert means with Leonides to demystify Salona's ethical objection, to lead us to the admission that whether we want to admit it or not, self-interest is inevitably the force behind all of our motivations. Even in the larger context of the romance as a whole it is difficult to decide which of these readings is more likely. We are probably supposed to notice that Leonides exhibits neither concern for his kidnapped child's suffering nor grief at his prospective death, but on the other hand his conversion to interested thinking is just what the romance recommends for its backward-looking sovereigns.

It seems significant in this regard that by comparison with the rapturous, identificatory friendship of *Argenis* or *Theophania* or even the heartfelt kind in *Parthenissa,* the relationships between princes in *Cloria* look markedly cool. When Arethusius and Narcissus meet for the first time, Narcissus deliberately mediates his response entirely through Cloria (the contrast with *Theophania*'s Demetrius at the same moment, described in Chapter 3, is dramatic), dismounting from his horse "with such a haste, as easily demonstrated what an humble heart, his intire affections to the fair Princess *Cloria* had created in his bosome," while Arethusius, for his part, rather than being struck by any natural affinity for his loyal ally and soon-to-be brother-in-law, merely "observ[ed] every rule of civility, as well as considering the extraordinary need he should have of [Narcissus's home country] *Cyprus* [*sic*] assistance," and "met him in the half way" (292). This is a meeting governed by courtesy and utility, not identification or even fellow feeling. And the narrator does not display any irony toward or dismay about the way interest trumps sympathy; one gets the sense, rather, that even in this situation conventionally expressive of love Herbert cannot muster much enthusiasm for relationship. The Farezius-Leonides episode does seem to be set up in such a way as to prompt us to think about Leonides' obligation to his son, but overall it seems to be Herbert's purpose to push such motivations into the background, as if to say that they do not truly govern behavior. If *Cloria* means to replace the solipsism of heroic ideology with recognition of the other, it is a recognition more Hobbesian than anything in *Theophania* or *Parthenissa*, one that construes other people according to the functions they serve for the self.[12]

There is a way, however, in which *Cloria* is not Hobbesian, in its tendency to avoid not only love but also the similarly intense connection forged by one person's exercise of authority over another. After angrily telling Leonides that in his resolution to sacrifice his son he is behaving as tyrannically as Farezius, Salona asserts that her rights as a subject are not being protected and that she therefore no longer has an "obligation to obey" either one of them (246). It is not made clear whether she is to be judged right or wrong because (characteristically for Herbert) she is not put to the test; in the end, independent of all the discourse meant to resolve the ethical dilemma, Leonides carries out a successful raid to rescue the child. Hobbes, of course, could not have let stand Salona's protest that she had been released from the obligation to obey her tyrant husband by his readiness to sacrifice her son, because by definition for him "every Subject is Author of every act the Soveraign doth" and therefore, as "may, and doth often happen in Common-wealths," the sovereign may put to death any subject, for any reason, without doing political wrong. To prove this point, in fact, Hobbes curiously cites the example of another father willing to murder his child, one who actually goes through with it—Jeptha in Judges, whose sacrifice of his daughter as recompense for triumphing over the Ammonites may have been in Herbert's mind as well when he devised the Leonides episode.[13] Central to *Leviathan* is the apparent paradox by which the primary drive toward, and right of, self-preservation on the part of every person leads to the absolute sovereignty of one, and Hobbes is resolute in his defense of the violence by sovereign against subject that the principle of self-preservation may thereby be made to sanction, with Jeptha's rash vow serving as a model.

Herbert, in contrast, is always setting up and then slipping out from underneath the moment of violent or catastrophic reckoning between sovereign and subject. And interest, of course, works analogously in *Cloria,* asking us to take account of the presence of others in a way that heroic and Stoic ideology did not, but at the same time insulating us from any direct affective confrontation between self and other. Arethusius's advisers cast his passion as distracting and infantile in their suggestions that he turn to the more pragmatic consideration of interest, but perhaps we should take passion in *Cloria* more seriously, as capable of frighteningly unreasonable damage. We might recall here the admonitory opening of Herbert's earlier work *Certaine Conceptions* (1650), ostensibly a moral guide for his son, in which two brothers imagining themselves lords of the sky on a starry night become so exercised in an absurd argument over who would have grazing rights if the sky were pasture that they murder each other then and there. In part, we can speculate, *Cloria* may ridicule heroic passion as a defense against the knowledge that in effect it may be anything but ridiculous. Rationalizing, temperate interest pulls us back from the passionate brink, and for Herbert that may be its most powerful claim to usefulness.

3. *ARETINA, ELIANA,* AND THE REFUSAL OF SOVEREIGNTY

Cloria is atypical of midcentury romance, I have suggested, in its use of interest as a tool for reform; it is also unusual in another way, in its vision of sovereignty achieved. Certainly Herbert, following in Sidney's and especially Wroth's footsteps, meant to criticize some of the individualist idealism attaching conventionally to notions of sovereignty in romance and in Royalist ideology, and perhaps too in the French *roman heroique,* but sovereignty's faith in its special and transcendent alliance with providence nevertheless won the day in *Cloria,* subsuming in retrospect most of the romance's conversation about interest. The romances first published after the Restoration, by contrast, though all in varying degrees Royalist, found themselves unable in the end to put the prince on the throne. This was not mainly a political failure—none of these romances offered political allegory in any detail—but rather one having to do with sovereignty's limitations in the moral-psychological sense, and one that was, for the first time, thical. Interest, I want to argue, newly opened romance after storation not only to the recognition of others' presence but the ways that the self, in its pursuit of individualist sovereignty, must necessarily violate the interests of others. If *Cloria* just barely intimated the ethical uneasiness that might accompany the drive to sovereignty, these post-Restoration romances expanded that intimation into a central preoccupation, to the point at which it became, as I will show, their governing formal principle.

George MacKenzie's *Aretina; Or, The Serious Romance,* published in Edinburgh in 1660, was in part a fictionalized account of the Civil Wars from a Royalist perspective. In his preface MacKenzie described romance in general and his in particular as a necklace on which the pearls of "moral Philosophy" were strung, saying (conventionally, but in up-to-date terms) that it was the task of romance to "strain the christal streams of vertue from the puddle of interest," to extract from the "servile, and lucrative imployments" of ordinary history those aspects of it that would teach us "what should be done."[14] As for Robert Boyle and John Crowne, romance was a youthful pursuit for MacKenzie (c. 1638–1691), who was best known as a judge and politician but was also a well-respected political and judicial theorist. A staunch Royalist, in the 1670s and 1680s he was Lord Advocate of the Scottish Parliament (with some interruptions for political reasons) until the accession of William and Mary, when his refusal to declare the throne of Scotland vacant upon the flight of James VII and II to France necessitated that MacKenzie flee to England. Among his most well known works besides *Aretina* were *Religio Stoici* (1663), denouncing religious persecution; *Institutions of the Law of Scotland* (1684), the main textbook for teaching Scots law until the middle of the next century; *A Vindication of his Majesties Government and Judicatures* (1683), which made a strong argument for the monarch's adherence to "necessity of State"; and *Jus Regium, or, The Just and Solid Foundations of Monarchy in General, and More Especially of the Monarchy of Scotland* (1684), an argument against resistance theory.[15]

One of *Aretina*'s most striking aspects is its extremely complex ending, which seems quite deliberately first to recapitulate and then to recast Herbert's central argument in *Cloria*. About forty pages before the romance's finish MacKenzie begins the process of closure by staging a fake ending, parodying romance's traditional idealist resolutions to uncover interest as his characters' true motivation. The prince Philarites, MacKenzie's main character, has just finished meeting all the conditions for assuming sovereignty, having secured his father's throne and rescued his beloved princess Aretina from a group of pirates who stole her from her father's palace, when a troop of masked gentlemen kidnaps the couple and deposits them on another pirate ship. At this inconclusive point the narrative seems to conclude, with a large "Finis" at the bottom of the page (408). But this is a false alarm, in both a thematic and a formal sense: the next page opens with the announcement, "Here is continued the History of Aretina, which was too abruptly ended in the former page" (409), and immediately Philarites' last protestations of love to Aretina, delivered while he is tied up on the deck of the ship awaiting murder by the kidnappers, are interrupted by the revelation that the ringleader of the troop of kidnappers is actually Philarites' best friend, Megistus. Megistus explains that he has staged the whole adventure to show Aretina's father, the king (watching from a hiding place on the ship), that the lovers really do care sincerely for one another in a courtly world filled with ambitious rivals, and the narrator adds that Megistus had his own reasons for the trick as well: "Man who placeth all vertue in advantage, would never put a true estimate upon friendship, if it were not seconded by reall advantages," he says, implying that such a favor as Megistus has just presented to his friend is sure to secure Megistus's own place in the soon-to-be king's affections (412).

MacKenzie stages a fake ending here for the same reason Megistus stages a fake abduction, because both know the value of heeding interest. Initially we are led to think that the (false) ending demonstrates the failure of romance's traditional heroics in their own terms: Philarites was hero enough to meet the conventional challenge of a kidnapped princess (a challenge that figures largely in, for instance, *Argenis, Cloria,* and *Parthenissa,* and to which their heroes always successfully rise), but when this second time around, much more unusually, the prince too is kidnapped, the predicament seems too much even for heroic agency, and the romance apparently has no choice but to come to a close. The narrative disqualifies this interpretation by its resumption, of course, and then reveals heroics to fail on a different ground. The second kidnapping turns out to be not an amplification of the first but a parody of it, a staged imitation, its thematic function to deliver the same lesson *Cloria* gives us, that what kings need in this newly interest-driven world is not heroic deeds but assurances that their allies are sincere. Megistus artfully adapts heroic ideology to prove both Philarites' loyalty and his own; MacKenzie, for his part, by melodramatically stranding his lovers and then demonstrating that he too was just kidding, acknowledges romance's tendency to be dated and false and suggests that his own romance is a different kind of narrative. Like the false kidnapping, the false ending stages the transition between old and new ways of seeing, the process by which character and reader alike come to understand that interest is the real governor of social and political transactions.

Megistus's trick and MacKenzie's parody would seem to have cleared the way for the conclusion that romance in this period finds so elusive, the establishment of a model of sovereignty that both retains some of its traditional idealism (Philarites is, still, a desperately loving and courageous hero) and also takes account of interest's influence and force. But Philarites and Aretina never make it all the way back home, and what MacKenzie offers instead, in a formal, much darker echo of Sidney's concluding technique in *Arcadia,* is an inset parable about interest's specifically ethical costs. As Philarites is headed back to Aretina's kingdom to claim her hand in marriage, he runs across a hermit who has dedicated his life to worshipping the memory of his dead wife. Piseta, the hermit recounts, was the peerless only daughter of a distant father and a malicious stepmother, who foiled her engagement to her virtuous suitor Ipsetus and drove her from her father's house. The play on "ipse," or "itself," in both names suggests not only that the two are so perfectly matched they are each other's "selves" but also, I think, that among the other characters in this roman à clef they are especially meant as self-images for its readers (in this instance ethical rather than historical images, although this story may also be an allegory for the Royalist abandonment of Charles I). In her naïveté Piseta unknowingly signed herself in service to a bawd, and her first customer was the hermit telling the story, who upon realizing her innocence, in an echo of the classic virgin martyr plot (also found, for instance, in *Theodora* and in Shakespeare's *Pericles*), offered to rescue her from the brothel if she promised to marry him. "After some reluctancie she at last condescended" (429), and the two had been living contentedly for only a few weeks when Ipsetus showed up at her door, full of reproach for her inconstancy, and stabbed himself to death before her. Consumed by guilt, and telling her husband that her fault "both in slighting my Oath, and in murthering the lovely *Ipsetus*" was so great that she would live "only to betray you," Piseta immediately died as well, leaving the husband, as he says in the last sentence of the romance, "as much grief in Legacie, as my never idle eyes shall be able to pay, although they imploy the whole stock of my moisture, for acquitting me of that obligation" (431–2).

If Wroth's heroine *Urania,* in the episode with which I opened my discussion of agency and self-interest in Chapter 1, could not quite say whether it was she herself or fate who bore the responsibility for releasing her from an impossible love, this story from *Aretina* might be read as an answer: yes, Piseta says, it is she herself who must be responsible in the end for transferring her love to another person, and this must be so even in the most impossible of circumstances,

circumstances far more difficult than Urania's own, when not to be inconstant must result in rape and possibly death. Not only that, but there is no avenue for Piseta to redeem her inconstancy; she stabs herself not, as Lucrece does, to prove her virtue but because if she lives, she says, she will only betray her husband in turn. Piseta can be said to have self-interest only in the most minimal and extenuating sense, in her desire to preserve her life and her virtue, and still she must bear the guilt for it—a guilt that in this late romance has specifically to do with relationship to others. Piseta's story differs from Urania's not only in that she has no choice but to bear responsibility for her change, but in the fact that what she violates is not constancy as a virtue in itself but her oath to Ipsetus and her responsibility for his wellbeing. This difference, in predicaments otherwise so oddly parallel, points toward the historical argument I made in the last chapter, that as interest became formulated more explicitly as a problem in midcentury romance, it was seen to threaten not a generalized good, nor the virtue of the individual, so much as ties between people. The result, in *Aretina,* is a standoff between interest and ethical obligation, the despairing perception that if interest renders obligation unmeetable, our recognition of obligation's ethical force at the same time makes our nature as interested beings impossible to bear.

Thematically Piseta's story does not really work as a political allegory; Piseta is as far from a sovereign as any romance character could be, and her narrative is about change in love, not the assumption of a throne. As if he has already conceded this, MacKenzie opens *Aretina* on Barclay's model, with an aging king no longer in political control, a single princess as heir, and two young, suitable princes as representatives of the next generation, but he then quickly provides an extra, unrelated princess to forestall Barclay's rivalry plot and casts Philarites' main rival instead as that conventional amalgam of interest discourse and heroic ideology, the scheming courtier, who is easily brought down by his own "ambition." Politically, these revisions intimate, the achievement of sovereignty is not as difficult as we have been led to believe. But formally Piseta's story does stand as a substitute for political closure, and as such it makes a surprisingly absolute ethical statement, that our drive to maintain or realize integrity must not supersede our obligations to others. To acknowledge interest may be a political necessity, MacKenzie seems to say, but when it comes to ethics, to return to his own metaphor, it is difficult to strain any virtue at all out of the puddle of interest or the kind of self supposed by it. It is not simply incidental, of course, that it is through a story of a young woman that *Aretina* makes this point. For MacKenzie as for Wroth, the factors that especially constrain women—their socially determined dependence on men and on the patriarchal structures men control (in Piseta's case, the household in which her stepmother must perceive her as a rival, as well as the brothel)—also privilege them as, or perhaps we should say doom them to be, representative ethical subjects, those who most starkly apprehend interest's terrible costs.

Eliana, I argued in the last chapter, explores in its narrative of Euripides' struggles with erotic love the conflict between love and interest, but in its other main plotline this anonymous romance also takes up the problem of sovereignty, and here too, as in *Aretina,* succession is a goal out of reach. *Eliana*'s main contribution to the discussion is to sharpen our sense of succession as an ethically problematic act, which it effects, quite innovatively, by recasting the ethical Oedipal story as a struggle between peers rather than father and son. The prince Lonoxia ends up as the elderly hermit companion of Euripides, the doomed lover whose narrative I described in Chapter 3, and Lonoxia's story functions as the political double for Euripides', a matching account of the impossible effort to escape self-interest without in the process becoming entirely the prey of others. The youngest of three brothers in line for a throne, Lonoxia is often the target of his brothers' envy and hostility, and in response to one of their attacks, in their parents' Edenic garden, he kills his eldest brother—an act that proves to him in retrospect that there is "no hatred . . . so strong as that between brothers" but that at the time seems entirely accidental to him, the mistake of someone who does not yet know evil (118). Despite his only dubious responsibility for this crime he is forced to flee his country, and in his wanderings he falls in love with Atalanta, who has secluded herself in the company of virgins. Learning of a plot by his middle brother, Marcipsius, to assassinate him so as to foreclose all rivalry for the succession, and also eager to insinuate himself into Atalanta's company, Lonoxia follows Sidney's Pyrocles and Barclay's Poliarchus in disguising himself as a woman. But when he gets to know Atalanta he learns that he has unwittingly trespassed on a brother yet again, and yet again on a brother who in some sense deserves the violation: Atalanta, still unmarried, is pregnant by Marcipsius, who has seduced and then abandoned her. Lonoxia initially recoils at the idea that she is no longer a virgin, then enters into a series of debates with himself about the ethics of his distaste and eventually decides that this new opportunity to love her as the sister she has proved to be offers him the chance to love "only for virtues sake" (150), "without ends" (151). His efforts to do this are the narrative version of the debates between Euripides and Argelois that I described in the previous chapter, about whether anyone can feel a truly disinterested love. Conveniently for Lonoxia, who cannot quite sustain his attempt to love her disinterestedly, Atalanta dies in childbirth, and Lonoxia fulfills his obligation to her by the less difficult proposition of raising her son and his nephew, Marinus. Eventually he and Marinus go to war against Marcipsius, now a tyrant, and after five "very Tragicall" years at war Marinus is killed and Lonoxia abjures his interest and retires to become a hermit (164).

In *Eliana* rivalry between brothers, like patrilinear rivalry in Sophocles' *Oedipus Rex,* is mainly structural rather than intentional. About the murder of his brother and his love for Atalanta Lonoxia has an Oedipal innocence, as if it has not occurred to him that the plot in which he is enmeshed necessarily casts him as an agent intent on securing by any means the political status that his virtue and prowess have earned him and that only his birth order continues to deprive him of. (Lest we miss the extent of Lonoxia's naïveté, *Eliana*'s narrator brings it home in his comical description of Lonoxia's "Metamorphosis" into a woman, during which he experiences such a narcissistic delight in his own "formosity" that he cannot believe he is not a woman—a luxury for which this romance, unlike *Arcadia* or *Urania,* does not condemn him in any way, but rather treats him as if he were so childishly devoid of shame for his self-interest as to be outside the ordinary moral economy [127].) To make sense of the ends toward which *Eliana* employs its Oedipal allusion we might recall Vladimir Propp's political version of the Freudian reading of the patricidal myth, in which he reminds us that there is no act of succession not implicated in violence, even when the central parties are simply father and son and much more overtly when a successor comes from outside to claim a throne.[16] But there is also a temporal necessity to intergenerational succession by which the violence is merely a cost of the process, not a real crisis; the father may resist, but whether he likes it or not, he and everyone else know that he must give up his throne to the son simply because he cannot live forever, and this provides the son a partial absolution for which Oedipus's ignorance is the symbol. In *Eliana*'s version of the story, however, the contestants are peers, and although Lonoxia clearly deserves the throne in the same way that Piseta deserved to marry and leave the brothel, his succession cannot be said to be structurally necessary in the same way as the son's. As in *Aretina,* we see here an ethical allegory, in which the agent cannot brook the costs to others, even evil others, of the self-interest that seems to dog him almost like an alter ego, and in response decides to bow out of the sovereignty narrative.

This scenario must have had obvious topical political significance, in a world in which at least outwardly peaceable hereditary succession seemed to have given way for two decades to violent competition for sovereignty between peers and in which Royalist supporters of Charles I, by the mere fact of surviving the king and adapting themselves to new political realities, revealed themselves as to some extent guilty of complicity in his demise. Suddenly, *Eliana* seems to say, succession has become a contest between brothers, and brothers not on the order of Barclay's Poliarchus and Archombrotus but rather with murderous intent, whose violent pursuit of their interests implicates everyone else as well.[17] In this light it is possible to read the entire Lonoxia narrative as a political allegory, in which Lonoxia represents the great majority of Charles I's subjects, killing their overreaching monarch almost before they know what they are doing, and Marcipsius Cromwell and his supporters, appropriating the almost-princess's symbolic body without contract or faith but only for their transient use. To distinguish himself from this wicked Cromwell figure and at the same time to prove that his earlier king-killing was an act of fate rather than a manifestation of his ambition, the basically well-intentioned Lonoxia must first show himself capable of loving Atalanta disinterestedly, without hope of any gain for himself. Eventually he does prove himself innocent of self-interest by becoming a hermit, but this conclusion seems to concede at the same time that there is little hope of achieving such a goal in a political context, in which the violent competition for sovereignty seems all but inevitable.

Eliana does offer one successful sovereignty narrative, but a compromised one that drives home the incompatibility this romance sees between sovereignty and sociality. Euripides has a cousin, Araterus, who disappears on the romance's fifth page as the result of the standard romance shipwreck (unlike *Arcadia*'s, this one has a permanently sundering effect on cousins) and is not heard from again until the romance's very last pages, when his squire wanders back to Euripides with a message. Araterus, we learn, was captured by pirates, whom he managed to escape by cannily inciting the pirates' other prisoners via the political principle of resistance to tyranny (while not believing any of it himself), then slipping away during the inevitable rebellion. Eventually he wandered to India, where (as if *Eliana* meant to make unmistakable the parallel with *Arcadia*'s concluding succession parable) he found himself in a situation similar to that of Sidney's reluctant young nobleman, wandering ostensibly by accident into the private garden of the young queen of India, who first furiously repelled and then suddenly desired him, demanding his hand in marriage. The marriage was opposed by members of the queen's council, but by circulating the lie that he was a prince at home in Europe and therefore had nothing to gain from the queen, Araterus eventually managed to effect his accession to the throne, and now he and the queen live in perfect accord with each other and the council. To the end he maintains the habit of portraying himself as a pawn of fortune, explaining to Euripides via his squire at the conclusion of his account that although "I should have preferred your company to all the Kingdomes of the East . . . I am enforced to abide where the gods themselves, as it were, have placed me" (287–8).

Unlike Lonoxia and Euripides, in his capacity to fulfill his self-interest even while disavowing both interest and agency Araterus is a perfectly politic agent. The reason he is eventually able to succeed, in a romance otherwise quite hostile to politic calculation, is because he has ended up in an entirely foreign world, one in which he has no peers, and his interest as an idea is virtually abstracted, outside the complex social network that usually gives it meaning. In India even such vestigial fathers as Basilius and Meleander are entirely missing, which means that Araterus's suit for the queen does not issue the conventional Oedipal challenge. The queen wants him only for himself, not for any goods, influences, or alliances he can convey—Europe is far too distant for that—and Araterus in turn is cut off so completely from his own social world that he can desire the throne only for his personal benefit in the most limited sense, because it is, after all, gratifying to be a king. Whereas Lonoxia goes out to make his way in the world, carrying the guilt of fratricide on his head, only to find that his surviving brother has always been there before him, Araterus is free of brothers, cousins, indeed all competition whatsoever; he operates, as it were, in a space that is politically and ethically empty, and he is therefore free to exercise his interest and claim his position as sovereign without social consequence. His success in India relies on the same untruth propounded by heroic ideology and identificatory friendship, that we are solitary beings in a world in which our interest impinges on no one but ourselves. Succession, his story suggests, is free from social violence only in a social vacuum; only here in this imaginary state can we achieve sovereignty uncompromised by our violations of others. And this fantasy, like Piseta's story in *Aretina*, is all the conclusion we get, the closest approximation *Eliana*'s narrator can muster of *Arcadia*'s concluding, perfectly balanced apology for self-interest.

4. RAPE AND THE FAILURE OF THE SYMBOLIC IN *PANDION AND AMPHIGENIA*

John Crowne's *Pandion and Amphigenia, or, The History of the Coy Lady of Thessalia* is impatient with the kind of wishfulness that characterizes *Eliana*'s and *Aretina*'s inability to conclude, which this relentlessly demystifying romance reads as a kind of bad faith, the genre's failure to have the courage of its convictions. *Pandion and Amphigenia* bows more completely than any other romance of the period to interest, which is shown to have such anti-idealizing force that it reduces the social world to a collection of objects, preemptively making impossible the ground from which *Aretina* and *Eliana* launch their ethical protest and draining sovereignty of all its symbolic value. Crowne's view of the relationship between romance and interest is one logical conclusion of politic ideology's trajectory in romance, the genre's surrender to its own insights about self-interest. As a conclusion to and also in sense a summation of the narrative I have been tracing throughout this book, I want to assess Pandion's sometimes comic but also excoriating cynicism as a willful recapitulation of romance's now decades-long history of conflict with itself.

Crowne is now known principally as a Restoration dramatist (his first play, *Juliana, or, the Princess of Poland* [1671], was dedicated to Roger Boyle), with at least fourteen plays to his name, the most successful of which, both in his lifetime and well afterward, was *Sir Courtly Nice; or, It Cannot Be* (first performed 1685). Crowne's father, William, was a successful politician throughout the 1640s and 1650s and a major landholder first in Nova Scotia and then in the Massachusetts Bay Colony, where he spent the last two decades of his life. His mother, Agnes Mackworth, was from Shropshire's most influential Puritan family. Throughout Crowne's long career—he published plays from 1671 through 1700 and died in 1712—he always remained in royal favor, though his politics were not always clear to his contemporaries. *Pandion and Amphigenia* was his first published work, appearing in 1665 when he was twenty-four years old, six years before his first play; in his preface he claimed that he had first "fancied" it when he was twenty, which would have had him beginning it either in Boston, where he spent three years with his father (and attended Harvard College, though he did not take a degree), or immediately upon his return to England.[18]

At the end of *Pandion and Amphigenia* Crowne tells us that he is unable to advance his princes to their thrones because of his contempt for romance's typical love plot, but love is hardly the only romance value demolished during the course of the narrative. *Pandion* opens with the usual weak king—Agis, who goes into the woods to lament the burdens of rule and all but hands his throne to the usurper Hiarbas, waiting to capture him behind a tree—and then quickly distributes his ineffectuality to just about every potential sovereign in the romance. Pandion, the true prince, whom Hiarbas fosters out to neutralize the threat he presents, has enough monarchical instinct to fall in love with Hiarbas's daughter and sole heir, but he has no talent whatsoever as a hero, and besides devising an elaborate private masque in which he descends from the ceiling on ropes in Amphigenia's bedroom (the only effect of which is to make the princess laugh), mostly he just moons around the edges of the royal household. Meanwhile, the ostensibly politic usurper Hiarbas fails to seize upon the tremendous political advantage to himself to be gained from this union because he does *not* have monarchical instinct enough to recognize the prince in disguise (Pandion has cleverly changed his name to Danpion), and so persists in his futile efforts to marry Amphigenia instead to the real Pandion's mirror image, an imposter hanging about court pretending to be the prince Pandion and himself in love with the ex-nun Glycera, escaped from a convent, who is without family, dowry, or any tolerance for his suit.

Although there is plenty of plot before we arrive at the end of Crowne's narrative, nothing changes sufficiently to repair this standoff. At the very end of the romance the two Pandions and Hiarbas do come to what promises at first to be a decisive confrontation: the false Pandion deposes Hiarbas and then puts the real Pandion up for execution as a political rival, at which point the old executioner, formerly in King Agis's employ, recognizes the true prince and proclaims publicly that "the highest soveraignty is your due by Descent and Desert."[19] But during the formal deposition ceremony happening at exactly the same moment, Hiarbas's naturally royal nature also makes itself apparent to onlookers, his eyes giving off "Beams of Majesty" that "seemed to unite and centre in his contracted brow, and with a strange kind of force to write a Law, not of pity, but of a reverential adoring a King though distrest." Hiarbas, the narrator confirms, is a "great Prince, one not undeserving that title and power, had he not used unjust means to entitle him to that power, one whose soul was richly furnisht with all those endowments of Fortitude, Justice, Prudence, and Temperance, which are the simples that constitute a true Princely mind" (298–9).

Crowne, by his doubling of hypothetically legitimate kings, has set up here an allegorical standoff through which the historical contestation over sovereignty is revealed to have devolved into a clash of interests, and his fittingly cynical response is to offer no resolution at all. Once they have disposed of the fake Pandion, Hiarbas proposes, remarkably, to take Amphigenia and go home, but Pandion will not hear of it, insisting that "the whole Kingdom should be as much at [Hiarbas's] command, as ever." Hiarbas accepts this offer of joint rule, "chiefly perswaded thereunto, by the hopes of having such an incomparable Prince for his Son in Law, by whose happy conjunction with his Daughter in marriage, the Soveraignty of *Thessalia* might run in his Reins [*sic*] which was ever the highest aym of his ambition" (306). But if this is his true desire he has nevertheless just kissed his daughter "with more fondness of affection than became a wise Father," the incestuous implication giving the lie to his protestations and to the Royalist paradigm of sovereignty, and Amphigenia for her part shows no signs of becoming more cooperative, receiving Pandion's kiss to her hand as payment for having released her from the fake Pandion "with a countenance that shewed rather how she hated her captivity, than loved her Captive" (305). Without Amphigenia's assent Pandion cannot fully effect the transition of sovereignty from usurper to prince, nor can Hiarbas gain the legitimacy he ostensibly craves. And meanwhile Crowne, in his travesty of the providentialist plot, has left several other characters not merely unfulfilled but in dire straits: the princess Amorosia is pining to death for the love of a nobleman who fruitlessly loves the ex-nun Glycera, Glycera herself is in prison awaiting death for having made the wrong powerful man fall in love with her, and another noblewoman has just been abducted by the evil ruler of Parrhasia.

In the last three paragraphs of the romance Crowne explains that he will not resolve these narrative problems, that he has left his "Lovers succourless in their miseries, not leading them out of their Labyrinths, by the Threed of my discourse," because "I esteem Ambition a more tolerable, and Masculine distraction than Love," and he therefore has little desire to "place my Hero . . . in the soft Effeminate Arms of a Lady; about which, I have not impertinent thoughts enow to spend." For those who are disappointed, he adds, "the vulgar Rule of *Romances* may salve all, That the Knight must kill the Gyant, and get the Lady"—a rule they must impose themselves, however, as his own pen is "now quite jaded and dull'd" (307). Crowne's disdain for love here is in striking contrast to Sidney's attitude at the end of *Arcadia;* instead of turning to love as ideological cover, Crowne denounces it as effeminate, artificial, and not worth his time, as if the idealist structures that Sidney could count on even while demystifying them were no longer available. And as Crowne well knows, masculine "ambition," whether of the heroic or the politic kind, offers no real alternative, since by the rules of romance it is not really separate from love; without possessing Amphigenia Crowne's prince cannot possess the throne. Romance, Crowne seems to argue here, should be abandoned, because it seeks a goal not worth attaining. Within the long history of romance's critical reception this may seem a commonplace view, one that does not require much explanation, but in Crowne's immediate context it is an odd argument, and in concluding this chapter I want to look more carefully at the nature of the goal Crowne means to reject, the women the possession of whom in *Pandion and Amphigenia* symbolizes sovereignty.

If neither Pandion nor Hiarbas is strong enough to command Amphigenia's love, for her part Crowne's usurper princess is the inverse of Sidney's princess of Cyprus at the end of *Arcadia* in her absolute aversion to all men except her father and her consequent refusal to legitimate anyone's claim to the throne. Each time the real Pandion wanders by accident into her walled garden she screams rape, and she also declines even to consider Hiarbas's attempt to marry her to the false Pandion. Refusing transfer in the end to the hereditary king, she serves as a symbol of sovereignty unachieved, the throne that still has not quite been claimed. Romance offers a couple of conventional ways to interpret her resistance, neither of which seems to work for *Pandion and Amphigenia*. Often, as I indicated in Chapter 2, incestuous relationships between kings and their daughters are markers of tyranny, but Crowne obviously disables this interpretation by portraying Hiarbas, even in his infatuation with his daughter, as also eager for her marriage to one of the Pandions or the other as a way to guarantee his legitimacy. We might be tempted to read Amphigenia's resistance to marriage as an attempt at liberation, in the same way that sibling incest in Wroth is an effort to secure exemption from an objectifying masculine economy, but this does not seem warranted by the narrative either, as Crowne never really dislodges us from the masculine point of view, according to which Amphigenia is an irrationally and sometimes comically unavailable prize.

A better context in which to make sense of Amphigenia's resistance is through her metaphoric relationship to Glycera, the escaped nun who is the object of the false Pandion's affections. Glycera would seem at first to be Amphigenia's opposite: whereas Amphigenia is excessively chaste, Glycera's symbolic punishment for leaving her convent is that she is actually raped, by an evil "Ruffian" (216) who happens across her when she is alone in the forest and "unloads his lust" into her body simply because it is female and available (218). It is difficult to emphasize enough just how exceptional an occurrence this rape is in a genre in which, as John Davies complains in the preface to his 1654 translation of Charles Sorel's *The Extravagant Shepherd,* it has become a universally observed cliché to bring the heroine to the brink of rape just so that she can be rescued at the last minute.[20] Glycera, it would seem, has fallen over the generic edge, and by the Renaissance logic according to which rape is defilement, she cannot help but become the chaste princess Amphigenia's antithesis. But if Glycera has been forced past romance's limit, so in a sense has Amphigenia, by her refusal to consider the erotic destiny that even Heliodorus's most chaste of heroines agrees to bow to in the end. In fact, the main effect of Glycera's victimization is to make her unmistakably Amphigenia's symbolic double, her soul similarly "hardned . . . to an impenetrability" by her suffering (231).

The most shocking and also the most significant aspect of Glycera's rape in its early modern context is not even that it occurs at all, but that once it is over it seems to have made no difference. It is impossible not to surmise at first that Glycera is murdered by her rapist, who after raping her "disenthrones those powers, that should govern her faculties, and seals pale death in the majestick throne of her Beauty" (218). When she is found, however, she is alive after all, and within a few days she is "restored . . . to her primitive health and beauty" (220). It might be tempting to read Glycera's ability to bounce back as a sign of feminist resistance to the prevailing ideology that rape takes away women's sole asset, their chastity, but it is fairer to the spirit of the romance, I think, to see it as proof of the non-eventfulness of her rape in a different sense. Crowne pushes Glycera off the conventional romance precipice so easily because she has nothing to lose—or more accurately, because no one else has anything to lose by her. As an ex-nun, completely devoid of kin and loved by a person whose entire identity is a pretense—in other words, as an absolutely unpropertied subject—Glycera already has no symbolic value in any exchange between men, and her rape by a nameless villain who means only to "pour out [his] lust into the kennel of [her] body" (218) does not change this status, only confirms it.

For a contrast we might return to the classic scene of near rape in Sidney's *Old Arcadia,* in which Pamela follows the conventional romance fate of being brought to the brink and then saved at the last minute. Pamela derives her enormous value from the fact that she is a princess, which in the context of the romance's succession narrative is to say(as Sidney keeps reminding us by emphasizing her "majesty")that she is an embodiment of Basilius's sovereignty. The odd thing about Musidorus's impulse to rape her, as I suggested in Chapter 1, is that such an act would represent not just the theft of a prize but also the destruction of it. Had Musidorus raped Pamela he would have removed her from the symbolic economy of *Arcadia*'s succession narrative and thus defeated his own purpose, by taking from her her value—her significance as a symbolic object to be traded between himself and Basilius—and reducing her to a mere body to be penetrated at will. That he is prevented at the last minute confirms Pamela's continued symbolic value in the narrative even as it predicts Musidorus's successful accession to Basilius's throne. When Glycera is raped it seems at first that perhaps this misogynistic text means to revalue rape in an awful way, as a symbol of the refusal by those who are inherently powerful to continue hypocritically to curb their power, a sort of triumphant Nietzschean accession to natural authority. The already-secure prince Musidorus might not have anything to gain by raping Pamela, but perhaps an evil ruffian, or a displaced heir manifesting an inexplicable reluctance to correct his fate, might accede through rape to his deserved status. Glycera, however, as Crowne shows us, is purely object, and if she does not have any symbolic significance, why then should the rape make any difference to either victim or perpetrator? After the rape the ruffian jumps off a cliff and vanishes from the narrative, and Glycera for her part is exactly as subject to victimization as she had been before (in the last of a series of subsequent indignities, when her narrative cuts off, as I noted, she is in a prison awaiting execution for being too desirable to another woman's husband), a fact we should read as proof that her postrape "impenetrability" is not really anything new. Glycera can never be invulnerable to literal penetration because she does not have Pamela's symbolic value to protect her; but within the same masculine context of the romance she is "hardened . . . to an impenetrability" in a symbolic sense, in that her rape has no meaning. Raped or unraped, from Crowne's perspective she is just the same, just a body.

If the designation of Glycera as impenetrable does not really mark any change in her own status, what it does do, as I have suggested, is link her to Amphigenia, establishing her as a type according to which we can interpret Amphigenia's refusal to consider marriage. And what Glycera tells us about Amphigenia is that it is not sex per se that is at issue in the princess's withdrawal, but rather symbolic significance. Like Glycera Amphigenia is a resistant body—not physically, but in the sense that she does not signify. Romance's most resonant symbol, the contested princess/throne, will not take up its function. I will speculate in a moment on the reasons for this resistance, but for now I want to suggest that this antisymbolic female body is the figure with which Crowne is really identifying his romance as a whole (not incidentally subtitled *The History of the Coy Lady of Thessalia*) when he jettisons the genre's traditional resolutions at the end. Certainly when it is violated but even when it is intact, Crowne has suggested, the female body is just a body, and now he argues that when romance elevates this body to an object of ritualized exchange, when it dignifies with the name of love what is really just a pragmatic trade or a self-interested act of appropriation, then it too becomes a ridiculously inflated story of giants and ladies. His own romance, in contrast, is analogous to Glycera herself, in that it refuses to signify, to deliver the symbolic closure by which its stories come to have meaning. This is not to say that Crowne has much respect for bodies in themselves, or for the women to whom they particularly belong; quite the opposite, as he conveys in the parodically pastoral interlude in the middle of the romance, which extends *Arcadia*'s contempt for real rustics into elaborate scatology so overbearing it is hard to believe Crowne even originally meant it to be comic. But at least, the romance seems to say, scatology is not a lie, at least when we are surrounded by the basest aspects of material existence (and by the kind of revisionary narrative willing to look them in the eye) we cannot take refuge in the bad faith of conventional romance's silly mystification of the feminine.

If we are seeking the logic behind *Pandion and Amphigenia*'s rejection of romance's traditional symbolic resolution, obviously it is based in part on misogyny, in particular on misogynistic attitudes toward women's relation to language and materiality. At several points Crowne sets up a connection between men as agents and as deployers of words, for instance in the inset narrative of Plivio, who is lord of "Parrhasia," the rhetorical term for freedom or boldness of speech, and whose main act in the romance is to abduct a princess under the rationale that "since (as the Philosopher saith) every one is the framer of his own fate . . . none should accuse his negligence for his infelicity" (258). Women in Crowne's romance, as we can gather from Amphigenia's and Glycera's stories, are not agents, nor are they wielders of language, because the communicativeness of their bodies trumps anything they might want to say: women's skin, for example, is "transparent Crystal" and "white paper where they pourtray the picture of their minds," and though they may try to maintain the integrity of their thoughts and feelings, to "Cloyster" them up "in the chast Nunneries of their hearts," it is their nature always to "suffer all such vain resolves to be ravished from them" (224–5). Women's thoughts in *Pandion* are like their bodies in being perpetually open to ravishment because they are what they mean, as if they were hieroglyphic signs. They seem to have no selves beyond those bodies or thoughts, selves that might deploy body or speech as instrument, and as a result it is not only the nature but also the essence of their bodies and thoughts to be available for use to others.

Crowne's chief precedent here was no doubt Ovid's well-known story of Procne and Philomela in *Metamorphoses* 6, to which the prince's name, Pandion, was a direct allusion. In Ovid's story, King Tereus of Thrace is sent by his wife, Procne, to her father, King Pandion of Athens, to claim his sister-in-law Philomela for a visit. Instead, Tereus rapes the younger woman, cuts out her tongue, and confines her in a hut behind a high stone wall. Philomela manages to weave her story into a tapestry and get it to Procne, who rescues her from the hut, and in revenge the two women slaughter Procne's and Tereus's son, Itys, and feed his body to his unknowing father. One of the moments of greatest pathos in the tale is when Philomela cries to Tereus just after he has raped her that he has turned her into "a concubine, my sister's rival," and himself into "husband to both," as if the rape were a symbolic act on the order of marriage.[21] In fact, as Tereus immediately confirms by cutting out her tongue, the rape entirely denies her social identity, taking her out of symbolic relation to others. Philomela is all body, Tereus conveys to her, so confined by her materiality that not only can she not use words, but she cannot, in effect, be as if she were a word, cannot signify even as an object of exchange. Philomela and Procne (who has her own powers of speech taken from her when she reads her sister's tapestry [6.579–81]) understand this lesson well, as they gruesomely demonstrate when they offer Tereus his son's body to eat: if in his rapaciousness Tereus has reduced Philomela merely to a body available for his use, they tell him, then Itys too to him will no longer be son or even person, only flesh.

Tereus, of course, is the original agent of this catastrophe, but Ovid implicates the women too : when Procne decides to "confound right and wrong" by picking up on Tereus's horrible cue (6.585–6), the "Thracian matrons" are in the midst of celebrating the festival of Bacchus, their revelry offering a context and maybe even part of an explanation for the brutality about to come (6.587–8). And Philomela's beauty already places her outside ordinary social structures even before she meets Tereus, with the naiads and dryads "in the deep woods," the narrator says, which is part of the reason that Tereus succumbs to lust for her in the same way that hay or dry leaves burst into flame (454–5). Women in the tale, with their propensity to hyperrealize that material aspect of their natures with which men identify them, represent at once the attractions and the horrors of pure bodiliness. From this point of view we might even see metamorphosis in Ovid as a curative force, liberating women's human identities into the symbolic register by bestowing on them a substitute, newly interpretable literality that is also more mundane and less threatening to men (that this is perhaps particularly to the misogynist point is suggested, for instance, by Andrew Marvell's revision of Ovidian myth in the lyric "The Garden," in which Pan's pursuit of Syrinx resolves itself by proving that what he really wants is a reed). In Crowne's revision, of course, there is no metamorphosis; what Ovid offers Crowne is only the idea that materiality and the bodily are both women's fate and somehow also their fault.

For Ovid the tale registers a problem confined mainly within the explanatory rubric of gender difference; Tereus violates Philomela but not really Pandion, even by extension, and there is no indication that Pandion, for his part, has done anything a more generous or prudent father or king might have avoided. Crowne, however, adds a political connotation to the narrative, by rewriting his Pandion as the forfeiter of a throne rather than a daughter. In the Newberry Library's copy of *Pandion and Amphigenia* an annotation by a seventeenth-century reader proves that this political connotation was quite clear to the romance's contemporary readers. Up the left margin and then again down the right margin of the two pages in which Hiarbas captures Agis, fosters out the boy Pandion, and seizes the throne, the reader traced the sentence "Pandion, comitem lacrymis commendat obortis. Ovid: met. lib. 6" ("Pandion handed over his companion with tears welling forth"), a direct quotation of line 495 of book 6 of the *Metamorphoses,* which refers specifically to Pandion's surrender of Philomela to Tereus. In other words, the seventeenth-century reader had perceived the obvious meaning of Crowne's allusion to Ovid—that Crowne's King Agis and, by extension, his son Pandion haplessly offer up their throne to be violated by the usurper Hiarbas in the same way Ovid's Pandion had surrendered Philomela to Tereus. If we follow the interpretation all the way through, then in Crowne it is the throne itself that has been wrested out of the symbolic register, and Amphigenia's and Glycera's resistance to symbolization is not only a cause but also a symptom of disordered rule, or perhaps better the allegorical representation of it. Like Tereus the incestuous Hiarbas eats his own young in this later version of the story, as allegorized by his failure to trade his daughter, to alienate her from himself in order to use her as a transferable object. Now that it has been violated, sovereignty can no longer authorize its holder, and as a result it has lost its function of putting people in orderly relation to one another, sorting out the distinction between ruler and ruled and effecting the transition from ruler to successor.

Certainly, Crowne's allusion to Ovid suggests that we should read *Pandion*'s failure to resolve the sovereignty contest as at least in part a political allegory, specifically as an argument that the Restoration had not really restored hereditary monarchy but only offered it one of several seats at the political table, and that when it was time for the transfer of power to the next ruler, it seemed unlikely that there would be sufficient principles or structures by which it could be effected. And yet *Pandion* also included elements that would trouble a strictly Royalist reading, making it difficult for us to claim that what Crowne meant to call for was greater authority for the hereditary sovereign. In Crowne's vision, the legitimate Agis, father of Pandion, is a clearly incapable king, and Hiarbas may be a usurper but he also, as I indicated before, displays a natural disposition to be a monarch, while Pandion's suit is not only markedly unconvincing to Amphigenia but often ridiculous. Crowne's nihilistic brand of satire, too, is a discouragement from reading elegiacally; perhaps he had concluded that meaning, and romance, had failed because England had entered on an age of weak kings, but it seems equally likely, maybe more so, that in Crowne's eyes romance (perhaps along with the kind of sovereignty it espoused) had always been wishful, conjuring up meaning out of nothing, and all that had really changed now was the extent to which people were willing to delude themselves.

In *Pandion*, quite unusually for midcentury romance, the word "interest" rarely appears, but as an idea interest has everything to do with Crowne's cynicism. Indeed, I want to insist, *Pandion*'s disenchantment of sovereignty and succession is a deep if also covert allegory for interest's trajectory in seventeenth-century romance. MacKenzie and the author of *Eliana* both point out self-interest's incompatibility with ethics, the tendency of the self-sovereignizing subject to violate the interests of others, but both at the same time assume the existence of an ethical ground separate from and resistant to interest, a different frame of reference in which our obligations to others can be assumed. Piseta and Lonoxia are heroic, in the only way romance still makes available to them, for mounting their ethical protest, for refusing to let romance proceed to its conventional conclusion. In *Pandion and Amphigenia,* by contrast, we are directed to disdain Hiarbas and Pandion for their inability to accept and act upon the truth that Crowne has by the end made abundantly clear: in a world demystified by interest there is no ground for ethical protest. *Pandion and Amphigenia* radically constricts its prince's options to only two: passivity or rape. Pandion can either dither forever while the throne, by all conventions rightfully his, hovers out of reach, or he can seize what he wants, and by doing so, as it were, put the object of his desire in her place, that is, force her to own up to her status as mere object. By Crown's misogynistic logic perhaps the object even deserves such a form of appropriation for turning out to be just an object after all, when it has so persistently and fraudulently presented itself as something more.

Pandion and Amphigenia marks a temporal end to the genre of original English romance I have been discussing in this book, and in conclusion I want to emphasize the central role that Crowne's misogyny plays in this victory of interest over romance. In the fable with which Sidney wraps up *Arcadia* the bemused prince is just as passive as Pandion, but for Sidney this passivity is not contemptible; on the contrary, it leaves a space to be filled by the "furiou[s] love" of the princess of Cyprus, which then takes on the role of bringing the princess's beloved over the morally perilous bridge to sovereignty. Romance for Sidney, as I argued in Chapter 1, becomes through its allegorical structure the perfect vehicle for bringing self-interest to light, but at the same time it absolves its main protagonists of self-interest by shunting agency to women, putting feminine desire behind its paradigmatic prince's accession to sovereignty. In effect Sidney brilliantly capitalizes on romance's long affiliation with love and the feminine to cover for the cultural anxiety about masculine self-interest. In the process, albeit with some irony, he offers women a power and centrality in romance narrative that could not but have been enabling to Wroth and later to Herbert and MacKenzie for thinking through problems of morality and ethics. In Crowne, of course, women never have any desire of their own; indeed, it is the function of the romance's governing rape narrative to construe feminine desire as an impossibility. The cost of this, within the conceptual scheme that romance has set up over the roughly seventy-year period from Sidney to Crowne, is precisely the cancellation of any ground for ethics, and the construal of interest as a relentlessly simplifying and culturally annihilative idea.

Conclusion

Early modern English romance was an intentionally allegorical genre in the sense in which I have been using allegory in this book, a genre that understood its literal representations, the stories it told, to be always in correspondence with other kinds of knowledge. As Francis Bacon argued in *De Augmentis Scientarum,* it was fiction's essential task either to narrate the events of history or to convey "objects of the intellect," philosophical precepts conducing to virtue.[1] If fiction thus conceived presents difficulties for the post-Romantic reader, accustomed to attributing to literature an integrity of its own, anyone familiar with early modern literary theory knows some of the more obvious arguments early modern writers and readers would have levied in allegorical fiction's defense—that it not only represented philosophy's lessons but also moved its audience to follow them, as Sidney had claimed in his *Apology for Poesy,* or that against the reality of censorship it was able to convey history's lessons more subtly and for the writer more safely than history itself. But it has been the argument of this book that romance's literal fictions also performed in the seventeenth century a more specific task: they provided a uniquely useful space for negotiation with what, at the time, was the culturally pressing problem of self-interest. From Sidney through Wroth and Barclay to the Boyles and MacKenzie, the allegorical middle space of fiction offered romance writers a resistant ethical hypothesis challenging their culture's dominant acceptance and accommodation of self-interest, a way, while acknowledging self-interest, also to hold it at bay. As such, I have claimed, romance opened a venue for moral and ethical exploration that history and philosophy could not.

Late sixteenth-century politic ideology, as part of its project of demystifying old humanist truths, raised with particular urgency the conflict between the ideal of commonwealth, long believed to be the ultimate goal of providential design, and the interests of the individual agent. Modern scholars of politic ideology have focused their attention on early modern historical writing, but Sidney, as a member of a political and literary circle with close ties to politic ideas, chose romance as the genre in which to explore them—in part because of the genre's long-standing aristocratic associations, and more centrally because romance's stories of thrones contested and achieved had for centuries played with the tension between supernatural and human agency, bringing forward but also often subsuming, in their providentialist conclusions, the force of individual interest. In *Arcadia* Sidney at once drew attention to self-interest's troubling tendency to defy conventional morality and violate social order while also asserting in his conclusion the power of romance's conventional narrative of love to cover for these threats, thus creating for his readers a kind of double vision. If self-interest in *Arcadia* was a demystificatory truth, it was also a simplifying one, and romance's literal fictions offered a more subtle counternarrative, one Sidney identified with what he understood to be the usefully oxymoronic quality of female agency.

Clearly in part as a retort to Sidney, Wroth's *Urania* took as its main subject the moral risks of female agency. Because of the ideological strictures on their agency, women labored under an even more complex and constraining imperative than men to avoid claiming self-interest outright, argued Wroth, and in response she developed a highly complex model of roman à clef, employing the space of the literal to devise a sort of compromise between hubristic self-consolidation (of the kind that might be achieved by, say, writing a story about oneself in order to proclaim and justify one's own desire) and conventional feminine silence and self-abnegation. As for Sidney, so also for Wroth romance made possible both a narrative and a moral freedom, by which the subject might be able to act without quite having to claim self-interest. As a consequence Wroth's subject might still be able to accomplish romance's traditional project—political, insofar as Wroth's characters were all princes and princesses, but also in *Urania* moral-psychological—of achieving sovereignty.

In foregrounding human agency at the expense of providential order and defining each person's interest as potentially distinct, the emergent politic ideology of the early modern period offered a threat not only to individual morality but also to social order, especially in its vision of the social world as made up by a large group of peers put in relation to one another not by hierarchical difference, nor by the humanist ideal of mutual service to a common good, but rather by individualized competition. At first romance responded defensively, by reasserting its traditional generic emphasis on chastity and singularity, in effect wishing the problem away. But in later romance this Heliodoran emphasis began to drop out, as if the tension between self-interest and social bonds had become increasingly difficult either to ignore or to reconcile, and by midcentury the genre found itself less and less able to enact the achievement of sovereignty even in its more idealist fictions. In response, romance sometimes looked for alternatives, mustering fiction for other kinds of ethical hypotheses, whether disinterested friendship or religious martyrdom or political utopia; more commonly, as time went on the genre staged explicitly its failure to achieve sovereignty and thus to come to narrative closure, as a form of ethical protest against interest's force. In these late romances, we might say, the space fiction had filled with its resistant hypotheses became preempted (or, in Crowne, entirely colonized) by self-interest, relegating ethical protest to the margins and rewriting the genre's Sidneian conflict with itself, traditionally ironic and covert, as newly blatant and disabling.

A large part of my goal in this book has been to give an account of romance's generic trajectory in the seventeenth century through a reading of its highly self-conscious manipulations and adaptations of its own allegorical form. But romance also tells another story in the seventeenth century, apposite but also distinct, of a shift in moral-philosophical habits of thought. To begin once more with politic ideology, most observers in the late sixteenth century seemed to agree that politic self-interest portended, if it had not already ushered in, political instability and fragmentation, but also that (perhaps because of its perceived seriousness, or its incendiary cultural associations) such a threat needed to be referred to only covertly, gestured toward as a not-quite-expressible secret. Not surprisingly, Jacobean romance took up its self-appointed task of trying to contain interest's more frightening social implications by way of entirely traditional strategies, engaging the old Stoic-heroic paradigm of the subject's struggle with her own passions in order to neutralize self-interest's force, or valorizing the metaphorical chastity and singularity by which the subject removed herself from competition with others. By the middle of the seventeenth century, however, interest was much more openly a subject of debate in romance and outside it. Certainly this was part of reason of state theory's long early modern trajectory toward conventionality; perhaps too the concept had been given new urgency by what Craig Muldrew calls the "culture of credit" requiring trust of strangers on an unprecedented scale, or by the growth in the 1640s and 1650s of factional politics. Whatever the exact configuration of reasons for the increase in its cultural currency, in the wake of the duc de Rohan's work in the early 1640s interest was increasingly seen as transparent and morally neutral, what it was the very nature of an object or agent to want, and with this growing rationalization the traditional drama of the self in conflict with its own passions seemed much less compelling. For those inclined to be sanguine, such as James Harrington, interest promised a newly reasonable political and social world; for the more skeptical among romance writers, interest had been liberated from all internal moral constraints and now promised to rage all but unchecked, susceptible only to the interest of someone more powerful. If politic interest inspired at first a story that I have called moral, the traditional Stoic-heroic psychomachia, now for the first time in romance it generated a different kind of narrative, one we can truly call ethical in the sense in which I have used the term, as romance writers trained their sights on the subsumption of one person's interests by another's and found it not only disorderly but wrong.

In 1673, looking back over his career, the publisher and bookseller Francis Kirkman claimed that after the Restoration romances were "thrust out of use . . . by the particular esteem of our late English stage plays."[2] Indeed Boyle, Crowne, and Samuel Pordage, possible author of *Eliana*, all turned decisively and exclusively to drama in this period, and although translation of Continental romance continued throughout the 1670s and 1680s, from about 1665 there were no new original English romances in the style of *Parthenissa* or *Cloria*. The traditional view of romance as an idealist genre preoccupied with the past might point to the conclusion that romance failed in the seventeenth century because its ideals were so out of date they could not be rehabilitated, and in a sense this is true. But I want to propose that it has been interest's essential function, not just in the seventeenth century but throughout its history as an idea, to construe idealism as inherently untenable or outdated. Interest finds its meaning by putting itself in a mutually constitutive, absolutely dichotomous relation with an ideal that it attempts continuously to usurp or dominate. So in early English politic ideology its function was to oppose absolutely the providentialist, old-humanist, vaguely communal ideal of virtue that seemed in that context its only alternative, and so at midcentury it came into focus as a failure of love. Interest challenges its opposite to maintain itself as viable and at the same time implies it never can, hence the assumption we see even, for instance, in contemporary Grotius scholarship, that the only real alternative to self-interest is the absolute and therefore rather unrealistic sacrifice of it. Through its failure in the 1660s, romance offers one object lesson for how limited the logic of interest is, and how difficult it is to think outside of it.

For a much more recent illustration of interest's intractability, and a way of suggesting why early modern romance's idealist formulation of the problem is perhaps less dated than it might at first seem, I want to conclude with a very brief reading of self-interest in the work of two contemporary philosophers. One of the central arguments in both Bernard Williams's *Ethics and the Limits of Philosophy* (1985) and Philippa Foot's *Natural Goodness* (2001) is that it is useless to challenge self-interest with a countervailing force or value; to open up its constricted view of social life we need not to concede or to deny it, but rather to think alongside it. In *Ethics and the Limits of Philosophy* Williams's goal is to trouble and ultimately to upset the dominance in ethical thought of the dichotomy between Kantian duty and self-centered desire, not in order to replace duty with some other counter for self-interest nor to shift our attention toward our responsibility toward others, but rather to suggest that ethical life is much broader than moral philosophy has painted it. It is a mistake, Williams says, to reduce nonethical behavior simply to egoism;[3] on the other side, any account of ethical behavior must acknowledge the ethical force of desire, of reaction as well as action, of the simple distinction between "what one has done and what one has not done" (38, 177). The problem with morality as obligation, he concludes, is that it justifies its existence by deluding us into believing that without it there is only "inclination" or "force," "efficiency, or power, or uncorrected luck," that a world without duty is essentially Hobbesian, governed only by self-interest and the simple exercise of power that belongs to it (196). A reconstituted ethics might open our eyes to the fact that we are driven not only by egoism but by many other kinds of motivation, some of which refuse to be categorized according to their adherence or resistance to self-interest, and in so doing might break the conceptual stranglehold imposed by the dichotomy between self-interest and its mirror opposite obligation.

In *Natural Goodness* Foot dismisses "psychological egoism" as already "thoroughly discredited," but other forms of self-interest seem to retain more cultural force for her. Two of her central tasks in this book, as in Williams's, are to confuse any easy distinction between self-interest and its opposites as they are traditionally construed and then to push both to the margins of ethical deliberation.[4] Foot decenters self-interest's role in motivation first by replacing desire with reason at the origins of behavior (it is only because most moral philosophy is "in thrall" to "a hydraulic picture of the psychological determinants to action," she says, that it grounds motivation in desire, something the agent "just wants" [21–2]) and then by separating reason from vulgar self-interest. Both traditionally self-interested human behaviors and those more commonly called "moral" in her terms, such as neighborliness or promise-making, are not much different from a tree's development of roots, in that all three obey the teleology of their respective species. Human behavior, of course, is self-conscious and volitional—that is, it is the outcome of "practical rationality"—but if it is "good," in Foot's meaning of the term, it is based on "the facts of human life" (for instance, that we look after ourselves in normal circumstances better than anyone else could do, and that we require the presence of others), which are as fundamental and indisputable to our existence as is a tree's development of roots (17–18, 33). If we mean by self-interest an agent's tendency to do what is most conducive to the thriving of itself and its species (roughly, close to what Herle means in the mid-seventeenth century by a stone's tendency to fall to the earth), then of course all behavior is self-interested, and the concept becomes so capacious as to be ethically meaningless, as Thomas Macaulay intuited long before. Conversely, if we define self-interest instead as an inexplicable and irrational desire, then it is a disorder in ethics and also in nature, and in Foot's view quite a rare one, without in the end much claim on our attention.

I do not mean to erase the substantial differences between Foot's and Williams's arguments, but I want to emphasize that in the view of both, ethical life should and indeed does happen to a great degree outside of self-interest traditionally construed, and to break its hold on our imaginations we do not need to come up with a great rival to it but rather to look elsewhere. Within the context of my reading of romance, to recognize the revisionary energy of this argument in Williams and Foot is to begin to perceive the historical power of interest's restrictive logic, how insistently it has claimed its own explanatory force. In the light of self-interest's long Enlightenment history of being more positively (some might say wishfully) valued, it is striking that already in the mid-seventeenth century romance had formulated it as a trap. In one sense we might see midcentury romance as ineffectual, clearly unsuited for the future in its refusal to accept an idea that would soon become a commonplace; but in another we might read the genre in the 1660s as quite radical, construing interest as an ethical impasse in a way that today seems oddly contemporary.

Notes

In the citations of modern translations of classical sources, the references in parentheses after the volume and page number from the modern translations are to book and section or line number from the original.

Introduction

1. See Michael McKeon, *The Origins of the English Novel 1600–1740* (Baltimore: Johns Hopkins University Press, 1987), 59, and Lennard Davis, *Factual Fictions: The Origins of the English Novel* (New York: Columbia University Press, 1983), 43, for both these claims. See also Nigel Smith, *Literature and Revolution in England* (New Haven, CT: Yale University Press, 1994), 241–6, for the argument that midcentury English romance is derivative of the French. *Pandion and Amphigenia* is sometimes alluded to in discussions of Crowne's much more well-known career as a Restoration dramatist; Paul Salzman's *English Prose Fiction 1558–1700* (Oxford: Clarendon Press, 1985) is the only critical work I know of even to mention *Herba Parietis* (which receives only two sentences, 288–9), though the romance was reissued in facsimile by Brummel Press in 1969. Salzman does not discuss Boyle's *Theodora* and characterizes it in his bibliography as a "Restoration novel" (375).
2. The most sophisticated example of this argument is McKeon's in *Origins;* see esp. 20–2 for a lucid summary. For arguments that romance at midcentury was outdated and naïve, offering "quasi-miraculous" and, by implication, unrealistic and simplistic answers to knotty new ideological questions, see Lois Potter, *Secret Rites and Secret Writing: Royalist Literature, 1641–1660* (Cambridge: Cambridge University Press, 1989), 109, and also 107–8, 150; and Smith, *Literature and Revolution,* 239. In the last few decades scholars have made some claim for the importance of prose romance, particularly its roman à clef form, though few take up in any detail the content of these admittedly enormous works: Salzman's useful classificatory survey includes romance, as do Potter, *Secret Rites;* Smith, *Literature and Revolution* (who devotes part of his chapter on heroic ideology in midcentury literature to romance, 233–46); and Annabel Patterson, *Censorship and Interpretation: The Conditions of Writing and Reading in Early*

Modern England (Madison: University of Wisconsin Press, 1984). Victoria Kahn offers a groundbreaking reading of sympathy and what she calls "aesthetic interest" in midcentury romance, first in "Reinventing Romance, or the Surprising Effects of Sympathy," *Renaissance Quarterly* 55, no. 2 (2002): 625–61, and then in *Wayward Contracts: The Crisis of Political Obligation in England, 1640–1674* (Princeton, NJ: Princeton University Press, 2004), 223–51.

3. For a discussion of the contemporaneous development of print culture and the emergence of popular literature, with particular emphasis on gender, see Wendy Wall, *The Imprint of Gender: Authorship and Publication in the English Renaissance* (Ithaca, NY: Cornell University Press, 1993).
4. For the Italian debate over romance see Bernard Weinberg, *A History of Literary Criticism in the Italian Renaissance* (Chicago: University of Chicago Press, 1961), 2:954–1073.
5. Even by the early seventeenth century this litany of complaints was conventional; it is somewhere behind Ben Jonson's famous dismissal of Shakespeare's *Pericles* as a "mouldy tale," and it reverberates in many of the prefaces to midcentury romance, for instance, in Percy Herbert's assurance to the reader in *Cloria* that he has been careful to maintain his focus on Cloria herself until the very end, an allusion to the common complaint that Ariosto should have named his romance after Ruggiero rather than the less central Orlando. See Jonson, "Ode to himselfe," in *The New Inne, The Complete Plays of Ben Jonson*, ed. G. A. Wilkes (Oxford: Oxford University Press, 1982 [1631]), 4:471–3, line 21. Weinberg discusses Giovanni Batista Pigna's justification in his *I romanzi* of Ariosto's title in *A History of Literary Criticism*, 2:964. For Herbert see *The Princess Cloria, or The Royal Romance* (London, 1661), "To the Reader," A2r.
6. Alex Davis, *Chivalry and Romance in the English Renaissance* (Cambridge: D. S. Brewer, 2003), 3.
7. For a fascinating discussion of the way romance—the category against which generations of readers differentiate their own reading matter and practice as sophisticated and serious—skillfully reshapes itself for a changing marketplace during the first few centuries of print culture even as it functions as elite literature's other, see Lori Humphrey Newcomb, *Reading Popular Romance in Early Modern England* (New York: Columbia University Press, 2002).
8. See, for example, *Birinthea, a Romance,* by "J.B." (John Bulteel) (London, 1664). The Newberry Library in Chicago holds at least two prose romances from the mid-seventeenth century in manuscript; one of them, *Rivall Friendship,* is currently being edited by Jean Brink for publication by t he Renaissance English Text Society.

   Aretina, published in Edinburgh, is the only non-English romance treated in this book; its inclusion among the other late romances I discuss is justified by its similarly central concern with monarchical prerogative as well as with interest. I chose not to describe the subject of this book as "British romance" so as not to connote an inaccurately broad cultural purview.

9. Probably the decline in the production of original prose romance in the 1660s had something to do with the remarkably abrupt shift in France around 1660 from the long historical romance to the *nouvelle.* The well-known seventeenth-century publisher and bookseller Francis Kirkman suggests that after the Restoration romances were "thrust out of use, by the present slighting and neglect of all Books in general, & by the particular esteem of our late *English stage plays*" (Kirkman, "To the Reader," in *The Honour of Chivalry: or, the Famous and Delectable History of Don Bellianis of Greece,* [an older romance with a continuation "Now newly written, by Francis Kirkman"; Kirkman first published the continuation in 1664, with a different note to the reader] [London, 1671], A4v). I argue in Chapter 4 that it was partly also romance's construal of the relation between interest and its own form that brought it to a dead end, at least in this particular manifestation.
10. In *Aretina* George MacKenzie offers a generic genealogy that consists of "Sidney, Scuderie, Barkley [John Barclay], and Broghill [Roger Boyle]," and before them Heliodorus (MacKenzie, *Aretina; Or, The Serious Romance* [Edinburgh, 1660], 6). This list is replicated closely more than a century later by Clara Reeve, with no hint that she knew MacKenzie, in her critical dialogue *The Progress of Romance,* further suggesting that we have lost the history of what at the time was a thematically and formally coherent group of narratives (Reeve, *The Progress of Romance* [1785] [New York: The Facsimile Text Society, 1930], xi, 71–80). Common to all the works on these lists is that they are prose, probably to contemporaneous eyes one of their most significant generic markers. Prose romance also signals its affiliation with a larger romance tradition not limited to prose: for example, the shipwrecked baby, Marinus, floating alone in a chest in *Eliana,* who owes a debt to Marina in Shakespeare's *Pericles* and before that to the shipwrecked prince in *Amadis de Gaule;* or the allusion by Bayly's *Herba Parietis* to *The Winter's Tale* in its relatively unusual narrative of a duke who casts out his daughter (usually royal children are stolen or lost in romance) and in the stage direction form ("Enter bear") with which it introduces a bear into a tragicomic moment in its plot.

    For the multiplicity of romance's form see MacKenzie's observation that "the judgement may pick more sound information" from romances because they are like laces on which the pearls of moral philosophy are strung (7), and the opinion of *Eliana*'s author that it is the particular virtue of romance to include "things *Oeconomical, Ethethical* [*sic*], *Physical, Metaphysical, Philosophycal, Political,* and *Theological* as well as *Amatory*" (*Eliana. A New Romance* [London, 1661], A3v).

11. Norbert Elias, *The Court Society*, trans. Edmund Jephcott (New York: Pantheon Books, [1969] 1983); 105.
12. See Martin Dzelzainis, "Bacon's 'Of Simulation and Dissimulation,'" in *A Companion to English Renaissance Literature and Culture*, ed. Michael Hattaway (Oxford: Blackwell, 2000), 233–40, 235, for the Italian and French origins of politic ideology in England.
13. For politic ideology, Tacitism, and affiliated modes of thought, see Alan T. Bradford, "Stuart Absolutism and the 'Utility' of Tacitus," *Huntington Library Quarterly* 46, no. 2 (1983): 127–55; Peter Burke, "Tacitism, Scepticism, and Reason of State," in *The Cambridge History of Political Thought 1450–1700* (Cambridge: Cambridge University Press, 1991), 479–98; Martin Dzelzainis, "Shakespeare and Political Thought," in *A Companion to Shakespeare*, ed. David Scott Kastan (Malden, MA: Blackwell Publishers, 1999), 100–16; Anthony Grafton and Lisa Jardine, "'Studied for Action': How Gabriel Harvey Read his Livy," *Past and Present* 129 (1990): 30–78; F. J. Levy, "Hayward, Daniel, and the Beginnings of Politic History in England," *Huntington Library Quarterly* 50 (1987): 1–34; J. H. M. Salmon, "Stoicism and Roman Example: Seneca and Tacitus in Jacobean England," *Journal of the History of Ideas* 50, no. 2 (1989): 199–225; Mary F. Tenney, "Tacitus in the Politics of Early Stuart England," *Classical Journal* 37 (1941): 151–63; and D. R. Woolf, "Genre into Artifact: The Decline of the English Chronicle in the Sixteenth Century," *Sixteenth Century Journal* 19, no. 3 (1988): 321–54, esp. 349–54 on politic history.
14. Levy, "Hayward, Daniel, and the Beginnings of Politic History," 9–15, and Salmon, "Stoicism and Roman Example," 204–8, each provide overviews of the association of Tacitean ideas with Sidney and Essex, as does Blair Worden, *The Sound of Virtue: Philip Sidney's* Arcadia *and Elizabethan Politics* (New Haven, CT: Yale University Press, 1996), 21, 255–63. See also Tenney, "Tacitus in the Politics of Early Stuart England." For the association of the Sidney circle with oppositional politics see David Norbrook, *Poetry and Politics in the English Renaissance* (London: Routledge and Kegan Paul, 1984), 93–5, 198–9. On Mary Sidney's circle, see Mary Ellen Lamb, *Gender and Authorship in the Sidney Circle* (Madison: University of Wisconsin Press, 1990), 115–41, and Alexander MacLaren Witherspoon, *The Influence of Robert Garnier on Elizabethan Drama* (New Haven, CT: Yale University Press, 1924, rpt. 1968), 67–83.
15. Tuck's is the most fully elaborated argument to date for the influence of the new humanism on seventeenth-century English thought. Richard Tuck, *Philosophy and Government 1572–1651* (Cambridge: Cambridge University Press, 1993), 63.
16. Maurizio Viroli, *From Politics to Reason of State: The Acquisition and Transformation of the Language of Politics 1250–1600* (Cambridge: Cambridge University Press, 1992), esp. 2–10.
17. Levy, "Hayward, Daniel, and the Beginnings of Politic History," 20.

18. Quoted in Bradford, "Stuart Absolutism and the 'Utility' of Tacitus," 132.
19. Quoted in Levy, "Hayward, Daniel, and the Beginnings of Politic History," 8.
20. In *The Sound of Virtue* Blair Worden provides a convincing account of Sidney's pull simultaneously toward republican ideology and toward the idea of a powerful monarch; see 239–47.
21. David Quint, *Epic and Empire: Politics and Generic Form from Virgil to Milton* (Princeton, NJ: Princeton University Press, 1993), esp. 9–10.
22. This argument for irony as always already present in romance goes against the dominant understanding of romance as by definition uniformly idealizing, an idea perhaps most influentially propounded by Northrop Frye's *Anatomy of Criticism* (Princeton, NJ: Princeton University Press, 1957), esp. 186–206; see also McKeon, *Origins,* 21, 131–3; Smith, *Literature and Revolution,* 234; and Robert Wilcher, *The Writing of Royalism 1628–1660* (Cambridge: Cambridge University Press, 2001), 25. J. G. A. Pocock's assumption, when trying to account for the romance elements of James Harrington's *Oceana,* that it is the function of romance as a genre to idealize, is evidence of the wide assent even in other disciplines to Frye's thesis; *The Political Works of James Harrington,* ed. Pocock (Cambridge: Cambridge University Press, 1977), 50, 74. The idea that antiromances such as *Don Quixote* signal the death of the genre is a truism; for *Don Quixote* as a "death knell," see Lennard Davis, *Factual Fictions,* 34.
23. Ann Astell, *Political Allegory in Late Medieval England* (Ithaca, NY: Cornell University Press), 1999, esp. chap. 5, "Penitential Politics in *Sir Gawain and the Green Knight:* Richard II, Richard of Arundel, and Robert de Vere," 117–137.
24. George Puttenham, *The Arte of English Poesie* (London, 1589), facs. ed. (New York: Da Capo Press and Theatrum Orbis Terrarum Ltd., 1971), 155.
25. Wayne C. Booth, *A Rhetoric of Irony* (Chicago: University of Chicago Press, 1974), esp. chap. 1, "The Ways of Stable Irony," 1–31.
26. For functional ambiguity, see Patterson, *Censorship and Interpretation,* 10–11.
27. McKeon, *Origins,* 59. McKeon is hardly alone in his sense that roman à clef makes for unsophisticated narrative, though he is one of the few critics to theorize about why this should be so. For a representative estimation of roman à clef's damaging effect on seventeenth-century romance in particular, see Smith's reading of Herbert's *Cloria,* in which he concludes that the romance's "fictionality" is "drained by allegorical pressure," paving the way for its simplistic providential conclusion (*Literature and Revolution,* 239). I am indebted in general to McKeon's powerful formulation of the "questions of truth" and "questions of virtue" that the novel eventually comes into being to express and mediate.

28. For a definitive account of *Arcadia* as political allegory, see Worden, *Sound of Virtue.* For Sidney's dedication to the Countess of Pembroke, in which he calls the work a "trifle, and that triflingly handled," see Philip Sidney, *The Countess of Pembroke's Arcadia (The New Arcadia)* (hereafter *NA*), ed. Victor Skretkowicz (Oxford: Clarendon Press, 1987), app. III, 506, and Sidney, *The Countess of Pembroke's Arcadia (The Old Arcadia)* (hereafter *OA*), ed. Jean Robertson (Oxford: Clarendon Press, 1973), 3. Sidney uses the term "stranger shepherd" in *OA,* 245. The lyric against tyranny is in the Third Eclogues of *OA,* 254–259; in the 1590 edition it was moved to the First Eclogues (see *NA,* app. II, 478–82).
29. For Rohan's influences, see Albert O. Hirschman, *The Passions and the Interests: Political Arguments for Capitalism Before its Triumph* (Princeton, NJ: Princeton University Press, 1977), 34.
30. Henri, duc de Rohan, *A Treatise of the Interest of the Princes and States of Christendome,* trans. Henry Hunt (Paris: 1640), 1; Rohan, *De l'intérêst des princes et des Etats de la chréstienté* (Paris, 1638), 1.
31. See Bernard Williams, *Ethics and the Limits of Philosophy* (Cambridge, MA: Harvard University Press, 1985), 6–7; Philippa Foot, *Natural Goodness* (Oxford: Clarendon Press, 2001), 68.
32. Williams, *Ethics and the Limits of Philosophy,* 12. For this use of Williams and also for this distinction between ethics and morality in general I am indebted to R. Clifton Spargo, *The Ethics of Mourning: Grief and Responsibility in Elegiac Literature* (Baltimore: Johns Hopkins University Press, 2004), esp. 6–9. Spargo draws on Williams and also especially on Levinas and Ricoeur to develop his own claim that ethics "is the inevitable and persistent fact of finding oneself in relation to the other" (7). This is a stronger and more explicit claim than Williams ever makes for the relational aspect of ethics, one that has colored my own reading of Williams and influenced my formulation of the distinction I see in early modern romance.
33. See Bernard Williams, "Utilitarianism and Moral Self-Indulgence," in *Moral Luck: Philosophical Papers 1973–1980* (Cambridge: Cambridge University Press, 1981), 40–53.
34. On the history of political uses of the concept of interest in seventeenth-century England, see esp. J. A. W. Gunn, *Politics and the Public Interest in the Seventeenth Century* (London: Routledge and Kegan Paul, 1969). Gunn cites Charles I's use of the term on page 49.
35. Rebecca W. Bushnell, *Tragedies of Tyrants: Political Thought and Theater in the English Renaissance* (Ithaca, NY: Cornell University Press, 1990), especially 38–9.
36. Craig Muldrew, *The Economy of Obligation: The Culture of Credit and Social Relations in Early Modern England* (New York: St. Martin's Press, 1998) locates the significant shift to a commercial society in England in the mid- to late sixteenth rather than the eighteenth century as is more common and shows that it precipitates a shift in conceptions

of society as unified through not just large, abstract concepts such as Christian love but also myriad individual economic transactions.

37. See Charles Herle, *Wisdomes Tripos* (London, 1655), 169–70.
38. See especially Colin Burrow, *Epic Romance, Homer to Milton* (Oxford: Clarendon Press, 1993).
39. See Catherine Belsey, *The Subject of Tragedy: Identity and Difference in Renaissance Drama* (London: Methuen, 1985) and Francis Barker, *The Tremulous Private Body: Essays on Subjection* (Ann Arbor: University of Michigan Press, [1984] 1995). See also Katharine Eisaman Maus, *Inwardness and Theater in the English Renaissance* (Chicago: University of Chicago Press, 1995), which, in keeping with the American New Historicist tradition with which it aligns itself, locates the emergence of the interiorized self on the Renaissance stage.
40. Stephen Greenblatt, *Renaissance Self-Fashioning: From More to Shakespeare* (Chicago: University of Chicago Press, 1980), 120, 203.
41. Tuck, *Philosophy and Government,* esp. 346–7. Worden, in *The Sound of Virtue,* makes the simpler but perhaps equally significant argument that one of Sidney's strongest responses to the corruption of the court (he understands this corruption as historical fact rather than as an aspect of ideology) is his recourse to a Stoic "inward self" (335–8).
42. See especially Pierre Force, *Self-Interest before Adam Smith: A Genealogy of Economic Science* (Cambridge: Cambridge University Press, 2003); for the rationalization of the economic sphere see Joyce Oldham Appleby, *Economic Thought and Ideology in Seventeenth-Century England* (Princeton, NJ: Princeton University Press, 1978); and Robert B. Ekelund Jr. and Robert D. Tollison, *Politicized Economies: Monarchy, Monopoly, and Mercantilism* (College Station: Texas A&M Press, 1997).
43. Worden's insensitivity to generic history leads him to find Sidney's treatment of providence at the end of *Arcadia* "thin" and "uncertain" (*Sound of Virtue,* 367); I would counter that Sidney's careful refusal either to embrace providence or to dispense with it signifies both as a break with convention and a brilliant ironization of it.
44. Smith, *Literature and Revolution,* 239.

CHAPTER 1

1. It is not known whether Sidney or his sister initiated these changes; see Jean Robertson's useful summary of *Arcadia*'s composition and publication history in her introduction to *The Countess of Pembroke's Arcadia (The Old Arcadia)* (Oxford: Clarendon Press, 1973).
2. Philip Sidney, *The Countess of Pembroke's Arcadia (the Old Arcadia)* (*OA*), 47; the matching scene in *The Countess of Pembroke's Arcadia (The New Arcadia)* (*NA*) is 112.

3. Here and in the text that follows I quote from *OA*, 406.
4. To clarify, although Musidorus's rape and Pyrocles' sex with Philoclea are removed from the 1593 edition, the ending of this edition is identical to that of *OA*. Perhaps Sidney would have altered Euarchus's judgment of the princes had he finished revising the romance, but even in *NA*, events in the third book (Pyrocles' night with Philoclea, though chaste; Musidorus's escape with Pamela after defeating Amphialus and Anaxius) are sufficient to merit the charge of "ravishment." In any case, given the extensive circulation of *OA* in manuscript, we are probably justified in assuming that Sidney's inheritors (certainly Wroth, at the very least) knew how Sidney had motivated Euarchus's judgment the first time around.
5. See *The Rape of Lucrece*, lines 731–2, in which after raping Lucrece Tarquin creeps away from her "Bearing away the wound that nothing healeth, / The scar that will, despite of cure, remain" (*The Norton Shakespeare*, ed. Stephen Greenblatt, Walter Cohen, Jean E. Howard, and Katharine Eisaman Maus [New York: W. W. Norton, 1997]). In his self-defense at the end of *Arcadia* Pyrocles asserts that if "in fine I offered force" to Philoclea, "love offered more force to me" (*OA*, 394).
6. For a concise expression of this paradox in ancient Greek thought as it was inherited by the Renaissance see Rebecca Bushnell, *Tragedies of Tyrants: Political Thought and Theater in the English Renaissance* (Ithaca, NY: Cornell University Press, 1990), 9–36. See also Frank Whigham, "Sexual and Social Mobility in *The Duchess of Malfi*," *PMLA* 100, no. 2 (1985): 167–86.
7. My sense of Sidney's purposiveness here differs from Blair Worden's reading (*The Sound of Virtue: Philip Sidney's* Arcadia *and Elizabethan Politics* [New Haven, CT: Yale University Press, 1996], 367) and also from that of Jean Robertson, editor of *OA*, who believes, following W. A. Ringler, editor of Sidney's *Poems* (Oxford, 1962), that the disregard of Euarchus's judgment on the princes after Basilius wakes up at the end of *Arcadia* must have constituted a "serious flaw" even to Sidney's own eyes, and that it is therefore likely that the Countess of Pembroke was following her brother's posthumous wishes in expurgating Musidorus's attempt at rape and the sex between Philoclea and Pyrocles for the 1593 edition of *NA*. Even if the desire to change these details was originally Sidney's, which there is no way of knowing, it seems unlikely to me that the ending of such a carefully crafted narrative as *OA* was a mistake, especially given the story of the potion that follows—nor that it could have been read as one in the seventeenth century, given Sidney's reputation and also, as I argue here, the romance's context in politic ideology. See Robertson, "Textual Introduction" to *OA*, lxi–ii.
8. The term "ravishment" in the early modern period does not always connote sexual intercourse and only sometimes, as here, connotes an action contravening the woman's will. See Carolyn Sale,

"Representing Lavinia: The (In)Significance of Women's Consent in Legal Discourses of Rape and Ravishment and Shakespeare's *Titus Andronicus*," in *Women, Violence, and English Renaissance Literature*, ed. Linda Woodbridge and Sharon Beehler (Tempe, AZ: Arizona Center for Medieval and Renaissance Studies, 2003), 1–28, esp. 4–8.

9. Miguel de Cervantes Saavedra, *Don Quixote*, trans. J. M. Cohen (New York: Penguin Books, 1950), 434.
10. Mary Wroth, *The First Part of the Countess of Montgomery's Urania*, ed. Josephine A. Roberts (Binghamton, NY: Renaissance English Text Society, 1995), 254.
11. See Jon Whitman, *Allegory: The Dynamics of an Ancient and Medieval Technique* (Cambridge, MA: Harvard University Press, 1987), 263, for a discussion of the etymology of the word "allegory."
12. Francis Bacon, *De Augmentis Scientarum*, trans. James Spedding, in *The Works of Francis Bacon*, ed. James Spedding, Robert Leslie Ellis, and Douglas Denon Heath (London: Longman, 1857–74), 4:315 (bk. 2, chap. 13).
13. Henry Peacham, *The Garden of Eloquence* (London, 1593), facs. ed., William G. Crane (Gainesville, FL: Scholars' Facsimiles and Reprints, 1954)], 13–14.
14. George Puttenham, *The Arte of English Poesie* (London, 1589), facs. ed. (New York: Da Capo Press and Theatrum Orbis Terrarum Ltd., 1971), 114–15, 155.
15. Quintilian, *Institutio oratoria*, trans. Donald A. Russell (Cambridge, MA: Harvard University Press, Loeb Classical Library, 2001), 3:451 (8.6.44); for irony see 3:457 (8.6.55). Gordon Teskey, in "Irony, Allegory, and Metaphysical Decay," *PMLA* 109, no. 3 (1994): 397–408, makes the nice suggestion that to make sense of the relation between allegory and irony here we should imagine a clock, the smaller hand declining progressively away from twelve as sense declines from words until at six o'clock sense becomes exactly Quintilian's "contrary thing" (398).
16. Wayne C. Booth, *A Rhetoric of Irony* (Chicago: University of Chicago Press, 1974), esp. chap. 1, "The Ways of Stable Irony," 1–31. See page 93 for Booth's opposition of his own notion of stable irony to Kierkegaard's and the German Romantics' conception of irony as "absolute infinite negativity."
17. Samuel Taylor Coleridge, *The Statesman's Manual, The Collected Works of Samuel Taylor Coleridge*, ed. R. J. White (Princeton, NJ: Princeton University Press, 1972), 6:3–52, 30. See also "Allegory," in "Lectures of 1818," *Coleridge's Miscellaneous Criticism*, ed. Thomas Middleton Raysor (Cambridge, MA: Harvard University Press, 1936), 28–32.
18. Angus Fletcher, *Allegory, the Theory of a Symbolic Mode* (Ithaca, NY: Cornell University Press, 1964); see esp. chap. 1, "The Daemonic Agent," 25–69. For this formulation of Fletcher's thought I am

indebted to Victoria Kahn, *Machiavellian Rhetoric: From the Counter-Reformation to Milton* (Princeton, NJ: Princeton University Press, 1994), esp. 41–2.

19. Edmund Spenser, *The Faerie Queene,* ed. A. C. Hamilton (New York: Longman, 1977), 2.12.86–9.
20. J. G. A. Pocock, *The Machiavellian Moment: Florentine Political Thought and the Atlantic Republican Tradition* (Princeton, NJ: Princeton University Press, 1975), viii.
21. Ibid., 350 (England does not manifest this polarity because of its Protestant conviction of election) and 371 (legitimation of authority over political action).
22. Nathaniel Ingelo, *Bentivolio and Urania, in Six Books,* 2nd ed. (London, 1669), B2r. The first four books were published under the same title in 1660, and the fifth and sixth books, or "Second Part," were first published separately in 1664.
23. I am indebted to Andrew Zurcher for this formulation of habitual practice in humanism.
24. Ingelo, *Bentivolio and Urania,* 91.
25. Not surprisingly, most critics have read Wroth's treatment of inconstancy mainly along gendered lines and within the relatively self-contained context of what has been called the Sidney family romance. See esp. Gary Waller, *The Sidney Family Romance: Mary Wroth, William Herbert, and the Early Modern Construction of Gender* (Detroit, MI: Wayne State University Press, 1993); Maureen Quilligan, "Lady Mary Wroth: Female Authority and the Family Romance," in *Unfolded Tales: Essays on Renaissance Romance,* ed. George M. Logan and Gordon Teskey (Ithaca, NY: Cornell University Press, 1989), 257–280; and Naomi J. Miller, *Changing the Subject: Mary Wroth and Figurations of Gender in Early Modern England* (Lexington: University Press of Kentucky, 1996). More recent work on subjectivity in Wroth has tended to focus on her sonnet sequence "Pamphilia to Amphilanthus," first published at the end of *Urania;* see, for example, Nona Fienberg, "Mary Wroth's Poetics of the Self," *Studies in English Literature* 42, no. 1 (2002): 121–36. To my knowledge there is no work on *Urania* that treats the formal structure of roman à clef as a mode of moral-philosophical inquiry as I attempt to do here, although recently critics have begun to argue for the compatibility of biographical with aesthetic as well as political approaches to Wroth; see particularly Christina Luckyj, "The Politics of Genre in Early Women's Writing: The Case of Lady Mary Wroth," *English Studies in Canada* 27, no. 3 (2001): 253–83, esp. 273–5; Marion Wynne-Davies, "'So Much Worth': Autobiographical Narratives in the Work of Lady Mary Wroth," in *Betraying Our Selves: Forms of Self-Representation in Early Modern English Texts,* ed. Henk Dragstra and Sheila Ottway (New York: St. Martin's Press, 2000), 76–93; and Michael G. Brennan, "Creating Female Authorship in the Early Seventeenth Century: Ben Jonson and Lady Mary Wroth,"

in *Women's Writing and the Circulation of Ideas: Manuscript Publication in England, 1550–1800,* ed. George L. Justice and Nathan Tinker (Cambridge: Cambridge University Press, 2002), 73–93.

26. My sense of constancy's qualified nature in *Urania* runs counter to Mary Ellen Lamb's argument (in *Gender and Authorship in the Sidney Circle* [Madison: University of Wisconsin Press, 1990]) for the romance's consistent championship of constancy as a form of heroism.
27. See Rudolf Kirk, introduction to Justus Lipsius, *Two Bookes of Constancie* (New Brunswick, NJ: Rutgers University Press, 1939), 9.
28. See *The Annals,* in *The Complete Works of Tacitus,* trans. Alfred John Church and William Jackson Brodribb, ed. Moses Hadas (New York: Random House, 1942), 393 (15.64), where the famously constant Paulina "sought the glory of sharing her husband's death" as long as she feared Nero.
29. See Richard Tuck, *Philosophy and Government 1572–1651* (Cambridge: Cambridge University Press, 1993), 63, and Martin Dzelzainis, "Bacon's 'Of Simulation and Dissimulation," in *A Companion to English Renaissance Literature and Culture,* ed. Michael Hattaway (Oxford: Blackwell, 2000), 235.
30. See Andrew Shifflett, *Stoicism, Politics, and Literature in the Age of Milton: War and Peace Reconciled* (Cambridge: Cambridge University Press, 1998), esp. 24–8.
31. James I, *The Basilikon Doron of James VI,* ed. James Craigie (Edinburgh: William Blackwood and Sons, 1944), 156.
32. Greenham and Hall quoted in Gilles D. Monsarrat, *The Light from the Porch: Stoicism and English Renaissance Literature* (Paris: Didier-Erudition, 1984), 104–5. Monsarrat gives many other examples of English disapproval of Stoicism (81–108). See also Gordon Braden, *Renaissance Tragedy and the Senecan Tradition: Anger's Privilege* (New Haven, CT: Yale University Press, 1985), 93.
33. Thomas Wyatt, "They Flee from Me," in *Collected Poems,* ed. Joost Daalder (London: Oxford University Press, 1975).
34. Bernard Williams, "Utilitarianism and Moral Self-Indulgence," in *Moral Luck: Philosophical Papers 1973–1980* (Cambridge: Cambridge University Press, 1981), 45–6.
35. Sigmund Freud, "On Narcissism: An Introduction," in *The Standard Edition of the Complete Psychological Works of Sigmund Freud,* ed. James Strachey and Anna Freud (London: The Hogarth Press, 1957), 14:73–102, 93.
36. Annabel Patterson, *Censorship and Interpretation: The Conditions of Writing and Reading in Early Modern England* (Madison: University of Wisconsin Press, 1984), 11 (emphasis Patterson's).
37. See particularly Christina Luckyj, *"A moving rhetoricke": Gender and Silence in Early Modern England* (Manchester: Manchester University Press, 2002).

38. Thomas Luxon, *Literal Figures: Puritan Allegory and the Reformation Crisis in Representation* (Chicago: University of Chicago Press, 1995), 12. Cranmer is quoted on page 6.
39. Paul de Man, "The Rhetoric of Temporality," in *Blindness and Insight: Essays in the Rhetoric of Contemporary Criticism* (Minneapolis: University of Minnesota Press, 1983), 187–228, 196.

Chapter 2

1. Vladimir Propp, "Oedipus in the Light of Folklore," trans. Polly Coote, in *Oedipus: A Folklore Casebook,* ed. Lowell Edmunds and Alan Dundes (Madison: University of Wisconsin Press, 1995 [1983; essay first published 1944]), 76–121, 110–12.
2. Fredric Jameson, *The Political Unconscious: Narrative as a Socially Symbolic Act* (Ithaca, NY: Cornell University Press, 1981), 118, emphasis Jameson's.
3. See, for instance, Maureen Quilligan, "Lady Mary Wroth: Female Authority and the Family Romance," in *Unfolded Tales: Essays on Renaissance Romance,* ed. George M. Logan and Gordon Teskey (Ithaca, NY: Cornell University Press, 1989), 257.
4. George MacKenzie, *Aretina; Or, The Serious Romance* (Edinburgh, 1660), 6. MacKenzie does not seem to have published a second part, though he promises one in the preface and ends his narrative in the middle of an episode.
5. Michel de Montaigne, *Complete Essays of Montaigne,* trans. Donald M. Frame (Stanford, CA: Stanford University Press, 1958), 291, in 2:8, "Of the Affection of Fathers for their Children": "Heliodorus, that good bishop of Tricca, preferred to lose the dignity, the profit, and the piety of so venerable a prelacy than lose his daughter—a daughter who still lives on, very nice, but for all that perhaps a little too curiously and loosely tricked out, and in too amorous a fashion, for the daughter of a churchman and a priest."
   Robert Burton, *The Anatomy of Melancholy* (New York: Da Capo Press, 1971 [Oxford, 1621]), Third Partition, Section 1, Memb. 1, Subs. 1, 496: "*Heliodorus* a Bishop, penned a love story of *Theagines* and *Cariclia,* and when some *Cato's* of his time reprehended him for it, choase rather saith *Nicephorus,* to leave his *bishopricke* then his booke."
6. There is another English translation, by William Lisle, published in 1638. Sidney mentions *Aethiopika* twice in his *Apology for Poetry;* see Philip Sidney, *An Apology for Poetry,* ed. Forrest G. Robinson (New York: Macmillan, 1970), 15, 21.
7. For Ovid's rendition of the Andromeda story, see *Metamorphoses,* trans. Frank Justus Miller, 3rd ed. (Cambridge, MA: Harvard University Press, Loeb Classical Library, 1977), 1:225–27 (4.663–764). Gazing down at the chained Andromeda, says Ovid, Perseus "would have thought her a marble statue" (227, line 675); he himself draws the

parallel between himself and the monster that Ariosto later calls an Orc, exclaiming, "those are not the chains you deserve to wear, but rather those that link fond lovers together!" (227, lines 678–9). Ariosto's versions of the story are in *Orlando Furioso* 10.92–11.9 (Ruggiero) and 11.30–77 (Orlando) (Ludovico Ariosto, *Orlando Furioso,* trans. Barbara Reynolds, 2 vols. [New York: Penguin Books, 1975]).

8. Eric Aversa, "Clorinda's Black Armor: Sacrifice and Substitution in *Gerusalemme Liberata* and Heliodorus's *Ethiopian Story,*" *Romance Languages Annual* 6 (1994): 208–12, 209. See also Richard Hunter's discussion of this argument in "The *Aethiopika* of Heliodorus: Beyond Interpretation?" in *Studies in Heliodorus,* ed. Richard Hunter (Cambridge: The Cambridge Philological Society, 1998), 40–59, 58. For Girard, see *Violence and the Sacred,* trans. Patrick Gregory (Baltimore: Johns Hopkins University Press, 1977), esp. chaps. 1 (1–38), 2 (39–67), and 10 (250–73).
9. *An Aethiopian History,* trans. Thomas Underdowne (New York: AMS Press, 1967 [1587]); "first fruits" 263; "father of the people" 273.
10. Ibid., 290; Moses Hadas, in his modern translation, renders the phrase "of the race of the Sun" (*An Ethiopian Romance,* trans. Moses Hadas [Philadelphia: University of Pennsylvania Press, 1999 (1957)], 277).
11. At the end of the romance King Hydaspes of Ethiopia extends extraordinary generosity toward his rival king Oroondates, refusing to enter the lands he has won from him in battle and deciding to return them to the aggressor— itself, of course, a metaphoric version of chastity.
12. Colin Burrow, as I suggested briefly in the introduction, argues that early modern romance turned increasingly away from the medieval romance ethos of pity (itself often a misreading of classic piety) (*Epic Romance: Homer to Milton* [Oxford: Clarendon Press, 1993], 61) back toward epic pietas rooted in righteous anger, a movement he sees as culminating with Milton. Burrow reads pity as "an attempt to comfort [others'] wretchedness" (61), which from the point of view of the seventeenth-century return to epic looks increasingly soft and even weak, and he sees *Orlando Furioso* as an exemplary text in this regard, its heroes driven by "compassionate amorousness" rather than epic's "centralized devotion to an imperial cause" (56, 53). Oddly, Burrow conflates this "compassionate amorousness" with attempted rape (see for instance 56, on Ruggiero's attempt to rape Angelica), the distinction between which, as I have just argued, Ariosto's irony makes very clear. Contra Burrow, I would argue that in Ariosto pity is already demystified, not as weak but rather as self-interested. In the historical narrative I am tracing in this book, this failing of pity dovetails with other aspects of politic ideology to give rise not to epic pietas, but rather in the romances I read to sustained ethical speculation about the relation between love or pity and self-interest. This is not to say that epic pietas was not reasserted in such seventeenth-century writers as

Milton, but rather that romance also took other routes, and that those routes were influenced by a line of argument in such figures as Ariosto that Burrow's narrative does not take account of.

13. John Milton, *Areopagitica*, in *The Riverside Milton*, ed. Roy Flannagan (Boston: Houghton Mifflin, 1998), 997–1024, 1006.
14. See Shakespeare's *A Midsummer Night's Dream*, in which Theseus indirectly asserts his dominion over the Amazon Hippolyta by characterizing Hermia's threatened punishment of being relegated to a convent where she will have contact only with women as a fate almost worse than death: "For aye to be in shady cloister mewed, / To live a barren sister all your life, / Chanting faint hymns to the cold fruitless moon." *A Midsummer Night's Dream*, in *The Norton Shakespeare*, ed. Stephen Greenblatt, Walter Cohen, Jean E. Howard, and Katharine Eisaman Maus (New York: W. W. Norton, 1997), 1.1.71–3.
15. See Josephine A. Roberts, introduction to *Urania* (Binghamton, NY: Renaissance English Text Society, 1995), vii–cxx, lxxii.
16. James Nohrnberg, *The Analogy of* The Faerie Queene (Princeton, NJ: Princeton University Press, 1976), 432.
17. John Webster, *The Duchess of Malfi*, ed. Elizabeth M. Brennan, 2nd ed. (New York: W. W. Norton, 1993), 1.2.44–5. Ferdinand and his brother the Cardinal are loath to see the Duchess's material wealth leave the sibling unit, but Ferdinand famously also cannot seem to stop imagining his sister in bed with other men.
18. Frank Whigham, "Sexual and Social Mobility in *The Duchess of Malfi*," *PMLA* 100, no. 2 (1985): 167–86, 169.
19. Philip Sidney, *The Countess of Pembroke's Arcadia (The New Arcadia)*, ed. Victor Skretkowicz (Oxford: Clarendon Press, 1987), 295. In response to Basilius's retirement his loyal counselor Philanax argues that Basilius's decision to withdraw his daughters to Arcadia where he can "keep them both unmarried" and "kill the joy of posterity" is a form of "unnaturalness" that "the god which is god of nature doth never teach;" "even the same mind hold I," he concludes, "touching your banishing them from company, lest I know not what strange loves should follow" (21–2).
20. Richard McCabe, *Incest, Drama, and Nature's Law 1550–1700* (Cambridge: Cambridge University Press, 1993), 30–3.
21. Ibid., 231.
22. Michel de Montaigne, *Essays*, trans. John Florio, ed. L. C. Harmer (London, 1912, rpt. 1965), 1:211.
23. Josephine Roberts, in her edition of *Urania*, emphasizes the story's dark tone, speculating that it has its "psychological genesis" in Wroth's "brooding" over her children with Pembroke, who conceivably, says Roberts, during their upbringing within the extended Sidney family might have become vulnerable to the same sin (781n524.11–12).
24. Early in the narrative Parselius falls in love with Urania, but he abandons her in the first enchantment because the tainted water has made

him forgetful. He marries Dalinea almost immediately afterward, in a private ceremony, then feels so guilty that he leaves her, pregnant, to find Urania again. When Urania is reborn, by being thrown off the cliff, into love for Steriamus, this relieves Parselius of his first obligation, but he does not then return to his wife, and Dalinea must bring her baby to court to prove her marriage and force her husband's hand.

25. Quilligan, "Lady Mary Wroth," 272.
26. Gayle Rubin, "The Traffic in Women: Notes on the Political Economy of Sex," in *Toward an Anthropology of Women*, ed. Rayna R. Reiter (New York: Monthly Review Press, 1975), 157–209.
27. See René Girard, "Myth and Ritual in Shakespeare: *A Midsummer Night's Dream*," in *Textual Strategies: Perspectives in Post-Structuralist Criticism*, ed. Josue V. Harari (Ithaca, NY: Cornell University Press, 1979), 189–212, and *A Theater of Envy: William Shakespeare* (New York: Oxford University Press, 1991).
28. For a brilliant extended reading of incest in *Measure for Measure* along different lines from my own, see Marc Shell, *The End of Kinship:* Measure for Measure, *Incest, and the Idea of Universal Siblinghood* (Stanford, CA: Stanford University Press, 1988).
29. *Measure for Measure*, in *The Norton Shakespeare*, 3.1.140.
30. Both the latter two translations were apparently at the request of the king; Charles may have wanted another translation in 1628, during the Petition of Right controversy, because he felt that the romance supported the prerogative of the monarch (though later Coleridge would celebrate *Argenis* for its republican sympathies). The verse translations in both the Long and Le Grys translations are by Thomas May, who was later to write a history of the Civil War (see *The Calendar of State Papers, Domestic*, 1627–8, February 21, 1628, for May's translation). *Argenis* was phenomenally popular on the continent, and in its first decade was translated into most European languages. Several epitomes and continuations exist (among them Nicolas Coeffeteau's epitome *Histoire de Poliarque et d'Argenis* [Paris, 1624]; Judith Man's English translation of Coeffeteau, *An Epitome of the History of Faire Argenis and Polyarchus* [London, 1640]; and Gabriel Bugnot's continuation *Archombrotus et Theopompus* [Rotterdam, 1669]). For Jonson's translation and the fire in which it burned, see *The Calendar of State Papers, Domestic*, 1619–23, May 11, 1622. *Argenis* has just received its first modern edition, in Latin with a lightly modernized version of Long's English translation on facing pages (*Argenis*, ed. and trans. Mark Riley and Dorothy Pritchard Huber, 2 vols. [Tempe, AZ: Arizona Center for Medieval and Renaissance Studies, 2004]). I have chosen to quote mainly from the Le Grys translation in this book, although Long's went into a second edition, because Le Grys follows the Latin original rather than adding, as Long does, the chapter divisions that first appear in the 1622 French translation,

and because Le Grys's translation is, if less elegant, simpler and more direct in following the Latin than Long's. For a discussion of the relative merits of the two translations see Riley and Huber, introduction to their edition, 1:31–3.

31. Le Grys, in the letter to King Charles prefacing his translation, emphasizes the romance's Englishness, citing "the Authors discent: his being so long bred under Your Royall Father." "For [although] it had a forraine birth," says Le Grys, "it was first conceived in this your Kingdome." John Barclay, *John Barclay His Argenis,* trans. Robert Le Grys (London, 1628), Dedication "to his Most Sacred Majesty," A2v. Although she mistakenly notes that Barclay "lived all his life in France" (180), Annabel Patterson responds to A. C. Baugh's judgment that *Argenis* "hardly belongs to English literature" with the objection that "we need to ask whether the phenomenon of three English translations of the *Argenis* in eight years can really be dismissed in this way" (*Censorship and Interpretation: The Conditions of Writing and Reading in Early Modern England* [Madison: University of Wisconsin Press, 1984], 183).

32. William Barclay, professor of law at Pont-a-Mousson in Lorraine, was the author of *De Regno,* a mainly historical treatise on Buchanan and Boucher. John, born about 1586 in Scotland to William and his French wife, Anne de Malleviller, had a mainly Jesuit education in France. After arriving at James I's court he wrote a *Carmen Gratulatorium* to James and published several indignant poems on the Gunpowder Plot, which along with other efforts to gain patronage resulted in his being made a Gentleman of the King's Bedchamber in 1606. For the next decade he received steady pensions from James and from the Earl of Salisbury, both of which he sought to increase, apparently unsuccessfully, on several occasions (see *Calendar of State Papers, Domestic,* 1603–10, January 7, 1610; December 21, 1611; Historical Manuscripts Commission, Calendar of the Manuscripts of the Most Honourable the Marquess of Salisbury [London, 1965], January 26, 1606–7). In 1605 Barclay published the second edition of the first part (no first edition survives) and in 1607 the second part of an autobiographical satire in Latin titled *Euphormionis Lusinini Satyricon* (*Euphormio's Satyricon*), which went through at least fifty editions in Europe before 1700. The pointedness of its social criticism inspired so much protest that Barclay had to write an *Apologia Euphormionis pro Se* in 1610. Barclay was in England with only a few interruptions, most for diplomatic missions, until 1616, when he left to go to the court of Pope Paul V. He probably began to write *Argenis* in 1618, and died only a few weeks after its publication in 1621. See David Harris Willson, "James I and his Literary Assistants," *Huntington Library Quarterly* 8 (1944–5): 35–57, 45; and David A. Fleming, introduction to *Euphormionis Lusinini Satyricon,* ed. David A. Fleming (Nieuwkoop, 1973), ix–xiv.

33. For some tantalizing evidence, see Albert Collignon's remark that he found several requests for keys to *Argenis* in the correspondence of Rubens, who evidently possessed one (Collignon, *Notes historiques, litteraires et bibliographiques sur* L'Argenis *de Jean Barclay* [Paris: Berger-Levrault & Co., 1902], 115).
34. One way to read Barclay's romance is as the *New Arcadia* minus the pastoral, what Sidney might have produced if he had flatly declared himself a courtier writing a popular fiction-cum-treatise on statecraft and political authority. Not surprisingly, without the pastoral influence *Argenis* also has less of *Arcadia*'s subtle irony; and thus, concomitantly, politic modes of thinking, rather than being the hidden agenda behind the surface romance plot, become entirely explicit. This is quite like Wroth's revision of Sidney, which I described in the last chapter as making manifest the notion of agency Sidney always portrays as a secret, except that for Wroth the politic becomes an object of moral investigation while in Barclay it functions largely descriptively.
35. For a list of Heliodoran conventions popular in Renaissance, particularly Italian, narrative, see Clotilde Bertoni and Massimo Fusillo, "Heliodorus Parthenopaeus: The *Aethiopika* in Baroque Naples," in Hunter, *Studies in Heliodorus,* 157–181, 157. The jesting, slightly adversarial relation between Arsidas and Gobrias, and Arsidas's tendency to put the responsibility for the tale's events with Gobrias rather than history, closely recall the encounter between Heliodorus's Cnemon and Calasiris.
36. Chariclea, as I noted before, glides untouched above the series of would-be rivals to Theagenes, all comic in their social insufficiency; Thisbe, the only young woman in the romance besides Chariclea, functions in her role as prostitute as Chariclea's negative double rather than any kind of rival; and the Ethiopian king Hydaspes, in the end, as if to show he is above the petty competitions that drive lesser kings, magnanimously restores to his rival Oroondates the territories he has just won from him in battle.
37. Musidorus is older, a bit more virile, and the prince of the relatively minor kingdom of Thessaly, while his cousin Pyrocles is younger, sweeter, and heir to the powerful Euarchus of Macedon, and hence Musidorus has claim to Basilius's heir Pamela, a princess who exudes "majesty," while Pyrocles can be content with the surpassing "sweetness" of the younger and less politically significant Philoclea.
38. While Archombrotus "doth many times celebrate *Poliarchus* his good hap in such a Love," says the narrator, "he began to like and admire those things, which he had before, without being moved by them, quietly beheld . . . This he considered not, as one that was falling in love, but as idle; yet not disproportioned, or unreasonable desires. Thus by degrees he was taken" (90).
39. *The Winter's Tale,* in *The Norton Shakespeare,* 1.2.77–88.
40. Polixenes and Leontes, as Polixenes says, are engaged before they become aware of women in "changes" (i.e., exchanges, 1.2.70). They

are thus in a symbolic sense not entirely chaste, but in their identity with each other they can enjoy a fluidity between the positions of subject and object, a fluidity necessarily disrupted by the arrival of woman as object, something to achieve or own.

41. Richard Brathwaite, *Panthalia, or the Royal Romance* (London, 1659), 29.
42. G. W. Pigman III, "Versions of Imitation in the Renaissance," *Renaissance Quarterly* 33, no. 1 (1980): 1–32, 23.
43. Jean Bodin, *Method for the Easy Comprehension of History,* trans. Beatrice Reynolds (New York: Octagon Books, 1966), 37; Percy Herbert, *Certaine Conceptions, or Considerations of Sir Percy Herbert, upon the Strange change of Peoples Dispositions and Actions in these latter Times* (London, 1652), 166–7.
44. See, for example, Cnemon's account of his "passing malicious" stepmother Demeneta, who tries to secure both father and son as sexual partners and in rage at Cnemon's refusal accuses him of a jealous attack on her pregnant body (presumably carrying a potentially threatening substitute heir), in response to which his father disinherits him (Underdowne, *An Aethiopian History,* 17–22); *NA's* account of Plangus's banishment by his evil stepmother, Queen of Iberia (*NA,* 215–22); and *Urania*'s narrative of the dire influence Prince Antissius's wicked stepmother has over his father the king and Antissius's own disinheriting (51–8). Aphra Behn's post-Restoration romance *Oroonoko, Or the Royal Slave* offers a fascinating variation on this story in its narrative of Oroonoko's elderly grandfather's knowing appropriation of his grandson's true love, Imoinda, an inversion of natural succession that signifies the corruption and exhaustion of Coromantien culture.
45. In the Clavis included in Le Grys' 1628 translation, for the most part cribbed from the "Discursus in Io. Barclaii Argenidem" that appeared in many Latin editions, Le Grys (like William Heywood after him in the Key that prefaces the second edition of Kingsmill Long's English translation [London, 1636], doubtless owing to the same source) finds it absurd to conclude that Barclay could have meant both Poliarchus and Archombrotus to represent Henry of Navarre, and conjectures that if Archombrotus is *not* merely a "supposed one" he may represent the duc d'Alencon (487).
46. See Rebecca Bushnell, *Tragedies of Tyrants: Political Thought and Theater in the English Renaissance* (Ithaca, NY: Cornell University Press, 1990), 1–5.

CHAPTER 3

1. James Harrington, *The Commonwealth of Oceana,* in *The Political Works of James Harrington,* ed. J. G. A. Pocock (Cambridge: Cambridge University Press, 1977), 198.

2. For Boyle's "raving" see *The Early Essays and Ethics of Robert Boyle,* ed. John T. Harwood (Carbondale: Southern Illinois University Press, 1991), xlviii–xlix.
3. John Barclay, *John Barclay His Argenis,* trans. Robert Le Grys (London, 1628), 131.
4. Thomas Hobbes, *Leviathan,* ed. Richard Tuck (Cambridge: Cambridge University Press, 1991), 16 (bk. 1, chap. 2).
5. Charles Herle, *Wisdomes Tripos* (London, 1655), 169. See J. A. W. Gunn, *Politics and the Public Interest in the Seventeenth Century* (London: Routledge and Kegan Paul, 1969), 37–41, for a discussion of English texts directly influenced by the work of Rohan. There is a modern edition of Rohan with a substantial introduction detailing Rohan's significance in political thought: *De l'intérêst des princes et des Etats de la chrétienté,* ed. Christian Lazzeri (Paris: Presses universitaires de France, 1995); I quote throughout from Henry Hunt's 1640 translation.
6. For Rohan's contribution to reason of state theory in France, see William F. Church, *Richelieu and Reason of State* (Princeton, NJ: Princeton University Press, 1972), esp. 349–56; Friedrich Meinecke, *Machiavellism: The Doctrine of Raison d'État and Its Place in Modern History,* trans. Douglas Scott (New Haven, CT: Yale University Press, 1957), 162–80.
7. For interest and individualism see esp. Gunn, *Politics and the Public Interest;* for the association of interest with the ideology of England's hereditary elites, despite its more modern associations, see Joyce Oldham Appleby, *Economic Thought and Ideology in Seventeenth-Century England* (Princeton, NJ: Princeton University Press, 1978), 10–11, and Stephen Holmes, "The Secret History of Self-Interest," in *Beyond Self-Interest,* ed. Jane J. Mansbridge (Chicago: University of Chicago Press, 1990), 267–286, 276.
8. Gunn, *Politics and the Public Interest,* 49. For the growth of factional, adversary politics in the 1640s see Mark Kishlansky, "The Emergence of Adversary Politics in the Long Parliament," *Journal of Modern History* 49, no. 4 (1977): 617–40.
9. Gunn, *Politics and the Public Interest,* 49, 15.
10. John Bramhall, *Castigations of Mr. Hobbes* and *The Catching of Leviathan* (London, 1658), 519.
11. Gunn, *Politics and the Public Interest,* 127–9.
12. Richard Brathwaite, *The Two Lancashire Lovers: or The Excellent History of Philocles and Doriclea,* ed. Henry D. Janzen (Ottawa: Dovehouse Editions, 1998), 216.
13. Francis Finch, *Friendship* (London, 1654), 23; Herle, *Wisdomes Tripos,* 25, 24.
14. Owen Feltham, *Resolves: A Duple Century,* 7th ed. (London: 1647), 136. For the publication history see the introduction to *Resolves, Divine, Moral, and Political,* ed. James Cumming, 2nd ed. (London:

John Hatchard and Son, 1820), which is unable to date the first edition but surmises that it is probably not more than twelve months earlier than the second and third editions, both of which are dated 1628.

15. Percy Herbert, *Certaine Conceptions, or Considerations of Sir Percy Herbert, upon the Strange change of Peoples Dispositions and Actions in these latter Times* (London, 1652), 139.
16. For "the application of self-interest to the psychology of individuals," see Pierre Force, *Self-Interest before Adam Smith: A Genealogy of Economic Science* (Cambridge: Cambridge University Press, 2003), 136; see also Force's discussion of the French development of the concept of disinterest as the possession of motives other than self-interest in the latter half of the seventeenth century and the subsequent English adoption of this idea on page 183. Force may be right to locate the origin of the term "disinterest" in 1660s France (although see my discussion of disinterest in Robert Boyle's *Theodora* below); his idea that the emergence of the concept marks also the emergence of the idea that it is virtuous to have motives other than self-interest, however, seems to me belied by the treatment of interest in English romance. For interest in 1690s English thought see also Appleby, *Economic Thought and Ideology*, 190–1.
17. Richard Hooker, *Of the Laws of Ecclesiastical Polity* [1593], ed. Georges Edelen (Cambridge, MA: Belknap Press, 1977), 1.3.5 (69).
18. Thomas Hobbes, *Philosophical Rudiments Concerning Government and Society*, published as *De Cive or the Citizen*, ed. S. P. Lamprecht (New York: Appleton-Century-Crofts, 1949), 1.7 (26).
19. Harrington cites this passage twice, once in the Preliminaries to *Oceana* (1656) (171) and again in *The Prerogative of Popular Government*, in *The Political Works of James Harrington* (1658) (414), a rebuttal of Matthew Wren's attack on the idea of the common interest in *Oceana*.
20. Albert O. Hirschman, *The Passions and the Interests: Political Arguments for Capitalism Before its Triumph* (Princeton, NJ: Princeton University Press, 1977), 50.
21. Marchamont Nedham, *Interest will not Lie. Or, a View of England's True Interest* (London, 1659), 3.
22. Thomas Macaulay quoted in Albert O. Hirschman, "The Concept of Interest: From Euphemism to Tautology," in *Rival Views of Market Society* (New York: Viking, 1986), 35–55, 48. The quote is from Macaulay's review in the *Edinburgh Review*, 1829, of Mill's "economic" theory of politics in his 1820 "Essay on Government." For discussions of interest as tautology, see Jane J. Mansbridge, "The Rise and Fall of Self-Interest in the Explanation of Political Life," in *Beyond Self-Interest*, 3–22, 6; Holmes, "The Secret History of Self-Interest," 269; Force, *Self-Interest before Adam Smith*, 110.

23. Hirschman, "The Concept of Interest," 36; the word "content" is Force's, in his illuminating summary of Hirschman's article (*Self-Interest before Adam Smith*, 110).
24. Force, *Self-Interest before Adam Smith*, 110.
25. Hirschman, *The Passions and the Interests*, 43.
26. Ibid., 20–31.
27. Mansbridge, "The Rise and Fall of Self-Interest," 6.
28. For trade as a zero-sum game in mercantilism, see Lars G. Magnusson, "Mercantilism," in *A Companion to the History of Economic Thought*, ed. Warren J. Samuels, Jeff E. Biddle, and John B. Davis (Malden, MA: Blackwell, 2003), 46–60, 47. On adversary politics, see Kishlansky, "The Emergence of Adversary Politics in the Long Parliament."
29. Craig Muldrew, *The Economy of Obligation: The Culture of Credit and Social Relations in Early Modern England* (New York: St. Martin's Press, 1998), 2–3.
30. See Holmes, "The Secret History of Self-Interest," 269.
31. Craig L. Carr and Michael J. Seidler, "Pufendorf, Sociality, and the Modern State," *History of Political Thought* 17, no. 3 (1996): 354–78, reproduced in facsimile with original page numbers in *Grotius, Pufendorf and Modern Natural Law*, ed. Knud Haakonssen (Brookfield, VT: Ashgate Press, 1999), 377n71. The authors are speaking in particular of the "Prolegomena" to Grotius's *De Jure Belli ac Pacis.*
32. Hugo Grotius, *Of the Law of Warre and Peace with Annotations* [trans. Clement Barksdale] (London, 1654). *De Jure Praedae Commentarius, Commentary on the Law of Prize and Booty*, trans. [of original MS of 1604–5] Gwladys L. Williams with Walter H. Zeydel (Oxford: Clarendon Press, 1950). For a translation and circulation history of *De Jure Belli ac Pacis* see Jacob Ter Meulen, *Liste bibliographique de 76 editions et traductions du* de jure belli ac pacis *de Hugo Grotius* (Leiden: E. J. Brill, 1925), which attributes the first English translation to Clement Barksdale and notes that Grotius refers in his letters to a different English translation circulating earlier. The Barksdale translation is reprinted in 1655 and a new English translation is published in 1682.
33. For a representative sample of scholars on both sides, see Haakonssen, *Grotius, Pufendorf and Modern Natural Law*, especially the following: Robert Shaver, "Grotius on Scepticism and Self-Interest," *Archiv fur Geschichte der Philosophie* 78: 27–47; Richard Tuck, "Grotius, Carneades and Hobbes," *Grotiana* N.S. 4 (1983): 43–62; Carr and Seidler, "Pufendorf, Sociality, and the Modern State"; and J. B. Schneewind, "Pufendorf's Place in the History of Ethics," *Synthese* 72 (1987), 123–55, esp. 139–41. See also Tuck, *Philosophy and Government 1572–1651* (Cambridge: Cambridge University Press, 1993). The argument I summarize from Tuck is in *Philosophy and*

Government, xvi; the formulation of the two questions about self-interest belongs to Henry Sidgwick, *The Methods of Ethics* (Indianapolis, IN: Hackett, 1981), and is quoted and discussed in Shaver, "Grotius on Scepticism," 47.

34. Grotius dispenses with any inconsistency by citing the maxim that to preserve the cargo one must preserve the ship, by which he means, he says, that the good of all by definition includes the good of the individual—not much of an answer to Carneades' famous question, familiar in the Renaissance through the work of Lactantius, about whether upon shipwreck one may preserve one's own life at the absolute expense of another who is weaker. Via Lactantius, Carneades in the Renaissance was considered the proponent of a version of self-interest so absolute that it precluded any system of social justice. See Lucius Caelius Lactantius, *The Works,* trans. William Fletcher (Edinburgh: T. & T. Clark, 1871), 1:328.
35. Probably one model for this book was the anonymous *Traité succinct des varies maximes et estats de l'Europe,* a collection of quotations from Rohan's work that appeared in Paris in 1647; see Lazzeri, introduction to Rohan, *De l'intérêst des princes,* 2.
36. *Politick Maxims and Observations,* trans. H.C.S.T.B. (London, 1654), 31–2.
37. Tuck, *Philosophy and Government,* 62.
38. William Sedgwick, *Justice Upon the Armie Remonstrance* (London, 1648), 11. See also Muldrew, *The Economy of Obligation,* 140, who claims (wrongly, by my account) that virtually all references to interest as self-interest were negative before the end of the eighteenth century (126) but that there was some sense outside of political discourse from the early seventeenth century on of interest as "mutual advantage, the benefit or profit of two or more parties" (140).
39. See esp. Appleby, *Economic Thought and Ideology,* 41, 191, 242 (the conclusion to her book is that "no more powerful notion came out of the seventeenth century than that of a natural order of economic relations impervious to social engineering and political interference," 242); also Magnusson, "Mercantilism," 54; Church, *Richelieu and Reason of State,* 350; and Anthony Brewer, "Pre-Classical Economics in Britain," in Samuels, Biddle, and Davis, *A Companion to the History of Economic Thought,* 78–93, 85.
40. On casuistical thought, see Thomas Wood, *English Casuistical Divinity during the Seventeenth Century* (London: SPCK, 1952); M. W. F. Stone, "The Adoption and Rejection of Aristotelian Moral Philosophy in Reformed 'Casuistry,'" in *Humanism and Early Modern Philosophy,* ed. Jill Kraye and M. W. F. Stone (New York: Routledge, 2000), 59–90; Barbara Donagan, "Casuistry and Allegiance in the English Civil War," in *Writing and Political Engagement in Seventeenth-Century England,* ed. Derek Hirst and Richard Strier (Cambridge: Cambridge University Press, 1999), 89–111.

41. In the *New Dictionary of National Biography* Nigel Smith notes that *Eliana* "has also been ascribed" to Samuel Pordage (c.1631–c.1691). If this attribution is correct, then the trajectory of Pordage's literary career closely followed those of Roger Boyle and John Crowne, who also wrote single romances in the 1650s or during the very early stages of the Restoration and then turned in the 1660s to drama, in Pordage's case heroic tragedies.
42. For the distinction between *l'amour d'élection* and *l'amour d'inclination* and the triumph of *l'amour d'inclination* in midcentury French romance see Mark Bannister, *Privileged Mortals: The French Heroic Novel, 1630–1660* (New York: Oxford University Press, 1983), esp. 72–3, 162–4. Ian Maclean, *Woman Triumphant: Feminism in French Literature, 1610–1652* (Oxford: Clarendon Press, 1977), discusses the association between marriage and *l'amour d'élection* and the shift from *L'Astrée*, 118.
43. The *New Dictionary of National Biography* entry for Bayly does not mention *Herba Parietis*, nor does Bayly or his romance come up in Annabel Patterson, *Censorship and Interpretation: The Conditions of Writing and Reading in Early Modern England* (Madison: University of Wisconsin Press, 1984), Lois Potter, *Secret Rites and Secret Writing: Royalist Literature, 1641–1660* (Cambridge: Cambridge University Press, 1989), or Nigel Smith, *Literature and Revolution in England* (New Haven, CT: Yale University Press, 1994). Paul Salzman, *English Prose Fiction 1558–1700* (Oxford: Clarendon Press, 1985), devotes five lines to the work (288–9).
44. This book by Lewis Bayly was one of two that John Bunyan's first wife brought to their marriage in 1648, with which, as he later noted, he retaught himself to read. See N. H. Keeble, introduction to John Bunyan, *The Pilgrim's Progress*, ed. Keeble (New York: Oxford University Press, 1984).
45. Thomas Bayly, D.D., *Herba Parietis, or, The Wall-Flower* (London, 1650), "To the Reader," no page sigs.
46. Midcentury romance seems to restrict its version of "true" friendship to the aristocracy even more firmly than had its early modern predecessors; see, for example, Anna Weamys's 1651 *Continuation of Sir Philip Sidney's Arcadia,* which demystifies the Strephon-Claius friendship from *Arcadia* by depicting the friends' mendacity and greed in their efforts to obtain Urania for themselves. Patrick Cullen reads this revision as progressive, in that by casting into question the friends' worship of Urania it frees her some space as an independent character, but it also identifies Sidney's pastoral plot more firmly with its "low" origins, restricting disinterested friendship more decisively than Sidney had as a possibility only for princes. See Anna Weamys, *A Continuation of Sir Philip Sidney's* Arcadia, ed. Patrick Colborn Cullen (New York: Oxford University Press, 1994); the account of Strephon's and Claius's struggle for Urania is on pages 187–94.

47. See Renée Pigeon's excellent introduction to her modern edition: *Theophania, Or, Several Modern Histories Represented by Way of Romance, and Politickly Discours'd Upon* (Ottawa: Dovehouse Editions, 1999), 12–13. All parenthetical references will be to this edition.
48. Victoria Kahn, in "Reinventing Romance, or the Surprising Effects of Sympathy," *Renaissance Quarterly* 55, no. 2 (2002): 625–61, argues that the sympathy between the two men "aestheticizes the political" and thereby combats the "jealousy and emulation that have given rise to civil war" (655); I am suggesting that in its suggestion of the relationship's implication in self-interest *Theophania* reveals itself to be more uneasy, if not about jealousy and conflict in this relationship then certainly about the motives that give rise to them.
49. For *Parthenissa*'s reputation, see bookseller Francis Kirkman's preface "To the Reader" to his edition of *The Honour of Chivalry: or, The Famous and Delectable History of Don Bellianis of Greece,* (London, 1671), in which he singles out *Parthenissa* in a group that includes *Bentivolio and Urania* and *The Princess Cloria* (which he writes "Clavia") as uniquely superior to French romance; George MacKenzie's Preface to *Aretina; Or, The Serious Romance* (Edinburgh, 1660); and Clara Reeve, *The Progress of Romance* (1785; New York: The Facsimile Text Society, 1930), 73–4.
50. Roger Boyle, *Parthenissa, A romance. The Last part, the Fifth Tome* (London, 1656), Preface (no page sigs). "I soone found," he recalls, "that he who was Ignorant of the Romances of those Times, was as fitt an Object for Wonder, as a Phylosopher would be, who had never heard of Aristotle, or a Methematician of Euclyd." For his time in France see also Kathleen M. Lynch, *Roger Boyle, First Earl of Orrery* (Knoxville: University of Tennessee Press, 1965), 38, and Eustace Budgell, *Memoirs of the Lives and Characters of the Illustrious Family of the Boyles* (Dublin, 1754), 29.
51. For an account of the history of Boyle's family in Ireland see also T. C. Barnard, "The Political, Material, and Mental Culture of the Cork Settlers," in *Cork: History and Society—Interdisciplinary Essays on the History of an Irish County,* ed. P. O'Flanagan and C. G. Buttimer (London, 1993), 309–52.
52. Roger Boyle, Earl of Orrery, *Parthenissa, that most fam'd romance, the six volumes compleat* (London, 1676), 566.
53. For this story, see Budgell, *Memoirs,* 34–9; Lynch, *Roger Boyle,* 67–8; *A Collection of the State Letters of the Right Honourable Robert Boyle . . . together with some other Letters, and Pieces of a different kind, Particularly The Life of the Earl of Orrery, by the Reverend Mr. Thomas Morrice, his Lordship's Chaplain* (Dublin, 1743), Preface, vi–vii. The *New Dictionary of National Biography* entry for Boyle notes that he was persuaded by Cromwell himself to join the revolutionaries "in circumstances which have always been surrounded by mystery and even fantasy."

54. An exception is Smith, *Literature and Revolution in England,* 246–9, to whose reading of Harrington I turn in note 60 below.
55. Harrington's separation of interest into two kinds was one of the more controversial aspects of his political theory: in 1658 he published in the *Prerogative of Popular Government* a lengthy and angry refutation of Matthew Wren's idea in his 1657 *Considerations upon Mr Harrington's Commonwealth of Oceana, restrained to the first part of the Preliminaries* that reason is the recognition not of one's interconnectedness with others but of one's power relative to others, and that therefore there cannot be any such thing as the interest of the whole; see Pocock, Historical Introduction, in *The Political Works of James Harrington,* 1–152, 87; and *Prerogative,* in *The Political Works of James Harrington,* esp. 413–19.
56. For the positive reading of Elizabeth's reign as romance, see Francis Bacon, "On the Fortunate Memory of Elizabeth Queen of England," trans. James Spedding, in *The Works of Francis Bacon,* ed. James Spedding, Robert Leslie Ellis, and Douglas Denon Heath (London: Longman, 1857–74), 6:317: Elizabeth's declarations of love for her people are "much like the accounts we find in romances, of the Queen in the blessed islands . . . But if you take them seriously, they challenge admiration of another kind and of a very high order; for certain it is that these dalliances detracted but little from her fame and nothing at all from her majesty, and neither weakened her power nor sensibly hindered her business."
57. This latter question is one of Pocock's central difficulties with *Oceana,* which he tries to answer first by suggesting that the romantic fiction is a simple mode of idealization (Historical Introduction, 74)—an explanation that does not seem likely, given the famous rhetorical and ethical ambiguities surrounding fictional utopias in Renaissance culture and romance's tendency in this period to qualify idealism. Pocock also argues, somewhat contradictorily, that Harrington fictionalized "defensively and evasively, in order to escape being taken too seriously" (75), but Pocock refutes this idea himself with the assertion that Harrington meant to be taken entirely seriously, as we can see from his repeated defenses of *Oceana*'s ideas in subsequent works (76).
58. Kahn, "Reinventing Romance," 628.
59. Gunn, *Politics and the Public Interest,* 144.
60. Smith, *Literature and Revolution,* in order to make this argument that romance provides for Harrington a model for good republican government, attributes to Harrington a view of romance that is the opposite of the one he in fact holds. After citing Harrington's observation that Elizabeth "converted her reign through the perpetual love tricks that passed between her and her people into a kind of romance," Smith says that "Elizabeth's politics had in Harrington's opinion attained the 'full perfection of the orders requisite unto popular government,' while soundly securing the status and means of the

monarchy, and giving to the English a key to future political peace. Sadly for the English, neither their two next kings, nor they, understood this prudence . . . Elizabethan government was the interplay of romance and pastoral, and it was a republic lost." This understanding of romance, Smith concludes, established for republicans romance's "usefulness and significance" (248). This reading rests in large part on a misquotation: in *The Art of Lawgiving,* Harrington says not that Elizabeth's politics *did* achieve the "full perfection of the orders requisite unto popular government," as Smith says, but rather, crucially, "*had* she introduced the full perfection . . . ," the stability of her state might have held (*The Art of Lawgiving* [1659], in Pocock, *The Political Works of James Harrington,* 599–704, 608; my italics). Following on this misreading Smith interprets Harrington's assessment of Elizabeth in *Oceana* as ruling "wholly (with an art she had unto high perfection) humouring and blessing her people" (248) as approval, but Harrington is here equating Elizabeth's "art" precisely with her "love tricks," by which, as I have already argued, in Harrington's view she fosters a direct affective relationship with her ordinary subjects while neglecting the landed nobility who are the real basis of stability in any sound government, as Harrington says subsequently in explicit terms. Similarly to Smith, David Norbrook, in *Writing the English Republic: Poetry, Rhetoric and Politics 1627–1660* (Cambridge: Cambridge University Press, 1999), argues that Harrington looked back to "an idealized Elizabethan age," and adds that "Harrington regarded Elizabeth's government as virtually republican" (363). Perhaps he is relying here upon Smith's evidence and his reading.

61. See, for example, a letter from December 1649 from Robert to Roger in which Robert calls Roger's military successes in Ireland "both much the difficulter conquest, and mor the usefuller" than his work on *Parthenissa* (Robert Boyle, *The Works of the Honourable Robert Boyle,* ed. Thomas Birch, 2nd ed. [London, 1772], 6:50).
62. Harwood, *The Early Essays and Ethics of Robert Boyle,* xliv; Harwood quotes Boyle on page xxvi.
63. [Robert Boyle,] *The Martyrdom of Theodora, And of Didymus* (London, 1687), A7r–A8r. Pierre Force locates the emergence of the term "disinterest" in France in the second half of the seventeenth century and says that the English use follows the French; he cites La Rouchefoucauld as one of the first to use the term, in 1665 (183–4). Force is not conversant, as I noted earlier, with romance, and I have argued for what he calls the use of interest in a "psychological" context, which he sees originating in France in the late 1660s, as already evident in English romance in the 1650s (*Self-Interest before Adam Smith,* 136). *Theodora* was not published until 1687, once Boyle had become a public figure for other reasons, and it is possible that his claim in the preface to have written and circulated the romance much earlier was a fiction. But details such as his remark that the romance

Raymond A. Anselment, *Loyalist Resolve: Patient Fortitude in the English Civil War* (Newark: University of Delaware Press, 1988) and Carol Barash, *English Women's Poetry, 1649–1714: Politics, Community, and Linguistic Authority* (Oxford: Oxford University Press, 1996).

8. Victoria Kahn, *Wayward Contracts: The Crisis of Political Obligation in England, 1640–1674* (Princeton, NJ: Princeton University Press, 2004), 230–1; the discussion of *Cloria* is on pages 227–34.
9. Ibid., 230.
10. For the new recognition among scholars of the importance of statecraft discourse to Royalist ideology see especially Victoria Kahn, "Reinventing Romance, or the Surprising Effects of Sympathy," *Renaissance Quarterly* 55, no. 2 (2002): 625–61; and also David Norbrook, "The English Revolution and English Historiography," in *The Cambridge Companion to Writing of the English Revolution,* ed. N. H. Keeble (Cambridge: Cambridge University Press, 2001), 233–250. The more typical view of an opposition between politic republicanism and the affective politics of royalism is held by, for instance, Derek Hirst, "The Politics of Literature in the English Republic," *Seventeenth Century* 5, no. 2 (1990): 133–155, which sets the republican insistence on "the prudential and comprehensible nature of politics" and the effort to "demystify statecraft" against the Royalist emphasis on "piety, mystery and art" (147) (Kahn takes direct issue with this article), and Raymond A. Anselment, "'Clouded Majesty': Richard Lovelace, Sir Peter Lely, and the Royalist Spirit," *Studies in Philology* 86, no. 3 (1989): 367–387. On the privatizing, mystificatory function of Royalist rhetoric see especially Lois Potter, *Secret Rites and Secret Writing: Royalist Literature, 1641–1660* (Cambridge: Cambridge University Press, 1989), 38–71. On the Royalist appeal to personal, affective loyalty see especially Andrew Lacey, *The Cult of King Charles the Martyr* (Woodbridge, UK: Boydell and Brewer, 2003). For an argument that midcentury romance's Royalist politics in particular are simple, see Potter, *Secret Rites,* 80; and Nigel Smith, *Literature and Revolution in England* (New Haven, CT: Yale University Press, 1994), 234, 243, 361.
11. Bernard Williams, "Utilitarianism and Moral Self-Indulgence," in *Moral Luck: Philosophical Papers 1973–80* (Cambridge: Cambridge University Press, 1981), 40–53.
12. I follow here Kahn, "Reinventing Romance," who calls *Cloria* "the most Hobbesian" of the group of romances she discusses, which also includes *Panthalia* and *Theophania* (629).
13. Thomas Hobbes, *Leviathan,* ed. Richard Tuck (Cambridge: Cambridge University Press, 1991), 148 (bk. 2, chap. 21).
14. George MacKenzie, *Aretina ; Or, The Serious Romance* (Edinburgh, 1660), 7.
15. For MacKenzie's biography, see A. Lang, *Sir George Mackenzie, King's Advocate, of Rosehaugh: His Life and Times* (New York: Longmans,

Green and Co., 1909), and Brian Vickers, ed., *Public and Private Life in the Seventeenth Century: The Mackenzie-Evelyn Debate* (Delmar, NY: Scholars' Facsimiles and Reprints, 1985). *Aretina* has received more critical attention than other midcentury romances in recent years; see esp. Irene Basey Beesemyer, "Sir George Mackenzie's *Aretina* of 1660: A Scot's Assault on Restoration Politics," *Scottish Studies Review* 4, no. 1 (2003): 41–68, for a discussion of MacKenzie's accommodation of law with contract in his theory of sovereignty. See also M. R. G. Spiller, "The First Scots Novel: Sir George MacKenzie's *Aretina*," *Scottish Literary Journal* Supplement, no. 11, 1979, 1–20, and Clare Jackson, "The Paradoxical Virtue of the Historical Romance: Sir George Mackenzie's 'Aretina' (1660) and the Civil Wars," in *Celtic Dimensions of the Civil Wars: Proceedings of the Second Conference of the Research Centre in Scottish History, University of Strathclyde* (Edinburgh: J. Donald Publishers, 1997), 204–25.

16. Vladimir Propp, "Oedipus in the Light of Folklore," trans. Polly Coote, in *Oedipus: A Folklore Casebook*, ed. Lowell Edmunds and Alan Dundes (Madison: University of Wisconsin Press, 1995 [1983; essay first published 1944]), 76–121, 110–12.
17. That *Eliana* means to draw attention to the shift by which succession is now between brothers rather than fathers and sons is confirmed by an almost comic moment at the end of the narrative, in which Lonoxia is begged by some mutinous forces of the evil Marcipsius to lead a military campaign against him but cannot quite bring himself to go to war against a man both "brother and king." Marinus, who is of course Marcipsius's natural son, acknowledges Lonoxia's reservations and then cheerfully volunteers instead, as if to say that father-son conflict has now become so obvious and conventional that it has lost its charge and, in contrast to fraternal rivalry, costs us nearly nothing to acknowledge.
18. Because of his work as a dramatist John Crowne's career is better known among literary scholars than that of any other midcentury romance writer I have discussed. For his biography see B. Neman, "John Crowne," in *Restoration and Eighteenth-Century Dramatists,* first series, ed. Paula R. Backscheider, *Dictionary of Literary Biography,* vol. 80 (Detroit, MI: Gale Research Company, 1989), 36–51; Arthur F. White, *John Crowne: His Life and Dramatic Works* (Cleveland, OH: Case Western Reserve University Press, 1922); S. Sengupta, "Biographical Notes on John Crowne," *Restoration: Studies in English Literary Culture* 6 (1982): 26–30.
19. John Crowne, *Pandion and Amphigenia, or, The History of the Coy Lady of Thessalia* (London, 1665), 292.
20. Charles Sorel, *The Extravagant Shepherd: Or, the History of the Shepherd Lysis. An Anti-Romance,* trans. John Davies (London, 1654), A2r.

21. Ovid, *Metamorphoses,* trans. Frank Justus Miller, 3rd ed. (Cambridge, MA: Harvard University Press, Loeb Classical Library, 1977), 1:325 (6:536–8).

CONCLUSION

1. Francis Bacon, *De Augmentis Scientarum,* trans. James Spedding, in *The Works of Francis Bacon,* ed. James Spedding, Robert Leslie Ellis, and Douglas Denon Heath (London: Longman, 1857–74), 4:315 (bk. 2, chap. 13).
2. Francis Kirkman, To the Reader," in *The Honour of Chivalrie: or, The Famous and Delectable History of Don Bellianis of Greece* (London, 1671), A4v.
3. Bernard Williams, *Ethics and the Limits of Philosophy* (Cambridge, MA: Harvard University Press, 1985), 15.
4. Philippa Foot, *Natural Goodness* (Oxford: Clarendon Press, 2001), 16.

Index

locate romance as part of a Foucauldian-inspired discourse — strictly taken over politics / tackle questions of agency + self-interest / self-fashioning

—

[illegible] against H — the issue of agency in [illegible] by [illegible] [illegible] — [illegible] [illegible], [illegible]

want to be part of my initial argument that romance tropes do textually / semantically to provide much of literary discourse

—

Check out [illegible] or Patterson on whether same as poetic discourse, being informed by theirs — just theory or own lit theory

—

using KM notions of function of allegory — & politic, coming [illegible] [illegible] merging politic philosophy & literary theory

i.e. allegory is part of interest or self-fashioning

—

RAC function of historical characters

virtue and agency

—

How do RACs prevent this from collapsing into sterile identification? — Smith says it's [illegible] [illegible] but they are larger selves [illegible] which doesn't [illegible] [illegible] [illegible]